Marcus Williamson

Modern diabolism

Commonly called modern spiritualism

Marcus Williamson

Modern diabolism
Commonly called modern spiritualism

ISBN/EAN: 9783337269326

Printed in Europe, USA, Canada, Australia, Japan

Cover: Foto ©Thomas Meinert / pixelio.de

More available books at **www.hansebooks.com**

MODERN DIABOLISM;

COMMONLY CALLED

MODERN SPIRITUALISM:

WITH NEW THEORIES OF

LIGHT, HEAT, ELECTRICITY, AND SOUND.

BY

M. J. WILLIAMSON.

NEW YORK:
PUBLISHED BY JAMES MILLER,
No. 647 BROADWAY.
1873.

LOVEJOY, SON & CO., STEREOTYPERS, 15 VANDEWATER ST.

PREFACE.

In the year 1867 a work written by the author of this, entitled "The Invisibles: An Explanation of Phenomena commonly called Spiritual," was published anonymously in Philadelphia.

That work professed, as does this, to be based upon information received from another world. It will be perceived, on reading the introductory narrative of the present work, that at the time the former was written, it was *extremely* difficult for the writer to procure the needed information; consequently, the work was not, even to the author, entirely satisfactory. The same difficulty, to some extent, has existed in the preparation of this work; but communication having become less difficult than formerly, and having received additional information, I decided to rewrite the former work, with the addition of such matter as would further explain the subject.

The narratives relating and explaining my own experience in the investigation of this subject to the date of the former publication, are—with an exception which will be hereafter stated—substantially the same in this as in the former work. The explanations of phenomena, and the reviews of other narratives bearing upon the subject, are also substantially the same. The brief description of the other world given in this work is here original; as are also the new theories of Light, Sound, etc., and the criticisms on the popular theories of these phenomena.

The exception above referred to, or difference between the narratives given in this and the former work, is this:—In the former work I carefully avoided giving any clue to the identities of the individuals of the other world who had been guilty of deceptions in their communications with me. It was very difficult for me to believe that these individuals had become such lying creatures; and I thought it possible that if communication was less difficult, some explanation might be given which would make their course appear less reprehensible. Having now learned, as I am convinced, all the important facts in the case, I see no reason why I should so carefully conceal the identities of these parties as to make the narrative appear like a fiction; especially as I have not hesitated to state that a relative of my own was one of the worst liars of the party—a fact, by the way, of which I was not aware when I wrote the former work.

In this work I have, therefore, stated such facts relative to these individuals, designated by initials, as were necessary to make the narrative intelligible; whether these facts make the individuals generally known to the readers of this work, or not, is a matter of indifference to me. It is somewhat unfortunate that, for reasons which will be apparent on reading the narrative, I must conceal the identity of the individual who, of the male persons, has communicated most frequently with me; and whom I have designated by the title of Count. A knowledge of the identity of this person would make the narrative clearer; still, I think the facts which I have given will make it, so far as relates to him, at least intelligible.

My reason for publishing the former work anonymously was, of course, that I did not wish to be known as a "medium;" I wished to avoid being requested to serve as such for communications to others, and also to avoid discussion of the subject, either with Spiritualists or those who believe the phenomena to be mere jugglery. The same reason for withholding my name still exists; but such withholding would now be useless; the narratives as now written would make the writer known to many of his acquaintances. Aside from this, however, as in some newspaper notices of the former work it was insisted, and perhaps with good reason, that the author's name should have been given as a voucher for such an extraordinary narrative, I had decided to give it in the present work.

The new theories of sound, light, etc., herein presented, should, and I hope will, be examined without reference to the source from which I profess to have have received them. I profess to have received them since I commenced writing this work, or less than six months since; and therefore have not had much time for considering them. Still, I have given to them as much thought as to those which I have criticised; and, while I readily perceived what to me seemed fatal defects in the latter, I do not perceive such in the former. But any theory of light requires for its demonstration experiments which I have no means for performing; I must, therefore, submit this for examination to those having such facilities.

These theories, I am well aware, do not harmonize with the belief of many—whether *most*, or not, I am unable to state— scientific men of the present day as to the nature of sensation. Sensation, and all the phenomena producing it, are now explained as being simply motion; sensation being, as I understand the theory, motion of particles of the brain. The theories I have received assume that all our sensations are of an electrical nature; and that electricity itself is not simply motion, but a substance; the theory of electricity differing but little from the single fluid theory as formerly held. The nature of sensation cannot, of course, be demonstrated; but the theory that it is motion—not a very satisfactory theory considered by itself—appears to have originated from the belief that all the phenomena producing it are simply modes of motion. I think if the belief had not been held that these phenomena are simply motions of particles, the idea would never have occurred to any one that sensation was such. Why theories of these phenomena are given in a work of this kind, is explained at the close of the introductory narrative.

I think most persons who have thoroughly and candidly investigated the phenomena generally termed spiritual, whether they became satisfied as to the origin of the phenomena or not, have, like myself, felt some disgust at the attitude assumed, in reference to the subject, by a certain class of, so-called, scientific men. The terms "science" and "scientific" have been made to play a very sorry part in this matter.

It has so happened that, in criticising the wave theory of sound, and the dynamical theory of heat, it has been a matter of convenience for me to review briefly the published lectures of one of these "scientific men." No criticisms of such nonsensical lectures, delivered by a professor of natural philosophy, could, under any circumstances, be too severe; but the language now employed is not such as was originally written, nor such as would now be used but for the supercilious attitude assumed by this professor, in connection with others of his class, toward all who express their belief in the genuineness of these phenomena.

When a crack-brained professor, having no knowledge of the subject, chooses to publish to the world his "despair for humanity," because people who have investigated the subject persist in believing the evidence of their senses, I do not feel called upon to be very guarded in my language when reviewing his idiotic lectures. And it does not appear to me probable that a man who is so ignorant on subjects which he professes to have made a study, can be so peculiarly gifted as to be able to decide authoritatively relative to phenomena which he has not investigated at all.

In this work I have used the words *death* and *died*, which Spiritualists carefully avoid, because they are generally understood, when applied to a human being, as referring only to the death of the body; and I can see no propriety in using several words to express a fact when one will equally well serve the purpose. On the other hand, I have, at some inconvenience, avoided using the term *spirit* or *spirits*, except when copying or reviewing other writings: for, as the inhabitants of the other world are not spirits, as the word is generally understood, the term, when applied to them, necessarily conveys a false impression.

It will, I trust, be understood that I give the somewhat lengthy narratives of my own experience in this matter solely for the purpose of illustrating the subject. I am as sensible as any one can be that, aside from this single object, they are not worth reading. The main object of this work is to explain what is termed Modern Spiritualism—a designation, however, which I now think a false one—and I have thought that a pretty full account of my own experience—a very unusual one from causes stated—would aid in making the subject understood.

I would here say a few words which in a work of a different character would be inappropriate. It will be understood, on reading the introductory and explanatory narratives, that, as at present situated, I should decline any request to serve as a medium for communications to others. But I wish to make it also understood that I should decline any discussion of the subject. I wish to avoid, as far as possible, talking or *thinking* about it; the reason for which will, I think, be perceived on reading the explanatory narrative.

I have, in this work, given all the information upon the subject which I am, at present, capable of giving. If, after reading the work, Spiritualists conclude that I have myself been deceived, and still think that they can receive communications from departed friends through the mediums, they, of course, can and will continue to visit them. If, on the other hand, others continue in the belief that no communications are, or can be, received from any of another world, and conclude that this work is the product of "nervous derangement," "reflex action of the brain," or something of the kind, they can continue to publish their "scientific" theories for the benefit of others; I only wish to say that any attempt to convince me that such is the fact would be a useless waste of time.

These remarks—more especially those referring to the latter class of individuals—prompted by past experience, are here made for the purpose of avoiding the necessity for any apparent rudeness hereafter.

New York, *October*, 1872.

CONTENTS.

MODERN DIABOLISM.

CHAPTER I.

INTRODUCTORY NARRATIVE.

ONE evening, in the year 1858, I received an invitation to accompany a party of acquaintances to a *séance* with a so-called spiritual medium. At this time I knew very little about spiritualism. I had accidentally, on two or three occasions, witnessed table-tipping, but, so far as I could perceive, the " mediums " moved the tables precisely as any ordinary mortal would have done ; and the answers to questions put by individuals present—which answers were limited to a simple affirmative or negative—appeared to be as often wrong as correct. In short, they were such silly attempts at imposition, that I did not myself think it worth while to ask any questions or make any investigations. Still, I did not conclude, as many do under such circumstances, that because what I had witnessed were silly attempts at imposition, all the phenomena reported as having been witnessed by intelligent individuals were of the same character. The time of which I am now writing was about ten years after the commencement of the Rochester knockings, so called ; and what little I had heard upon the subject had produced a vague impression on my mind that, in the presence of certain individuals, phenomena did occur which were not yet fully understood. But I concluded that if spirits had any agency in the phenomena, and were able to communicate by means of the "raps," as pretended, something would have been communicated tending to establish the fact; and I had neither read nor heard anything of the kind.

The medium at the *séance* above referred to was Mrs. Brown, a member of the celebrated Fox family; and she, as I am now convinced, was the first real medium I had seen. On this occasion I witnessed phenomena which puzzled me, and excited sufficient interest to cause my further investigation. I, therefore, visited Mrs. Brown alone, as I could thus more satisfactorily investigate the phenomena. I also visited other mediums, and sat in "circles" with acquaintances who were also interested in the subject. There is such a uniformity in these phenomena, and they have been so often described, that I shall not detain the reader with a repetition. It will be sufficient to state that I became fully convinced the phenomena occurring in the presence of Mrs. Brown, her sister, Miss Fox, and some others, were genuine, and not jugglery; and that is all of which I was convinced. I was unable to arrive at any conclusion, satisfactory to myself, as to the origin of the phenomena.

The fact that sounds resembling raps were heard, and furniture moved, without any visible cause, did not, of course, necessarily indicate that spirits had any agency in the matter; but there was a certain degree of intelligence manifested, independently of the medium, for which it was difficult, if not impossible, to account upon any other hypothesis than the presence of invisible beings. On the other hand, there was not sufficient intelligence manifested to warrant the assumption that any one possessing the intellect of a rational human being was an agent in the matter. The idea at once naturally occurred to me, that if the disembodied spirits of human beings were the agents, the spirits could explain how they produced the phenomena. But I was unable to obtain any rational explanation ; and on conversing with Spiritualists, those who had "investigated," as they stated, for years, relative to this point, I found they had not even a sensible idea upon the subject. They had an undefined theory that the raps were, in some way, caused by discharges of electricity; and as for the moving of furniture, they found, as they said, no difficulty whatever in understanding it. "Spirit moves ponderable matter when you raise your arm," they said ; "why, then, can't a spirit move a table ? " I felt it would be a hopeless task to seek information from such people, and soon abandoned the investigation, without having satisfied myself any further than as above stated.

The question was suggested to my mind whether there might not, after all, exist such beings as the demons once believed in, and described in the New Testament ; and who, through their connection with individuals of our world, learned so much of the English language as to be able to spell out sentences ; but this idea was not seriously entertained. I now know, however, that the idea was not very far from the truth ;

but the demons are men and women, once inhabitants of our world.

Another idea which occurred to me was, that certain individuals of the invisible world, and only these, might have the power of producing the phenomena through certain individuals of our world; and that all the communications purporting to be from departed friends of the visitors, might be made by one, or more, constantly with the medium. But this theory appeared unsatisfactory, for the reason that I could perceive no inducement for such beings to remain *constantly* with the medium. If the communications had been of a nature calculated to work evil in the recipients, then I could have perceived a motive for the personations; but they were, so far as I had any knowledge, not calculated to produce any result, either good or bad. Aside from the "tests" relative to identity, occasionally given, the communications were mere platitudes, having such an air of uniformity as almost to appear like sentences given off by machinery. Now, I could not conceive that the disembodied spirit of a man or woman—assuming such to exist—would stay with a medium day after day, waiting for some visitors to whom these platitudes might be communicated.

In the autumn of 1863, having no particular occupation for my evenings, I determined again to try if I could not settle the point in my mind as to whether the phenomena were caused by beings of another world; and I may as well confess that my object was to satisfy myself that we continue to exist after the death of the present body.

Mrs. Brown was now married, and not a public medium.; Miss Fox I was also unable to see, as she was unwell; I visited two or three mediums, but the result was even more unsatisfactory than my former investigations. Having been told by, or through, one of these mediums that I would receive more satisfactory communications direct, by sitting alone in my room, than through others, I concluded to try this plan. The mode of communicating, I was told, would be by writing with my hand. I, therefore, sat at a table in my room, holding a pencil on paper, but could not perceive the slightest tendency in my hand to move in any direction. Partly by accident, however, I discovered that if I moved my hand as passively as possible, there was a slight foreign influence exerted upon it, guiding it either to the right or left. The influence was *very* slight, almost imperceptible; but by watching it closely, and permitting my hand to be guided by it, letters and words were formed. To write a word or a name was, at first, a difficult and tedious task; one great difficulty being that my hand would sometimes move backwards, or from right to left. The first name—and in fact the first words—written, was that of an intimate acquaintance who died at Cleveland, Ohio, my former residence, a little more than a year previous.

In the hope that the writing would become less difficult, I sat, for a short time, nearly every day for the purpose. For some time nothing but names were written, most of these being the names of former residents of Cleveland. Of the decease of most of these individuals I had learned, but not of all; nor do I now know whether all whose names were then written had left our world, or not; some of them not having been intimate acquaintances of mine. Some of the names were not written correctly, being apparently spelled in accordance with the pronunciation.

Several days after I had commenced sitting, the name "Ella" was written, and repeated continuously, nothing else being attempted during the sitting. The same was repeated the next day; I could get nothing written but "Ella," although I requested that Ella would let some other person write. As I never had any intimate acquaintance, so far as I could recollect, of that name, I ceased sitting for communications. About a month afterward I again sat down to see what would be written, when, to my great vexation, the name "Ella" was again given. Then I concluded to endeavor to ascertain who this Ella was. It would, at this time, have been tedious, if not impracticable, to have an explanation written out; I therefore asked questions to which a simple affirmative or negative would be an answer. In this way, after asking several questions, I learned that Ella claimed to be a sister of mine. It then occurred to me that the last four letters of Isabella, the name of a deceased sister, formed the name Ella. The former name was then written, and on asking this person pretending to be my sister, if she had forgotten her name, she replied that she had. This was, upon any hypothesis, the more inexplicable from the fact that the name of this sister was correctly given at Mrs. Brown's during my former investigations.

In the succeeding spring the facility in writing had become such that short communications were given. But it was still a tedious process; not more than one brief communication being, as a rule, written at a sitting   As soon as it became feasible to write sentences, one individual appeared to have the entire control. This person gave the name of, and pretended to be, an acquaintance of mine who died at Cleveland more than twenty years previous. He was an educated gentleman; this invisible being, pretending to be him, was an illiterate and vulgar creature ; the sentences being generally ungrammatical, and the language co arse. All my efforts to induce this person to let others write were ineffectual.

In May, 1864, I left New York for Trenton, New Jersey. On resuming my sittings at the latter place, the communications for several days all purported to be from soldiers who had lived in that vicinity, and who had been killed or died from sickness during the war. They wished, as was stated, to send messages to their friends through me, but I took no steps to ascertain whether such persons had lived there or not.

On the evening of the fourth day after my arrival at Trenton, the name of a gentlemen who had boarded during the past winter at the same hotel in New York as myself, and whom I will designate as Mr. A., was written. As I had seen the gentleman the day previous to leaving New York, this purported to have been a very sudden death. But as Mr. A. had recently received a severe injury, from which he had not entirely recovered when I last saw him, and the statement, in reply to my inquiry, being that he had taken a severe cold, which, in connection with his injury, had caused his death, the suddenness of the death did not seem so very improbable. I put a few questions to test the identity, though not expecting to be convinced by the answers, as I could only put questions the correct answers to which I knew, and I was aware that the personator, if it was such, might obtain the answers from my mind. But the next morning I found New York papers, and examined the obituary notices from the date given as that of the death, which was the day following that on which I left New York, without finding any notice of the death of Mr. A.

A day or two afterward I was visited by one giving her name as Ellen ——; the surname I could not read, and, as she did not pretend to have been an acquaintance, did not ask to have it rewritten. This Ellen appeared to have no definite object in coming. She was excessively vulgar; admitted having lived a depraved life in our world; said she was the same kind of a woman now, and had no intention or desire to reform. The one claiming to be Mr. A. continued to visit me and assert the identity; and for two or three days he and Ellen performed all the writing. Then Mr. A., as I will continue to designate this visitor, made what seemed to be a very good suggestion, namely, that I should not permit Ellen to write—that I should stop as soon as I detected her vulgar style, which I could generally do as soon as a few words were written.

At the sitting when the above suggestion was made, Mr. A. stated that he had brought a young lady who had been an acquaintance of his in our world, and who wished to communicate with me. The young lady then gave her name as Miss Annie Allen. She stated that Mr. and Mrs. A. were acquaintances of the family of which she was a member; that the latter resided at

No. 84 East Twenty-second street, New York, and that her father was a banker, dealing in foreign exchange. The name of the firm of which her father was a member she could not give, nor the precise location of the office, though she said the latter was in one of the streets near Wall street. Subsequently she gave what she thought was the name of the firm, one I had never heard of. Miss Allen appeared to have no object in visiting me, other than to unite with Mr. A. in urging that I would send a letter from the latter to Mrs. A., which I had no intention of doing until I had learned of his death from some other source.

Shortly after the first visit of Miss Allen, one giving her name as Mrs. Arnold came. She had lived and died, as she stated, at South Bend, Ohio. I told her I was a native of Ohio, and that I was quite confident there was no such place in the State. She, however, insisted she was correct, but was unable to state where South Bend was located, further than it was upon some river. This female also continued to visit me, apparently without any definite object in view.

After being urged for some time to permit a letter to be written to Mrs. A., I recollected that there was an acquaintance of Mr. A. then in Trenton, who would probably be advised of the death if it had occurred, and I concluded to inquire of this gentleman when I met him. Miss Allen then said that she had been acquainted with this gentleman; and a day or two afterward she informed me that he was then in the street near my hotel, requesting me to go out and make the inquiry. I should state, to make this understood, that at this time these invisible beings could write with my hand about as rapidly as I could by the exertion of my own will; and they were able to make me understand that they wished to write something when I was not sitting for the purpose. This intimation was given by producing the sensation of being taken by the hand by some one. At the time I was requested to go out and make this inquiry I was not sitting for communications, but feeling the signal that some one wished to write, I granted the request.

Not seeing the gentleman when I went out of the hotel, I was informed in the same way that he had gone into a bank in the same street; and a gentleman soon came out of the bank who, as intimated, was the one thought to be the acquaintance of Mr. A. There was considerable resemblance in the two individuals, though not a very striking one, and this gentleman was several years younger than the one I was looking for. On returning to the hotel Miss Allen urged me to go to that in which the gentleman was boarding, and make the inquiry. I told her that if she would go to his hotel and ascertain that he was in I would do so. I had no reason for supposing that she could do this, other than what had just occurred. She replied that she would go, and in a few minutes, feeling the signal, I was told that she had been to the gentleman's hotel and saw him there. I asked her what the gentleman was doing, and she replied that he was sitting at a small form, but that she could not see, or did not notice —I do not recollect which phrase she used—what he was doing. This hotel was in a street crossing that in which mine was situated, and the distance between the two hotels—following the streets—was about one hundred and fifty yards. I went to the hotel and looked in the two principal rooms without seeing the gentleman; then passed out, but stopped at the door to let Miss Allen write. She wrote that the gentleman was in a small room in the rear of the one I last looked in. Entering this small room, I saw a gentleman, the only person in the room, seated at a small plain desk, reading a newspaper. This individual did not at all resemble the one I was looking for, and was as much older as the one first mistaken for him was younger.

Two or three days afterward I met Mr. A.'s acquaintance, and made the inquiry, but without telling him how I had heard of the death. He said the report was not true: that he had just returned from New York, and when there called at Mr. A.'s office to see him, when he was told that Mr. A. had just gone out.

To my great surprise, the invisible being claiming to be Mr. A. still insisted that he was that individual, and gave the following as an explanation of the mistake of this acquaintance: He said he had a cousin in New York of the same name (surname) as his own; that when his acquaintance inquired for him, the one of whom he inquired must have supposed his friend knew of his death, and thought the inquiry was for his cousin. I was no longer urged to send a letter to Mrs. A. until I had learned of the death of her husband; and I could perceive no possible motive in urging me to satisfy myself as to the fact if the death had not occurred. Finally, although still suspecting that it was a personation, I wrote to the proprietor of the hotel in New York, and learned that Mr. A. was still boarding there.

This terminated, for a time, the communications of

Miss Allen; but Mrs. Arnold continued to visit me. She said that the individual who personated Mr. A. was a man, and that she supposed he was Mr. A.; that she had herself been deceived. She stated what she now supposed was the object in the deception; but her explanation was not very lucid, and is not worth repeating.

About this time, which was the latter part of May, I became unwell, and stopped sitting for communications; in fact, I had pretty much stopped before this, as few visited me at Trenton but these women, and I could learn nothing from them. During this illness, however, I acquired the faculty of hearing these beings. At first the sensation did not resemble sound, but was rather as though words were, in some way, impressed upon my mind. Gradually this sensation changed, and soon became the same as hearing one of our world speak.

A short time after I had been advised by the personator of Mr. A. not to let Ellen write, I had received two or three electric shocks which I was told at the time were caused by Ellen; in fact, the statement to this effect purported to be by Ellen herself; and the reason for causing the shocks was stated to be my refusal to let her write. These shocks caused me considerable uneasiness and apprehension at the time, though they were not renewed. But during my illness, and after I had become able to hear these beings, I was awakened one night by feeling a hand grasping my throat and trying to choke me; at least, such was the sensation. As soon as I awoke, Ellen said she was the one performing this, and that she intended to choke me to death. I soon perceived, however, that she could not affect my breathing, and, aside from the annoyance, cared little about it. This attempt to choke me was renewed during the two or three succeeding nights, and was an annoyance, as it prevented me from sleeping soundly. I found that I could stop it by placing my hands around my throat, but, as I could not keep them there when asleep, I concluded the best course would be to pay no attention to it, and try to make Ellen believe that I cared nothing about it; though she asserted that she would persecute me while I lived, and torment me in my "dying agony."

A short time after the above annoyance commenced, I awoke in the middle of the night with a violent palpitation of the heart, and feeling that my limbs were partially paralyzed. Ellen said, as soon as I awoke, that she had been operating upon the action of my heart while I was asleep, and that if she had had one hour more—that is, before I awoke—"she would have stopped its beating forever." This, I confess, frightened me. The attempt at choking, after I became satisfied she could not compress the windpipe, merely annoyed me, as a similar attempt of a child would have done; but this operation upon my heart I could not understand; and the idea that this creature might have power to affect its action while I was asleep, was horrible. The violent palpitation continued, and on the two succeeding nights when I went to bed Ellen said she should renew her operations as soon as I fell asleep. On the fourth evening, about bedtime, Mrs. Arnold, who continued to visit me, said that if I would sit up awhile she would bring my father and other male

friends, and that if Ellen did not then leave they would
kill her. In a short time I was told she had brought
my father and a former male acquaintance, and I was
directed to fix my mind intently upon the former. It
was the warmest night of an unusually warm summer,
and I should not have slept much if I had gone to bed.
I did not intend, however, to sit up very late, but I
dozed in the chair, and it was daylight when I went to
bed. I was then told that Ellen had been killed. Although too sleepy to think much about it, I noticed
that her talking had ceased, and I never afterward
heard anything purporting to be spoken by her.

About a week after the above affair, and when I had
nearly recovered my health, I was visited by one who
said his name was M——, and that he was formerly
president of the M—— Bank, in New York. I had been
engaged in the banking business in New York, but was
not acquainted with the officers of this bank. I thought,
however, that I recollected the name given as being that
of one of the officers, but whether president or cashier I
could not recollect. I had not heard of the death of
either officer, and on inquiring of the visitor, he stated
that his death occurred in the year 1860 or 1861—I am
not certain which of these dates he gave. He said that
when in our world, he had been somewhat interested in
Spiritualism, and had, to some extent, investigated the
subject; that since he had left it, he had visited several
mediums, but that I was the first one he had found with
whom he could communicate. On asking him how he
had found me, I noticed some hesitation in the reply,
but finally, he said that my sister had told him about
me.

On the succeeding evening this individual came again; but in the meantime I had examined a bank-note reporter and found that a Mr. M—— was then president of the M—— Bank. On stating this at the second visit, the visitor said that the directors of the bank had told him, before his death, that they would continue his name as president, whether he was alive or dead, and he supposed they were doing so. This reply did not indicate much knowledge of banking; however, perceiving that he understood me to refer to the reports, or statements of the bank, I told him that what I had examined was commonly called a counterfeit-detector. He then said that it must be his son who was president; that he had a son who was a director of the bank, and who must have been elected president, though he had not supposed he would be. This visitor had not, at this time, given his first name, and I believe I did not tell him the first name of the president; he afterward gave his, which was not that of the president.

By this time, which was four or five weeks after I had gone to Trenton, I had become convinced that if any relative or acquaintance had visited me at all, they had more often been personated by others. As I have stated, as soon as it became feasible, in New York, to write sentences of any length at one sitting, one illiterate individual appeared to be able to prevent all others from writing. In Trenton, the only visitor, previous to my illness, pretending to have been an acquaintance, was the personator of Mr. A. During my illness I was visited, as represented, by my sister and other friends; but I was not then in a condition to take any steps to satisfy myself as to the identity. These visitors spoke of former residents of Cleveland, but mostly of persons who had died or left the place when I was quite young, and whom I had almost forgotten. Mrs. Arnold now admitted that she had frequently personated my sister; but as she did not pretend to have ever lived in Cleveland, her personation did not account for the knowledge evinced of that place. I had received no communication from any one pretending to be a relative or acquaintance for some time previous to the visit of this late bank president, as the individual styled himself.

This Mr. M., as I will designate the visitor, stated that I differed from all other mediums; and that people of his world who could not communicate with any other medium could do so with me. He urged me, therefore, to go to New York and act as a medium for communications to wealthy individuals; stating that I could make more money in that way than in the business in which I was engaged; and he wished me to permit him to act in some way—how, I did not inquire —as a manager of the business. He also stated that he had engaged Miss Allen to remain with me, and prevent, in future, the personations which had been practiced. Now, this Miss Allen, it will be recollected, had been connected with the personation of Mr. A., since which I had heard nothing from her; but Mr. M. said she had been drawn into that by others, and much regretted her connection with it; and that as she had become so much *en rapport* with me, it would be better to engage her for the purpose than to bring another person.

As I had been unable to learn anything about the

other world from the females, I attempted to do so from
Mr. M.; but he wished to postpone entering upon that
subject until I went to New York. I told him, however, that I should not act as a public medium; that
I intended to pass the coming winter in New York,
and would, perhaps, serve, in a few instances, evenings.
With this he was obliged to be content; but said he
wished to have some one of our world interested in the
matter, and would like to make arrangements at once
for this purpose. He requested, therefore, that I
would permit him to write, through me, a letter to a
gentleman in New York, and have a reply sent to me
at Trenton. This I refused, recollecting the recent attempt to have me send a letter to Mrs. A.; and although
Mr. M.'s communications differed very much from those
of the personator of Mr. A., I was not satisfied that he
was the late bank president.

At one of the visits of Mr. M.—to state the matter in
its sequence—I asked him if he had met in the other
world a Mr. W., late a prominent New York banker,
with whom I had been slightly acquainted. This Mr.
W. died four or five years prior to the time of which I
am writing; and it is unnecessary to state why the visit
and conversation of Mr. M. recalled the former to my
recollection. Mr. M. replied that he had not met him,
and asked when he died, thus intimating that he had
not been aware of his death. The name of Mr. W.
was not again mentioned until as will be hereafter
stated.

At another time Mr. M. brought, as stated, a large
party to see me. I was told the party consisted of
about forty persons; but the names of only five were

given me. These were Howard, the English philan-
thropist; Daboll, author of an arithmetic; Dudley M.,
of whom I knew very little; Mr. T., late president of
a New York bank, who died the preceding winter; and
Mr. K., late a New York stock-broker, with whom I
had been acquainted—rather a queer collection. ·

Dudley M. I knew nothing about, further than that
he was a resident of one of the Southern States; but I
had seen in a newspaper, at the commencement of the
late war, a statement that he had gone to Europe as an
agent of the Southern Confederacy. On mentioning
this, I was told that he died in Paris.

The death of Mr. K. occurred in the preceding summer; but not having been in New York at the time,
I did not learn of it until autumn, when I was told
that he had committed suicide. He inquired if I had
heard of his death, and I repeated to him what I had
been told. At this he professed, at first, to be very indignant, asserting that his death was accidental. Before the meeting adjourned, however, he confessed that
he had committed suicide in consequence of pecuniary
embarrassment; but as the gentleman who gave me the
information was not an acquaintance of his, and knew
very little about the matter, he requested that I would,
when next I went to New York, ascertain whether his
acquaintances believed that he had committed suicide.
My business called me frequently to New York, and I
promised to make the inquiry, which I did, and learned
there was no doubt that such was the fact.

I had not sufficient confidence in the identity of the
individual claiming to be the late bank president to give
my address to any one to whom he might wish to write;

but, finally, I consented to send his letter, and call for an answer in New York. Accordingly, one day, about the first of July, I held the pencil for him to write, as he seemed to prefer this course to dictating orally. I had not previously been informed, or inquired, who the letter would be written to. It was addressed to David A. L——, and reminded him that he and the writer had together investigated Spiritualism about four years since; stated that the latter had at last found a medium through whom he could communicate; and inquired if he, Mr. L., would not co-operate with him in what he was about to undertake. The letter was signed, "Jos. M——, late of the old M—— Bank." Mr. M. did not state definitely what the undertaking was, or what co-operation on the part of Mr. L. was desired; nor did he state anything, beyond the fact of their having investigated Spiritualism in company, calculated to make Mr. L. believe in the genuineness of the letter. When the name of Mr. L. was written, I thought I had seen it with the prefix of *Reverend;* and on asking Mr. M. about this, he said he believed Mr. L. had been a clergyman, but that he was not now usually addressed as Reverend, and directed me to omit the title. This letter I enclosed with a copy, fearing Mr. L. would not be able to read the original.

A few days afterward I went to New York, accompanied by Mr. M., and called for the answer, but received none, at which the latter expressed great surprise. Mr. M. then requested me to go into Wall street, and I visited, with him, several places, one of which was the M—— Bank; but it struck me as a little singular that he said nothing about visiting the latter

until I asked him if he wished to go there. Then he
replied, "O yes, go there next." On leaving the cus-
tom-house Mr. M. inquired what bankers and stock-
brokers I was acquainted with. I named, among
others, a prominent banking firm in Exchange place.
Mr. M. requested me to visit this firm and en
gage the senior member in conversation on business
topics, saying he wanted "to hear him talk." I entered
the office, and, after conversing a few minutes with the
banker, Mr. M. said, "Ask him if it is my son who is
now president of the M—— Bank." Rather thoughtlessly I put the question as requested, asking the banker
if the Mr. M. now president of the M—— Bank, was
a son of the former president. The banker replied,
"Why, it is the same man—there has been no change;"
from which I inferred that no president of the bank had
recently died, and that this was another silly personation now ended. But on leaving the office, the invisible person, still claiming to be Mr. M., asserted that the
banker was mistaken, and requested me to make another inquiry. In Wall street I met another banker
of my acquaintance, and, putting the question properly
this time, learned that a president of the bank had recently died, but that his name was H——, and that
Mr. M., the present president, was formerly cashier.
On learning this, which he did without my repeating
it, the personator of Mr. M. seemed to be really confused. He said, "We will have to give it up, won't
we, sir?"—a remark I could not understand, as I could
perceive no room for doubt that he would have to give
up personating Mr. M. He said he was going to leave,
and bid me good-by in Wall street.

I supposed this personation had ended like that of Mr. A. ; and it was impossible for me to perceive any amusement in such deceptions. But on the same evening, while I was sitting on the piazza of the hotel at Trenton, this invisible being came again. He now said that he had forgotten what his name was in our world, but that he had been " home " and learned it was H——. I reminded him that on leaving the M—— Bank, he said he saw his son there. He replied, " Well, I suppose I must have been mistaken about that, too." He expressed himself gratified at finding me so calm ; said that if he was in my place he should be in a terrible passion ; and only requested that I would suspend my judgment as to his being Mr. H. until I went to New York in the autumn, when he would fully satisfy me.

As to suspending my judgment, it made no particular difference, so far as I could perceive, whether I did or not; but as Miss Allen continued with me, and talked as though she expected me to act as a medium when I went to New York, I told her that I should not do so, even if I became satisfied that this visitor was Mr. H. ; for, if they forget their former names, they certainly could not satisfactorily identify themselves to their friends in our world. To this she replied that Mr. H. was a singular man in that respect ; that she could recollect every incident of her former life, and that most persons of her world could do the same. But she added that, as they had now discovered how forgetful some persons were, when I acted as a medium, every one who came to communicate would be cautioned to refresh their memory before coming, and, consequently, there would occur no more mistakes of the kind.

Mr. H., as I will now designate this individual, visited me occasionally after this, but without urging me
to take any further steps in reference to acting as a
medium; everything being postponed until I went to
New York to pass the winter. At one of these visits
Mr. H. inquired of me as to my acquaintance with Mr.
K., the stock-broker, who, it will be recollected, he had
brought to see me. He said that Mr. K. had represented himself as having been an intimate acquaintance of mine before either of us went to New York to
reside. This, I informed Mr. H., was not the fact, stating the commencement and nature of our acquaintance.
He then said that in consequence of the representations
of Mr. K. as to our intimacy, it had been decided to
have him connected with the business—that is, in some
way connected with my agency as a medium.—but that
he had known Mr. K. in our world, and considered him
then a great rascal; that he was now " a poor miserable creature," and, therefore, as I said he was not an
intimate acquaintance, he would have no connection
with them. Miss Allen subsequently spoke of Mr. K.,
in reference to his present character, in the same terms;
but how she happened to know anything about him
she did not state, and I did not inquire.

About the middle of July I went to Long Branch.
In the morning of the day I left Trenton, Miss Allen
said she was not going with me, but that she should
go there in the evening; and before I left, Mrs. Arnold,
from whom I had not heard since about the time of
the first visit of Mr. H., came and said that she was to
accompany me at the request of Mr. H.

When informed, in New York, of the death of Mr.

H., I made no inquiry as to the date, presuming that ended the matter; but when again in New York, on my way to Long Branch, I made this inquiry of a bank cashier, and was told that the death occurred in the year 1860 or 1861, the cashier was not certain which of these dates was the correct one. I also learned that a Mr. H. was a director of the M—— Bank; but whether a son of the former president, or not, I did not learn, and have not since inquired.

On the boat I was annoyed by a man of the other world, who talked like one of the lowest and vilest class of ours. When I requested him to leave me, he replied, " D—n you, sir, do you know that I could pick you up and throw you overboard?" During the succeeding night at Long Branch I was further annoyed and prevented from sleeping soundly by this person's constant talking. I heard nothing from Miss Allen this first night, but in the morning she came, and accounted for her absence by saying that she thought I was going to Newport, and that she had gone there. The annoying talker continued with me, talking in the same coarse style, all this second day. Miss Allen said there were three men present, and that the object of their visit was to induce me to act as a medium for them, instead of Mr. H. I never could distinguish any difference of tone, or quality, in the voices of these invisible persons, and therefore could not tell whether there was more than one or not; but the repeated and silly threats to kill me did not indicate much expectation that I would act as a medium for them.

When I went to my room, the second night after my arrival, I perceived that I was again to be prevented from sleeping by this talking. Miss Allen then said, that if I would go out and walk awhile, fixing my mind intently on her, *she would kill these three men.* This, taken literally, was rather a strange proposition. I had not been able to learn the nature of the operation by which I had, as I supposed, got rid of Ellen. It had never occurred to me when Mr. H. was present to make the inquiry of him, and neither Miss Allen or Mrs. Arnold would make any other reply to my questions on this point, than that she had actually been killed. Whatever the operation might have been, I believed that by means of it I had been relieved, either of Ellen's presence, or from her power to annoy me if she was present. I judged so, not merely from the fact that physical annoyance had then ceased, but also because I had since heard nothing purporting to be spoken by her. And I inferred, also, that the action of my mind, or will, must have had an important agency in affecting the deliverance.

It being a fine moonlight night, I went out and walked on the bluff, thinking as directed, until Miss Allen said two of the men were killed, and the other had left. I then returned to my room, when the talking was as incessant as before; but Miss Allen affirmed that those now talking were not the three men, but females. No further attempt was made to kill any one, and, after this night, I suffered no further annoyance during my stay at Long Branch. But Miss Allen informed me that, as her talking increased the power of others to talk, she would thereafter make her communications by writing. And from this time there was constantly some one with me who appeared to be acting ın opposition to Miss Allen, and interfering when the latter attempted to communicate. Miss Allen said this was a female who came the second night after my arrival there. Mrs. Arnold, on the second morning, said she was going to leave me, and I never afterward heard anything from her.

At Long Branch I did not sit for the purpose of receiving communications, in fact I had ceased doing so before leaving Trenton; but at the former place I would occasionally be told that a visitor from the other world was present. One of the names thus given me was that of Mary M——, an individual I could not at first recollect, and, finally, only remembered having heard, when quite young, of the death of such a person at Cleveland. She had no communication to make, and appeared to have merely come from curiosity. Another visitor there was an acquaintance who died in New York the preceding spring, and whom I will designate as Mr. B. Before leaving Trenton I had been told Mr. B. would be associated with Mr. H. in the proposed business; that he had left his family in rather needy circumstances, and wished his daughter—a young lady I had met several times, but with whom I had not much acquaintance—to be associated with me. The idea I received was, that it was still expected I would be induced to act as a public medium; that, as I would be visited by ladies, it would be proper there should be a lady present to receive them; and that Mr. B. wished his daughter to have this position. It was, as represented, to converse upon this subject that Mr. B. came to see me at Long Branch; but, according to my recollection, there was very little said about the matter.

About the middle of August I returned to Trenton; and on the third of September came to New York, with the intention of remaining here during the autumn and winter. Mr. H., who had not visited me at Long Branch, now came, but made an excuse for not attempting to identify himself, as promised, of the difficulty in communicating, owing to the interference of the female who had followed me from Long Branch. It really seemed to be difficult at this time even for Miss Allen to communicate; whether she exaggerated the difficulty or not, it was impossible for me to determine. This female had become somewhat of an annoyance to me, and Mr. H. stated that steps were being taken to have all such interferences and annoyances prevented.

On the 14th of September I was obliged to return to Trenton. Before leaving New York I was assured by Miss Allen that as soon as I returned I would be relieved of this female. This word *relieved*, which was subsequently often used, and which for brevity I will also use, meant sometimes one thing, and sometimes another. Sometimes it meant the removal of two females; sometimes of three; sometimes of only one; sometimes it meant they were to be removed bodily, and by force; at other times, merely that their power of annoyance and interference was to be overcome, it being stated that those of the other world had no power to move each other against the will.

I returned to New York on the 29th of September, and again excuses were offered for the delay in removing this female. All doubts as to the individual representing himself to be Mr. H. being a personator were soon removed from my mind, and I also soon became convinced that Miss Allen had never lived in New York, as represented when she first visited me. And I now doubted whether I had received a single communication from a relative or friend in the other world. Whether this was owing to the fact that my friends knew nothing about my situation, or that being with me they were unable to communicate, I had no means of determining. But, as the action of my will seemed to have great effect, I adopted the plan of sitting at a table, holding a pencil on paper, and thinking intently of a relative as being present, trying the effect with different ones. This Miss Allen urgently opposed, asserting that if she did not constantly exert herself to prevent, the other female would write, and thus her power would be increased.

To induce me to stop this practice, my father, as represented, was brought; and, as tests of identity, several incidents were narrated which, at the time, appeared to me satisfactory. I was assured that I would soon be "relieved," and advised to wait patiently; and when I requested that a period should be named within which I would be "relieved," this was done. But this time passed without my being "relieved," and I then concluded my father had been personated. The incidents given as tests of identity I had frequently thought of since their occurrence; and, although I was not aware of having done so for many years prior to this time, I now felt it would be strange if my father happened to narrate only the same trivial incidents I had recollected. I concluded the incidents must have been obtained from my mind; but inasmuch as I could not recollect having thought recently of them, how this was accomplished was to me a mystery.

I resumed the practice of sitting for writing; for although I could perceive there might be some force in the argument urged against it by Miss Allen, I also knew that she was, for some purpose, attempting to deceive me, or she would have my friends brought, and permit them to communicate with me. Mr. B. next came, as represented, to induce me to be patient. Although Mr. B. was not an intimate acquaintance, I felt it would be some satisfaction to know that any one of the other world with whom I had been in the least acquainted had visited me, and I requested this visitor to identify himself. For this purpose, he stated that he had visited me at Long Branch. I replied that that might be true, but how it identified him as Mr. B. I could not perceive. "Oh, well, I will satisfy you of that," he said, and narrated an incident which did satisfy me, for I felt confident this could not have been obtained from my mind. Mr. B. named another period within which I would be "relieved," which period also elapsed without anything being done. I then concluded Mr. B. must also have been personated; but was completely mystified as to how knowledge of the incident related could have been obtained. I ought to have required more than one incident to be given; but as the one pretending to be Mr. B., as soon as I appeared to be satisfied of the identity, commenced conversing on the subject of his daughter being associated with me, I neglected to do so.

About the middle of November, my father, as represented, came again; but I instituted no further tests as to identity. Frivolous excuses were given for the delay, but it was now stated that I would certainly be "relieved" on or before the second Monday in December. As the word *relieved* is so frequently used, I would state that at this time the annoyances caused by the female said to have followed me from Long Branch were not very great; but her interference was assigned as the reason why none of my friends could communicate with me, further than to the extent of a very few words at a time ; and as, so far, I had learned absolutely nothing about the other world, and was not satisfied that any friend of mine there had communicated with me at all, I was desirous that this difficulty, or excuse, whichever it might be, should be removed.

Several days prior to the expiration of the period last named, Mr. H., as this person still called himself, said it was desired that I should go to England as soon as "relieved;" and a day or two after speaking of this he came again in the morning and informed me that a certain individual, late of high rank in our world, and who died in England about three years prior to the time of which I am now writing, was coming to see me at an hour then agreed upon in the afternoon of the same day. The revelations made by this individual when he came, and which I am now informed were substantially correct, implicate persons now living in England as having been connected with him in the perpetration of a fraud of so very grave a character that I must suppress his late title, and will designate him as the Count. The Count was a German by birth, but married an English lady of high rank, and passed the last twenty years of his life in England.

Mr. H., as for convenience I will continue to designate
this individual, at his visit in the morning stated that
the Count wished me to go to England as soon as "relieved;" that it was desired Miss B. should go with me;
and that, as a matter of propriety, a lady would have to
accompany her.   Mr. H. wished that the daughter of a
friend of his—a New York banker with whom I had no
acquaintance—should be this companion; but he preferred that I should name the lady to the Count, when
he spoke about the matter, as being my own selection.
I did not like this proposition, and asked Mr. H. what
he expected me to say in case the Count inquired if the
lady was an acquaintance of mine, or why I proposed
her.   "In that case," he replied, "tell him that I
suggested her."   I saw no particular objection to this,
and agreed to do as requested.

The Count came at the hour appointed, and at once
entered upon the subject of my going to England, of
Miss B. going with me, and inquired who I would like
to have accompany her.   I named the daughter of Mr.
H.'s friend—provided, of course, I went; but, as yet, no
reason for expecting me to go to England had been
given.   The Count said he got the impression from my
manner that there was something wrong about this lady,
and inquired as to my acquaintance with her.   I told
him that I had no acquaintance whatever with her, and
that she had been proposed by Mr. H.   The Count then
expressed dissatisfaction with my course in the matter,
when I told him he might as well drop the subject of
my going to England, for that I had no desire to go.
After a little delay, he said he had received the impression from my manner that the lady was a bad character;

but that the matter had been satisfactorily explained by Mr. H.

The Count then made a statement, of which the following is the substance, given in as few words as possible:—Soon after his marriage he received an injury—the nature of which will be understood from what follows—for which he was under the care of surgeons about two years. During these two years his wife, with his assent, cohabited with another man. The first child of his wife is legitimate, the two second children are illegitimate; the first is a daughter, the second a son, and the latter, therefore, is acknowledged as the heir.

He then proposed that I should go to England, and, without making the facts generally known, make use of my knowledge of the same for my own benefit. The utter absurdity and impracticability of the scheme he proposed, assuming his statement to be true, I did not at the moment perceive; for, in consequence of the interference of the unknown female, it was so difficult for him to write that, in order to enable him to do so, I was obliged to fix my mind intently on him, and could not think much about what was written. However, I told him that I should not enter into the scheme, when he expressed himself as being very much gratified with my decision; and stated that he wished to have the facts made known, and the matter rectified as far as possible. As I was the only one of our world through whom he could communicate, he wished me to go to England and place him in communication with the widow, that the matter might be adjusted as peaceably as possible. The condensed statement I have given hardly explains why

I should be expected to go to England on this business; but there is a fraud on the British nation connected with the matter, which I cannot state without naming the parties.

The Count wrote for more than two hours, and until I refused to sit any longer; he then made an appointment for the next afternoon at the same hour. At the appointed hour he came again and wrote for about the same length of time as before, when I again told him I could sit no longer. Most of what he wrote was nonsensical and incoherent; but the language indicated the writer to be an educated man; the phrase *educated fool* will express with tolerable accuracy the impression I subsequently received from what he had written; at the time of writing, as I have stated, I could not fairly exercise my judgment. During the two sittings I fully believed the writer to be the Count; and my impression that the writer was the person he represented himself to be was much stronger than it had ever been before when receiving a communication from one of these invisible beings. This *impression* I was never afterward able wholly to shake off, though my judgment was that the visitor was another personator.

When I inquired why he wished Miss B. to go to England, he replied, in substance, that he wished to have the matter adjusted without a resort to legal proceedings; that Miss B., by means which it is not necessary to state, was to prevail upon the eldest son to relinquish his rank and title. A few minutes before, he had expressed dissatisfaction at the idea of a female of doubtful character accompanying Miss B. At the first sitting he stated that the father of the two illegitimate children was a certain individual, late of high rank in our world, at this time in his, who accompanied the eldest son on a visit to the United States a year or two previous to the Count's death. At the second sitting he retracted this statement, and said, first, that as his wife had cohabited with several individuals during the two years, he could not tell who was the father; but al most immediately retracted this statement, and said he would rather not give me the name of the father. At the first sitting he said his widow would soon give birth to a son of whom he was the father; and offered me, as an inducement to go to England, the position of tutor to this baby, with a salary of eight thousand pounds per annum. That is, a boy of whom he was the father was to be born about three years after his death; and as I was only requested to agree to remain in England four years, the child of whom I was to be tutor, with a quite liberal salary, would be about four years of age when I left. At the second sitting, an inducement of a different nature was offered, and the proposition was that I should remain permanently in England. What this second offer was it would be improper to state, especially as I am now informed it was made in good faith, and that others besides the Count believed the scheme to be practicable. The proposition appeared to me about as absurd as any other of his statements. No decision was expected of me until I had been relieved of the interfering female, and my friends of the other world had satisfied me as to the identity of the visitor, and that his proposal was made in good faith.

During these sittings the interference was constant, and so great that, although each sitting lasted for about two hours, the amount of writing executed by the Count was small. Now, as it was stated that this female was to be removed, I could not understand why they did not remove her, at least for the time, when one of them wished to write; and on this point I could get no satisfactory explanation. Miss Allen, in reply to my question as to why they did not keep the woman away from me when they wished to write, said, "We don't pull and haul as you do," but would not attempt to explain what the nature of the operation, in effecting her removal, would be.

The second sitting with the Count was on the Sun day preceding the second Monday in December; and the expiration of the last-named period within which I was to be relieved would occur on the latter day. I reminded the Count and Mr. H., who was also present, of this, and was told that my friends would come in the afternoon of the next day, and that the female would then be removed. On Monday afternoon, at the hour previously named, I was informed that several of my relatives were present; and brief communications were written purporting to be by my father and mother. They gave no tests of identity, and I did not ask for any; but was informed that the removal would be effected during the night. I went to bed at my usual hour, and during most of the night was kept awake by talking and magnetic operations causing twitchings of the muscles and limbs, stated to be in some way connected with the removal of the female. In the morning, finding she was not removed, I pondered long as to what could be the object of these invisible beings, if they had any object in view, but was unable to arrive·

at any satisfactory conclusion. It appeared to me that they must have some scheme in view, but what it was I could not imagine. In the afternoon the Count came again, and stated that after I had been told in the preceding afternoon the removal would be made that night, they had decided to postpone it, not being quite prepared, but on leaving had forgotten to inform me of the fact; and he confirmed the previous statement of Miss Allen that the female, taking advantage of my expectancy, had produced the disturbance. There were contradictory statements during the night, which gave an air of plausibility to this explanation.

A few days afterward, being in a public library, I examined the "Peerage of Great Britain"—I believe this is the title of the work—to see how certain statements made by the individual calling himself the Count compared with the facts. He had perceived about what age I supposed the Count to have been at the time of his death, and said that I was mistaken on that point; but instead of stating in the usual manner his age, gave the date of his birth and of his death, which would make him, if the Count, to have been a younger man than I supposed. I knew nothing about the age of the Count, but knowing very nearly that of the widow, assumed the husband to have been, as usual, several years older. I found the dates given of birth and death to be correct, and that the Count and his wife were born in the same year. But other statements I found to be incorrect. I had somewhere seen it stated that the Count and his wife were cousins. This the visitor claiming to be the Count denied; affirming that there was no blood-relationship whatever between him and his wife; but the "Peerage" informed me that the Count and wife were first cousins. The visitor claiming to be the Count stated that his wife had, in all, six children, of whom one had died; but the "Peerage" stated the number of children to be more than six, none of whom had died. Of course I concluded the visitor was not the Count, but as he evidently knew something, and more than I had previously known, about him, and also about Englishmen, it seemed to me strange that he should not have informed himself, before undertaking the personation, of facts easily obtained, and as to which I could readily ascertain whether his statements were correct.

Soon after the last visit of this individual, Miss Allen admitted that none of my friends had visited me, and said they did not know where I was. She still asserted, however, that the visitors claiming to be Mr. H. and the Count were those individuals; and that they were endeavoring to carry out a plan which would be for my benefit. The difficulty she now stated to be with my father, who had been informed I was a medium—though not where I was—and who wished himself to be manager. It would be much more for my benefit, she said, to let the Count have the management; and when I asked why my friends were not brought, and I permitted to decide for myself, she replied that it was desired to spare me the pain of deciding against my father, and that an arrangement would soon be effected. As I have stated, strange as it may seem, I never could entirely rid myself of an *impression* that the visitor claiming to be the Count might really be that individual; but if the one claiming to be Mr. H. was not a personator he could easily satisfy me of the fact; and Miss Allen eventually admitted that Mr. H. had never visited me, but continued to assert that the Count had.

Since the night when I was to have been relieved, and was greatly disturbed, the annoyances at night, though not so great as during the one named, were much greater than they had been from the time of the operation called killing Ellen up to that date; and I soon began to feel very much exhausted and worn out from want of sleep. I received twice, at night, electric shocks which, for a moment, almost paralyzed me. I soon began to suspect that Miss Allen was engaged in creating these disturbances, notwithstanding her assertions that they were caused by the opposing female, and that she exerted her power to prevent them.

The assertions now made by Miss Allen to the effect that my friends were unable to find me, were, of course, no evidence that such was the fact, inasmuch as she had previously asserted that they had visited and communicated with me; and, thinking they might be present, I continued to sit occasionally for communications; my principal encouragement for doing so being the anxiety of Miss Allen to prevent the practice.

One Sunday morning in May (1865), Miss Allen said the Count was coming to see me at three o'clock in the afternoon; that she would have Mr. B. brought with him, and I might test the identity of the latter in any way I pleased; her idea appearing to be that if I could be fully satisfied Mr. B. was connected with the party, I would wait for their scheme to be perfected, and cease sitting for communications from my relatives. The test of identity formerly given by one claiming to be Mr. B was still a mystery to me, and I now determined to ask questions, the correct answers to which I had never known. As I wished to ask only questions the correct answers to which I could readily obtain, it was necessary that I should think beforehand what they should be; and I wrote out a few, the correct answers to which I could obtain with little inconvenience.

But before the hour named had arrived, Miss Allen informed me that Mr. B. could not be present; she said he thought that he had sufficiently identified himself already, and that it would be inconvenient for him to come that day. The Count came, as represented, and with him Mr. W., the late banker, about whom, it will be recollected, I had inquired at Trenton of the visitor claiming to be Mr. H. As I had not since inquired or thought about him, and he was never an intimate acquaintance, I could not understand why Mr. W. should be brought; and no particular reason for bringing him was given. In fact, neither Mr. W. or the Count appeared to have any definite object in this visit, and very little was written by either. The one claiming to be the Count said that, as I doubted his identity, he would, if I wished it, give me the name of the father of the illegitimate children of his wife; but added that he disliked doing so, as the father was a relative of his wife, and it was, therefore, a painful subject. Giving me the name, or title, of some one who might be such a father, would indicate nothing more than that this visitor had lived in England, or had some means of acquiring information about Englishmen, as to which I was satisfied already; I therefore replied that I did not care about the name being given.

When the Count had finished, I was told that Mr. B. had come, and that I might test the identity. Mr. B. had retired from business some time previous to his death, and the first two questions on my list were, as to the number of his late place of business, and the name of his successor. It appeared to be so very difficult for him to write that, when I had obtained answers to these two questions, I concluded not to ask the others. The store was in Broadway, about one mile from my hotel; and although I did not know the number, I knew the locality. On going to the office of the hotel and examining the City Directory, I found that the number given was in the square next south of that in which Mr. B.'s store was situated, and that there was no such name as the one given at either locality.

Some time previous to this I had discovered that these invisible beings were able to exert a powerful influence upon my mind; and in the evening of the same day, I felt that, although nothing was spoken, this power was being exercised to make me believe there was, after all, something in this pretended scheme. Presuming this attempt to be by Miss Allen, I told her it was useless, when the influence instantly ceased. This will, doubtless, appear very strange; but such were my sensations, namely, that a foreign influence was being exerted to induce belief in something which my judgment decided must be false.

Miss Allen then made a lengthy statement, purporting to be a confession, the substance of which was, that her real name was Annie Morford; that she had been

acquainted with Mr. and Mrs. A. at Auburn, N. Y,
and had visited me for the purpose of communicating
with them, but had been drawn into the personations
and deceptions by Mrs. Arnold; that Mr. W., the
banker, hearing of me, had, with his friend the other
banker, whose daughter was to have accompanied Miss
B. to England, invented a scheme which she stated, but
which is too lengthy, as well as silly, to be here given.
In attempting to carry out this scheme, she said, Mr.
W. and the other banker had personated Mr. H. and
the Count, neither of the two latter individuals having
ever visited me. The failure of the scheme was owing to
their inability to effect an arrangement with the Count,
who had finally decided not to enter into it. Nothing
was said as to how she had rid herself and me of Ellen,
and it did not occur to me to inquire. She concluded
by promising to bring my father next morning at nine
o'clock.

In the morning as soon as I awoke, my mind reverted
to the matter of the communication made the preceding evening, and I was not fully convinced that the
Count had never visited me; perhaps it would be more
correct to say that the *impression* that he had visited
me was very strong. Miss Allen—by which name I
will continue to designate this female always with me
—then said that her statement of the preceding evening was false; and again asserted that the Count was
endeavoring to carry out a plan which would be for my
benefit. She requested that I would allow them three
days more in which to complete the arrangements; that
is, that I would refrain for three days from sitting for
communications. As my sittings had resulted in noth-

ing, and were very tedious, I readily granted this request, on the promise being given that at the expiration of the time my friends should be brought. The mode of communication this morning was by speaking; but generally, at this time, and always when the communications were lengthy, it was by writing.

When passing down Broadway the day on which the above occurred, I looked for the number which had been given as that of Mr. B.'s store, and found that there was no such name as the one given at this number; neither were the goods here dealt in the same as those dealt in by Mr. B. But I noticed over the entrance of an adjoining store a name resembling, though not the same as that given me; and the goods here dealt in were also dealt in by Mr. B., but the latter dealt in two kinds of goods, this store in only one.

And being in the public library a day or two afterward, I had sufficient curiosity again to examine the "Peerage" to ascertain what male relatives the wife of the Count had. I found that she had another first-cousin, of about her own age, residing in England, who, upon the unreasonable assumption that the story given me was true, must be the relative referred to as the father of the illegitimate children.

On the evening of the succeeding Sunday, as my friends had not been brought, 1 determined to see if I could not learn something from the female opposing Miss Allen. I had nothing definite as to her appearance or idiosyncrasies upon which to fix my mind so as to aid her in writing against the opposition of Miss Allen; but finally received the impression that she was a girl of fifteen or sixteen years of age. I learned nothing, however, from her. Some time previous to this, I had inquired why this female, who appeared to be opposed to the party with which Miss Allen was connected, did not bring my friends, and thus defeat their scheme: and the reply was to the effect that she was not permitted to leave, being held a prisoner. On now asking her if this was true, she replied that it was; and affirmed that if I would continue the writing, thinking of her, she would soon be able to release herself, and would then bring my friends. Of course I could see no sense in the idea that writing would release her, or that, if a prisoner, she would be kept so near me as to enable her to interfere with Miss Allen and her friends. I therefore rose from the table as much in the dark as to what the plot could be, if there was any, as before. When I sat down for the purpose of getting information from this female, I began to feel an undefinable dread, or *horror*. It was not precisely fear, for I would have continued to sit if there had been any prospect of learning anything; but appeared to be an impression which my will was unable to overcome. I supposed this feeling was produced by Miss Allen, and she admitted such was the fact. I did not get entirely over it until I had gone to bed and fallen asleep.

As sitting for communications from my friends had produced no result, I did not feel sure that the statements that they were unable to find me might not be correct. Whether there was so wide a difference between myself and other mediums as Miss Allen and her associates asserted, or not, I did not know; but I did know that one portion of their statements on this point must be true, namely, that only the lowest and most stupid class of their world could communicate through other mediums. I presumed that I must have been seen by many of this class, as was stated, but had no reason for supposing that any of these would bring my friends. It occurred to me that some of the better class, although unable to communicate, might occasionally visit the most celebrated public mediums, owing to the interest they would naturally feel, knowing that their friends of this world visited them. I thought, therefore, that I might, by visiting these mediums myself, through these casual visitors of the other world, make my situation known to my friends there, in case they had not found me. Whether, if they came, they would be able to remove the individuals with me, or to communicate at all, I, of course, had no means of determining ; but I decided to make the experiment. About the first of June, however, I left for Trenton without having put this plan in execution.

At Trenton I wrote a condensed narrative of the communications received from these invisible visitors from the time I commenced sitting for the purpose in the autumn of 1863. This narrative has been continued up to the present time, and from it the one here given to the public is prepared. My purpose in writing it up to the date above given (the summer of 1865) was, to compare the communications, and endeavor to satisfy myself whether the strange visitors had any scheme in view, and if so, what it was. But on reviewing the narrative, I was unable to arrive at any satisfactory conclusion. I could not feel at all certain as to how many persons had communicated with me. That

Ellen and Miss Allen were distinct females I had no
doubt; but as to whether Miss Allen and Mrs. Arnold
were not *aliases* for the same individual, I was not satisfied. Thaᴛ aᴛ least two male persons had communicated with me I was also certain, but not as to whether
more than two had. Then the next question was,
Were any of these parties acquaintances of mine? I
saw no reason for supposing that any female of my acquaintance had communicated with me; but from the
way in which Mr. W.'s name had recently been used,
in connection with what I recollected of past conversa-
tions, I now strongly suspected that he was one of my
visitors. At the sitting in Trenton when the visitor
pretending to be Mr. H. called Mr. K., the late stock-
broker, a "rascal" and "poor miserable creature,"
something was said about an Ohio railroad with which
I had been connected, and in the stock of which Mr.
K.'s firm had dealt more largely than other brokers.
Mr. H., or the one personating him, evinced a knowledge of the affairs of this railroad which I could not
understand; and I asked him how he happened to know
so much about that railroad. The only reply he made
was, "Oh, I knew a good deal about it." If Mr. W.
was the personator, the matter was clear, for his house
was the financial agent of the company. A short time
either before or after—I do not recollect which—the
visit of Mr. W., as represented, with the Count, I was
asked if I would assist in making a medium of Miss
B.; she to be under the charge of her father, another
and more intimate acquaintance of mine, and Mr. W.
I could understand why the first two names should be
given, but not why Mr. W.'s was; and this incident

now confirmed my suspicions. But, on the other hand, it was difficult for me to believe that Mr. W. had fallen so low as to be a lying personator of other individuals, attempting to deceive a person in my situation.

Then as to the visitor calling himself the Count: The reader will not understand, from what I have written, why I should have hesitated in deciding that this visitor could not be the Count. But there were several reasons for hesitation in coming to such a conclusion. I knew from the language that this visitor had never before communicated with me ; and, in short, the language, or style, as well as the substance of a portion of what was written, indicated that the visitor might be the Count. I thought, also, that he manifested a little shame in telling his story. Of course I have given but a small portion of what was written during nearly, or quite, four hours. In these remarks I refer only to the first two visits ; nothing was subsequently said, or written, tending to produce conviction that it was by the Count. But at these two sittings I had an impression, such as I never had before, that the writer was the individual he claimed to be, and not a personator. On the other hand again, if any reliance whatever is to be placed in obituary notices, and newspaper articles relative to a deceased person, the Count is, in England, thought to have been a man of prudence, honesty, and sense ; this visitor is a lying fool, one who does not even know how to lie to advantage.

It appeared to me, on reviewing the narrative, that there must have been some scheme in view from the time Mr. H. was personated ; and I also concluded that this attempt at personation was the first communication

I had received from any male visitor. Up to that time, the females wished to be writing or talking almost constantly; after that date, or at least after my return to New York, neither Miss Allen or her associates wished often to say anything, and all they did say had reference to some scheme. I concluded, however, that the scheme, whatever it might be, must be an impracticable one: and the important question with me was as to how much more time must elapse before it would be abandoned. Of late, the only suggestions made were that I should aid in developing another medium; and it did not appear to be expected that I would do this until "relieved" and visited by my friends. The persecutions at night had nearly ceased prior to this time; but the constant presence of these two females was, in itself, an annoyance; and, besides, I wished to learn something about the other world, which I had not as yet succeeded in doing.

I returned to New York in October, determined to carry out the plan, formed before leaving, of visiting other mediums. Not knowing who were at this time the most noted ones, I had an interview with one of the most prominent Spiritualists in New York, a lawyer, to ascertain, and told him something of my experience. On mentioning the personation of Mr. A., the lawyer admitted that the "spirits" did sometimes lie; but said the fact that Mr. A. was still living in our world did not prove that he was personated at Trenton by some other spirit, for it might have been his own spirit that visited me there. This gentleman held the theory, common, I believe, with Spiritualists, that the "spiritual body" of a man may leave the "physical body," go to any distance, and return at will. As this gentleman was, at the time, residing out of the city, and apparently not very well informed about the public mediums, I called on another prominent Spiritualist, a physician. The physician agreed with the lawyer that the spiritual body of Mr. A. might have visited me at Trenton : but he did not agree with him that the spirits sometimes lie. "In an experience of thirteen years," he said, "I have never known an instance of the kind;" and he requested that I would not accuse them of lying. This nonsense, coming from Spiritualists, did not at all surprise me, and I visited the gentlemen only for the purpose of inquiring about mediums, not with the expectation of learning anything in explanation of my own experience.

I visited several mediums, but learning nothing through them—as, in fact, I expected would be the case—and nothing new occurring from the visits, I concluded the only judicious course for me to take would be to endeavor to divert my mind as much as possible from the subject. I had relinquished all hope of learning anything from Miss Allen or her associates, and had ceased making inquiry of them. At this time I seldom experienced any annoyance, either in the daytime or at night, and in a short time was able to forget, except at brief intervals, that invisible beings were with me.

But on the night of November 23d, as soon as I went to bed, I experienced a new and violent attack, differing from anything before felt. The sensation was as though a powerful electric current was passing through my head, producing twitchings of the muscles of the face, and even the brain seemed to be actually in motion.

This continued during the whole night, in consequence of which I did not sleep for a moment.

The operation thus affecting my brain was continued every night for a long time; gradually, however, becoming less violent. For more than a week, I was able to sleep only about every alternate night, and even then far from soundly. I inquired of Miss Allen the cause of this, though without much expectation of learning the truth. She said that she had left me for a short time, and thus the opposing female had obtained power to produce the strange effect. This reply, I felt, threw no light upon the subject; but a remark which she made some time afterward did, as I thought. One night, when I was feeling very much exhausted and manifested the same, she said, " Then tell your friends to let you alone ; " from which I inferred that my friends were present, and that some kind of a contest was going on between them and Miss Allen.

About the middle of January (1866), as the contest appeared to be still going on—though I was much less disturbed—I prepared a series of questions which I thought it would be impossible to answer without giving me some information, or some clue by means of which I might arrive at a definite conclusion upon this subject, and visited a noted medium named Mansfield. But stupidity beat me; the questions, without having come to the knowledge of the medium, were all replied to without giving any information whatever. The following, given in reply to the question as to why Miss Allen and the other female remained with me contrary to my wishes, is a sample of the answers :

" Because they find in your magnetism something

that attracts them; you do not desire them to come to you, and yet they do; alike attracts alike, be it in that or in this world. You desire not their counsels, and consider them fantastic spirits; they feel indignant."

This is also a fair sample of the communications received by myself and others during my first investigations. And it was partly owing to the fact that all who had communicated directly with me, excepting Ellen, had conversed more rationally, or, at least, more like the men and women of our world, that I was inclined to believe the assertion that my condition differed from that of other mediums, and that, in consequence, Miss Allen and her associates might have some scheme in view.

About two weeks later, I again attempted to learn something from the female opposing Miss Allen. Believing one or more of my relatives to be present, I asked the girl why they could not communicate with me. Her reply, written with much difficulty, was, "Because they are so much better than you." This was, to a certain extent, in accordance with the repeated assertions of Miss Allen and her associates, namely, that only a certain class of their world could communicate through *other* mediums; but if my friends could not communicate with me, it was impossible to imagine what the plot could be. I afterward endeavored to learn something more definite from this girl, but became convinced that if the writing was executed by her she was as great a liar as Miss Allen. I also, at various times, attempted to get communications from my friends, fixing my mind sometimes on one, sometimes on another. Communications were written purporting to be by my

friends, generally by my father, advising me, as formerly, to wait patiently; but I concluded they were
written by Miss Allen.

On Sunday, May 6, (1866), I again made the attempt
to get a communication from a relative. As I had tried
only once or twice *thinking* of my mother, I decided·
this time to fix my mind on her. It was with the utmost difficulty that anything was written; but I finally
became fully satisfied that my mother was present, and
that the incidents given to satisfy me on this point came
from her; for I had, by this time, so much experience
with these invisible persons that I knew what could be
obtained by them from my mind and other sources,
and what could not.

I now devoted a portion of nearly every day to sitting
for writing by my mother—fixing my mind on her—
presuming from my past experience, and being also informed, that this would increase her power. After
sitting a few times, I determined to endeavor to get from
her an explanation of my extraordinary experience; as
she might as well, for the purpose of increasing her
power, write about this as anything else. I was told
that Mary M., whose name was once given me at Long
Branch, was one of the females with me, and would
assist my mother in writing, but that I must fix my
mind on the latter. This Miss M. died at Cleveland,
aged about seventeen years, and when I was about ten
years of age. Her father was one of the wealthiest men
in the place, and Cleveland was then so small a village
that, young as I was, I must, probably, have seen every
resident; but all that I can now recall to recollection in
reference to Miss M. is the fact of being one day told

that she was dead. With other members of the family I became well acquainted.

The undertaking proved to be an excessively difficult and tedious one, and when at last the narrative was completed, I found it to be incoherent in some points, and improbable in others. Suspecting that Miss M. had been treacherous, I endeavored to get corrections of these points, but found that my mother was unable to write them. Then, fixing my mind intently on her, I endeavored to get an *impression* as to the fact in each case, and, when I thought I had received this, would get by a movement of my hand a simple affirmative or negative as to whether my impression was correct. In this way I succeeded in getting an explanation which was coherent and plausible, and which, as I am now informed, was substantially correct, though there were some unimportant errors. I next attempted to get explanations of the several phenomena, such as rapping, table-tipping, etc., and in this Miss M. again assisted.

It was not, at first, my intention to publish anything upon the subject; but understanding that my friends in the other world desired I should publish the facts I had learned, which, to a certain extent, showed the evils of so-called Spiritualism—though not the full extent of these evils—and finding that the power of my mother to write did not increase, I decided to prepare, to the best of my ability under the circumstances, a work for publication. The manuscript was finished and delivered to the publishers in March, 1867.

CHAPTER II.

IN order that what follows may be understood, it is necessary here to state a portion of the information received when preparing the former work. I have given in the preceding narrative only such names as were frequently used, and but a small portion of the communications received. I can now recollect the names of more than thirty individuals who, as represented, visited me once or twice.

In the explanations received, I was informed that, until my mother succeeded in writing, only seven individuals had directly communicated with me. These were, the female called Ellen, whose surname was McCauley; another female of whom I never before heard; Miss Mary M.; Mr. K., the late stock-broker; Mr. W., the late banker; and the two individuals designated as Mr. B. and the Count. The three females, as I was informed, had been with me from about the commencement of my experience as a medium; the power of Miss McCauley had been partially overcome by the other two females, but she had never been removed; and the idea I received was that those of the other-world had no power to move each other against the will.

The statement given me in reference to the Count, and which I am now informed was correct, was as follows: Shortly after his marriage, when riding on horseback, he received the injury alluded to, which his surgeons pronounced incurable. The rank of his wife, being much higher than his own, gave him, as her husband, a position which he would not otherwise have had. I state this simply as a fact, without asserting that the Count was influenced by it, which he denies: the reader can draw his own conclusion. At any rate, it was his suggestion that the wife should select some one for, what I will call, her husband; the legal connection between her and the Count to continue, and the matter to be kept a secret if possible. The surgeons, on being spoken to, said that professional etiquette required' them to keep such things secret if the patient so desired; but the English cousin of the wife—the one who I ascertained on examining the "Peerage" must be the father of the illegitimate children, if the story was true—would be the heir in case she died without leaving issue; and the surgeons demurred at conniving at what might be a fraud upon him. It was finally agreed, and arranged, that this cousin should be the husband; and he was to remain (legally) unmarried. The result of this arrangement is, that the first child, a daughter, is legitimate, and all the other children are illegitimate. The second child is a son, and is, of course, acknowledged the heir.

The story as now given, although rather "tough," seems more probable than the version given me by the Count; and reflects less dishonor both on himself and wife. I will state the few facts I have learned tending to corroborate the story. From a book published in London, according to my recollection in the year 1867, I learned that the Count met with an accident when riding on horseback about two months after his marriage. From the "Peerage" I learned that the English cousin would be the heir under the circumstances stated; and this work gave no account of the marriage of the cousin. From other sources, however, I have learned that he is married, but there is something unusual about the marriage. In one work I have seen it stated that the marriage is a *morganatic* one; in another, that there is a difficulty in the matter owing to the opposition to it of the Count's wife.

On the completion of the former work, I was directed to cease sitting for writing, but to think, as constantly as convenient, of my sister as present with me. In about two weeks from the time I commenced doing so, this sister became able to talk with me; but it appeared to be a matter of great difficulty; she pronounced each word, apparently, with as much force as possible, pausing between each, as one does when speaking to a person partially deaf, or at a distance. I supposed, and she appeared to think, that her power to converse orally with me would rapidly increase, as had that of the other females; but in this I was destined to be disappointed.

When I commenced the former manuscript the annoyances at night again commenced; and when my sister attempted to acquire and increase the power of oral conversation, the annoyances greatly increased. It was, however, represented to me that my sister, with the aid of my mother and Miss M., hoped soon to overcome the power of the other two females, so that they would be unable to annoy me; though I am not certain that I inquired, or was told, whether both of the other females, or only one, was engaged in causing these annoyances. At this time, these females appeared to be unable to talk much; but they, or one of them, had the power of operating on my muscles so as to cause involuntary movements, or twitchings—not of the whole limb, but solely of the muscles—which prevented me from sleeping soundly. One great annoyance at night was this operation upon my eyelids; and I was for a long time, on going to bed, obliged to place my hand over my eyes and hold it there until I fell asleep. My hope of being soon relieved from these persecutions was also destined to terrible disappointment.

After *thinking* a long time of this sister, I was directed to think of another sister, then of my mother, and again of the first sister. All seemed to be of no avail; after the first few months the power of my relatives did not appear to increase. One great difficulty was that, from some cause which I could not understand, when they attempted to increase their power the annoyances increased; while when they made no efforts of the kind, I was not disturbed at night.

Without detaining the reader with repetitions of the same occurences and disappointments, I will pass on to the spring of 1869. Then I was informed that, although one of the three females with me was Miss M., as had been stated, one of them, and the one who had at times assisted my mother and sisters, was Mrs. S., a cousin of mine. This cousin, a daughter of my father's sister, visited Cleveland once when I was seven or eight years

of age, and again ten or eleven years later; except at
these two visits, I never saw her. I had not heard of
her death, or, in fact, heard anything about her for
many years; but she states that her death occurred in
the year 1843.

As I now understood the matter, the three females
were, Miss McCauley, Miss M., and Mrs. S.; and the
first was the principal, if not the sole persecutor. And I
inferred from what was said, though it was not distinctly
stated, that the difficulty and disappointment my mother
and sisters had experienced were owing to the course
taken by Mrs. S., who would sometimes aid them, and
at other times refuse to do so; and I also understood
that it would be very difficult, if not impossible, for them
to succeed without her assistance. A proposition was
now made by Mrs. S. that I should agree to aid in developing another medium with whom she could communicate and be connected, as soon as I was relieved
from the power of the other two females. On my
agreeing to this, she would, as she stated, give her
assistance to my mother and sisters. Of course I now
knew, not only from this proposition, but also from the
fact that she was one of the three females with me from
the commencement, that Mrs. S. was literally a devil;
and I could not conscientiously enter into an agreement to aid in placing another individual in her power.
This proposition was made by writing, for it seemed at
this time difficult for either of them to talk.

About the first of May I was again requested to sit
for writing. The Count, from whom I had not heard
for a long time, now came again—at least he said he
had been absent—and I was told that he would write,

but that I must fix my mind on my mother, as heretofore. The Count now renewed the proposal that I
should go to England; but he soon commenced telling
such absurd and egregious lies as to what great things
he would do for me there, that I refused to let him
write longer, insisting that my mother should write.
He stated that if I would go to England, and agree to
the plan he proposed, Mrs. S. would assist my friends,
and I would be "relieved" of the three females. Mrs.
S. had previously made a similar statement, but she insisted that I should enter into a positive agreement to
aid in developing another medium when "relieved."
If there was any practicable plan by which I could be
"relieved," I wished to be informed of it; but was unwilling to hold my hand for the Count to write nonsense. My mother then attempted to write, but found
it so difficult that I again permitted the Count, on condition that he would confine himself to the subject of
relieving me.

The sittings upon this subject continued for nearly
two weeks; finally the following agreement was entered
into: I was to go to England, place the Count and
others in communication with certain individuals there,
and thus aid in rectifying as far as possible, and as
peaceably as possible, the wrong which had been committed. I use the phrase "as far as possible," because
it is one of those frauds which cannot be entirely rectified. The eldest son is married, himself and wife believing he is the legal heir. Several of the illegitimate
daughters are also married; but so far as they are concerned the parentage is of less importance.

While performing the above, Mrs. S. was to aid in

"relieving" me; and when this was accomplished, so that my friends and acquaintances in the other world, upon whose advice I could place reliance, would be able to converse freely with me, it was to be left to my own decision whether I would aid in developing another medium. It was represented that the medium would be a female, and that although Mrs. S. was to be in some way connected, she would not have the same power as with me; a male relative of the medium being the one to be placed intimately *en rapport*. About all these matters, however, I was to be definitely informed when "relieved."

Inasmuch as the medium was not to be developed until after I had been relieved, the reader will not understand why the latter might not as well have been performed in New York as in England. I cannot state the reasons advanced why I should at once go to England; some of which I still consider valid, others I do not. It is sufficient to say that I am now informed if the plan had been carried out Mrs. S. would have lent her assistance, and I should in a short time have been "relieved." I was under great depression in consequence of my situation, and would have been willing to go round the world if there had been a reasonable probability of being "relieved" by so doing. As to whether I would be relieved by going to England, I was, in a great measure, obliged to rely upon the judgment of my friends in the other world. I should not have placed much reliance upon the judgment of my mother or sister (the only friends who could communicate directly with me) in such a matter, any more than if they had been in our world; but I understood they had male advisers, who coincided with them in the opinion that I had better go. Moreover, I wished to visit Europe, which I had never seen, and thought it would be less convenient to go for several years to come than it then was; still my depression was so great that I should not have thought of taking a pleasure trip if I had not hoped to be " relieved " in England.

I sailed for England on the 26th of May, and two or three days after my arrival in London went to my room for the purpose of having a letter written ; the understanding having been that on my arrival the Count was to write a letter to the widow, identifying himself and requesting for me an interview. When I sat down at the table I experienced, though in a less degree, the dread, or horror, once before felt and described ; and it appeared to be unusually difficult for any one to write. I persevered, however, until a few lines were written, when I perceived the writing was not by the Count, but by Mrs. S. Then I at once suspected that so far as being " relieved " was concerned, I had made the trip in vain. However, as it was stated that in a day or two the letter would be written, at the expiration of the latter period I again went to my room for the purpose. This time I was informed that the mother-in-law of the Count would first write a letter. Writing was again difficult, and I again soon perceived from the style that the writer was Mrs. S., when I stopped. The Count then *spoke* nearly as follows : " So long as this opposition continues the letter will not be written ; when it is written it will be dictated orally; for the present you may consider the expedition a failure." I inquired the cause of the opposition, and why the expedition was a

failure, but he would give no explanation, merely repeating, "For the present you may consider the expedition a failure." My own conclusion was that Mrs. S.
was the cause of the difficulty, and that the others did
not like to acknowledge they had been deceived by
her; and yet, as she appeared desirous of having the
letter written, I could not understand what the nature
of her deception was. I left for Paris without again
sitting for a letter to be written.

A day or two before leaving Paris, I was sitting in
my room, thinking whether I should return home by
way of England, or not—a point I wished then, for a
certain reason, to decide—when Mrs. S. commenced
talking. She said that the letter would be written during my journey at some point where it would be convenient for me to sit for the purpose. It was as convenient for me to sit then as it would be at any future
time, but she said there was a dispute between the
Count and my friends which would soon be settled.
In the following night, my mother, after great efforts,
succeeded in giving me, partly by words and partly by
impression, a brief communication, the purport of
which was, that I must constantly bear in mind how
very difficult it was for her to communicate; that I
must not send the letter even if the Count was willing
to dictate one, or, in short, take any important step in
the matter without first ascertaining that my friends ap-
proved of it, and the manner of ascertaining this would
be by having her identify herself. This brief communication, much briefer than what I have written, cost
me nearly half the night's sleep; it was some time after
she commenced the effort before she could speak dis-

tinctly, and the effort so affected my nervous system that I did not fall asleep until long after the communication was ended. I inferred from this that the difficulty in London had not been entirely, if at all, with Mrs. S.; but that the Count had in some way been treacherous.

In October of the same year I was again in London, and, finding the letter would not be written, at once engaged my passage home. Knowing that it would be difficult for my mother or sister to inform me, against the will of Mrs. S., I had not attempted to get an explanation of the difficulty; but after I had engaged my passage home I thought there could no longer be any motive for concealment, and therefore made the inquiry. The reply, purporting to be by my sister, was to the effect that the Count, after I had sailed from New York, renewed the proposition that I should remain permanently in England, and refused to carry out his part of the plan unless it was agreed to. This did not make the matter very clear, inasmuch as I was the party that must enter into such an agreement, if it was to be binding; and besides, it did not explain why my mother, at Paris, made so great an effort to caution me against sending the letter in case the Count was willing to dictate one. However, I concluded the Count had made some unreasonable demand, and inquired no further. This communication was oral; and as soon as my sister ceased speaking, the Count said that his story about the illegitimacy of the children of his wife was a fiction. This was instantly contradicted by my sister, who said I had received a correct statement of the matter; and the Count did not repeat his assertion.

For some time after my return to New York nothing more was said about "relieving" me; and I had
arrived at the conclusion that I must abandon all hope
of its accomplishment. During the journey, and since
my return, I had suffered so little annoyance that, but
for past experience and the fact that at rare intervals a
few words were spoken, I should not have been aware
that invisible beings were with me. But I had never
been able to understand, or to get an explanation of,
what I understood to be the physical inability of my
friends to remove these females. I had understood that
all my friends were aiming at was to overcome their
power, so that if they remained they would be unable
to annoy me, or to interfere with communications from
others; and that there was no power to remove them
bodily. I supposed, at first, that such must be the fact;
but it was a fact, if such, which I could not reconcile
with others given me when writing the former work;
and the more I thought upon the subject, the more
irreconcilable the statements appeared to be. I had
repeatedly requested a definite explanation, but it had
always been postponed, and I began to suspect that
there was something connected with this matter which
my friends did not like to inform me of.

About two months after my return, as I was sitting
one day thinking about this matter, my sister, as I understood it to be, commenced speaking. She said there
was no difficulty in removing the females other than
the effect it would have upon me; and added that they
were prevented from leaving, as the effect of their leaving voluntarily was feared. Some time after this I was

informed that my friends were preparing to effect their removal.

On the night of January 26 (1870), when I went to bed, I was directed to fix my mind on my sister, as Miss McCauley and Miss M. were then to be removed. Mrs. S., as I understood, was expected to aid my friends. I experienced no unusual sensation for fifteen or twenty minutes, then I began to feel very faint. This faintness soon passed away, when I was informed that the operation had been postponed. In the morning I was told that it was thought the operation might have been safely completed, and that it would soon be performed. On the second night following, I was again told to fix my mind on my sister, and the removal would then be made. This time there occurred violent palpitation of the heart, at least I know not what else to call it, but my whole breast heaved with *terrible* violence and rapidity. Some one said, " You are going, sir," and, for a few moments, I thought I was dying. When I had partially recovered, I was informed that the two females had been removed. But during the succeeding day I perceived that there was some one still with me acting in opposition to my friends. This, I was told, was Mrs. S. ; and it was stated that she had agreed to leave after the other two females had been removed, but now refused to do so, and that her removal must be effected by force, as had been that of the other two. On going to bed the following night, I was directed to fix my mind on my sister when I awoke in the morning, as Mrs. S. was then to be removed. Her removal, I was informed, would affect only my head, not the action of my heart as that of the two others had. In the morning I fixed my mind on my sister, as directed, but experienced no unusual sensation, either in my head or any other part of my system. In a short time I was told that Mrs. S. was removed; but while dressing she commenced talking; at least the talking purported to be by her, and I knew that if not by her, it must be by one of the other two said to have been removed. It was then admitted that neither of the three had been removed; and from a remark made by the Count I inferred that he had done the lying; though why he was now staying with me I could not imagine.

No further attempts to relieve me being made, on the 30th of March I sat down to learn, if possible, the truth about my situation. I told my friends that I wished to know whether they did, or did not, feel sure that they could ever remove the females; and if they felt certain it could be done, then I wished to know within what time it could be accomplished. The reply was that they felt confident it could be done within a year from that date. To make it certain that this came from my friends, and not from Mrs. S., I requested my mother to identify herself in certification; this being done, I felt that the only course for me to take was to be patient, and assist my friends as much as possible by the exercise of my thinking faculty as directed.

I perceived no particular effect from the efforts of my friends until about six months after the above date; then, although not sick, I became very weak. After this latter date, I was repeatedly told that I would be relieved before the close of the year 1870; but believing these assertions to be made by Mrs. S. I did not place much reliance upon them. The course now taken by Mrs. S. was to me a constant mystery. She, as I understood my friends, was to be removed, as well as the other two; but she constantly talked as though she was assisting my friends against the others. In talking, she always endeavored to give me the impression that my sister was speaking; but the mystery was that her constant admonitions about *thinking* were, so far as I could judge, correct; and the impression she gave that it was my sister who was speaking increased, as I understood, the power of the latter. The only objection I made to her admonitions was that they were so frequent as to be annoying. She constantly warned me not to think of past occurrences connected with this matter, and, especially, not to think of myself, or exercise self-consciousness. "Don't think of that," and, "Don't think of yourself," were so frequently repeated as to become wearisome.

On the afternoon of the 31st of December (1870) my sister informed me that Miss McCauley and Miss M. were to be removed during the following night; and she said that if I felt very weak after rising in the morning, I must lie down again; the principal object of the communication was, however, to advise me that she should not again speak to me until some time after the operation had been performed; and she told me to recollect if there should be any talking during the night, it would not be by her.

Nothing unusual occurred during the night, and at the moment of waking in the morning my sister informed me, in three or four words, that the removal had not been made. Later in the day Mrs. S., personating my sister, attempted to make me believe that the

removal had been made, and that the one then acting
in opposition to my mother and sister, and interfering
with their communications, was herself. This attempt
failing, the Count said my friends ought to inform me
that the removal was an impossibility. Afterward,
when I attempted to learn the cause of the non-re-
moval, I was told that the difficulty was with the
Count; that at the last moment he had made a demand
which could not be granted, and he, therefore, had refused to assist. This purported to be spoken by my
mother; and I inquired if, when told that I would be
"relieved" within a year, she had relied upon the assistance of the lying Count. She replied, "I don't wish
to talk more than is necessary, but we did rely upon
his assistance." As it appeared to be difficult for her
to talk, I made no further inquiry. On thinking of
the matter afterward, however, I became convinced
that it made little difference whether the Count assisted
or not, as he could not have much power in the matter; and that the above must have been spoken by
Mrs. S., who was the real cause of the failure. What
she was aiming at I could not imagine; but it was evident that if this was the fact my friends must have relied upon her assistance; and, therefore, after this date
my hope of being "relieved" was not very strong.
The reader will understand that, from first to last, I
knew it was almost impossible for either my mother or
sister to communicate with me when Mrs. S. opposed.

I was told subsequently that my friends still hoped
to "relieve" me within the period first named; but
whether the statement was made by my mother or sister, or by Mrs. S., I made no attempt to ascertain. It

was now stated that there was only one, namely, Miss McCauley, the effect of whose removal was feared. As I had been informed that Mrs. S. and Miss M. had overcome her power at Trenton, I could not understand this.

The year within which I was to have been " relieved " passed away without any renewal of the attempt. After the expiration of that period the persecutions increased so much that one night—about the middle of May, 1871—after several nearly sleepless ones, I felt that I could not stand it much longer, when my mother said, "Bear it one month longer, and then, if we are unable to relieve you, we will stop the persecutions." When the month had expired, or about the middle of June, the persecutions nearly ceased, and I was not " relieved." I was then told that an attempt would be made to place the mother-in-law of the Count intimately *en rapport* with me. I understood there was a plan connected with this movement which would be explained when this measure had been accomplished. About the middle of July I learned that this plan was a failure, and that my friends saw no other course than the one they had been pursuing by which to " relieve " me. The disturbances at night were then renewed, though I rested a little better than formerly.

I was repeatedly told by Mrs. S. that I would certainly be " relieved " before the close of that year (1871) ; and one night near the close of December, my mother, as I felt confident it was, confirmed this statement. I understood they had, as before, decided upon the last night of the year as the time for performing the operation. I went to bed that night expecting, or at least

hoping, the removal would be made; but nothing unusual occurred, and at the moment of awaking in the
morning my mother said the removal could not be performed. I had requested that the removal should be
made this night, or that all efforts for the purpose should
then cease; and I supposed, when told the above,
that the latter course had been decided on. But I
knew, from past experience, that if my mother and
sister abandoned the idea of removing the females the
disturbances at night would cease. These did not
cease, and I soon learned that the idea of removal
had not been abandoned. I also learned that the difficulty was, as I had suspected, with Mrs. S.—though
her course was still to me an impenetrable mystery—
and that the next move would be her removal.

Nothing unusual occurred until the night of the 14th
of January (1872), when I was awakened by a peculiar,
sharp, and piercing pain in the head. The sensation
was as though a dagger had been driven into my brain.
This was momentary, but it was succeeded by a dull
pain lasting until the night of the 18th of the same
month. On the latter night, soon after going to bed, I
was attacked by a *terrible*, and almost unendurable pain
in the head, which continued, without the slightest
abatement, until daylight; then there was a little miti-
gation of the pain, and I slept for about half-an-hour.
A dull pain succeeded this, which continued until the
night of the 24th of the same month, when the occurrence of the night of the 18th was repeated, except that
the pain this time was not *quite* so severe. As before,
the terrible pain came on soon after I went to bed, in
consequence of which I slept none until daylight, when

I again slept for about half-an-hour. This attack was also succeeded by pain of less intensity, which continued for several days, gradually passing away. I understood that this pain was caused by efforts to remove Mrs. S. ; but, knowing that at such times my mother and sister were unable to converse, I asked no questions. When the pain had left me, I learned that this attempt was also a failure.

In the year 1868, I was told that as I thought of writing a new work, I might commence it, and that by the time it was so far completed as to require the additional matter my friends in the other world were to furnish, they would be able to give it. I therefore prepared the manuscript as far as possible; but when I attempted to get this additional matter, I found that, for some reason, it could not, or would not, be given. Then came the proposition to go to England, and I took the unfinished manuscript with me, expecting to complete and publish it in London.

When I learned that Mrs. S. could not be removed, I abandoned all hope of being " relieved ; " and then made another attempt to get the matter required for completing the work. I found that my sister was willing to make the attempt to furnish it ; and, although the undertaking has been attended with great difficulty, I persevered until I have, as I believe, obtained it so far as is absolutely essential.

When, in 1868, I commenced this work, I was told that new theories of Light, Sound, etc., would be given me. I inferred that these theories must have a very important bearing upon my subject; and therefore wrote brief criticisms upon the popular theories of these phenomena. On receiving the new theories, they do not appear to me of quite so much importance, in reference to my subject, as I had supposed would be the case. Still, they have a bearing; and, as I have received them, I give them for consideration, with the criticisms upon other theories which I had previously written. One reason for giving these theories here is, that they are positively the only evidence I have received, or am able to offer the reader, that there are in the other world any who in ours would be considered intellectual and intelligent men.

CHAPTER III.

ONE of the delusions of Spiritualists is the belief that the "spirits" have superhuman means for knowing the movements of the inhabitants of this world. They must have this belief, if they have any definite idea upon the subject; for otherwise they would not think it at all probable that they could, at any time, receive a communication from a friend in the other world by visiting a medium. The truth is, however, Spiritualists do not much trouble themselves with questions of this nature. During my earlier investigations, I never knew an instance of a Spiritualist, when receiving through a medium a message purporting and believed to be from a friend in the other world, inquiring how that friend happened to be present.

When I was requested to act as a medium, the idea advanced was, that engagements for the meetings must be made, and those of the other world sent for; precisely as if both parties were in this world. It is true that the movements of those of the other world are, compared with ours, exceedingly rapid ; and that, there-fore, they can more readily find an individual of their own world. But when they undertake to find one of this world whose location they do not know, they, of course, lack one great opportunity which we possess, namely, that of inquiring of others personally, or by mail or telegraph.

I resided at Cleveland, Ohio, until the year 1855, when I changed my residence to New York. All the relatives referred to in the preceding narrative, with the exception of my cousin, Mrs. S., died at Cleveland. In New York, after the first year, I boarded at the same hotel until the year 1862; and my friends in the other world had learned where I was boarding. In the spring of 1862 I left New York, and was absent most of the time until autumn of the following year. When I returned in the autumn of 1863, the hotel at which I had formerly boarded being closed, I was obliged to go to another; my friends thus lost track of me.

All public mediums are surrounded by a considerable number of the other world, besides those intimately *en rapport* with the mediums, and who give the communications. Some of the former always attempt to become *en rapport* with the visitors; and in a large proportion of cases the attempt is more or less successful. If the reader has ever received through a medium an answer to a mental question, then in his, or her case the attempt referred to has been, to a certain extent, successful; for in no other way could the question have been learned.

As a general rule in such cases, those intimately *en rapport* with the mediums become, for the time being, *en rapport* with the visitors, in order to learn the questions; as they can more readily effect this than others. But when one of these becomes *en rapport* with a visitor, it increases the facility of others present to accomplish the same; and when one of the latter succeeds in this, he, or she, frequently follows the visitor when he leaves. Even if the one of the other world does not become able to communicate with the visitor, as is hoped, something of what passes in our world can be learned through him, which is a gratification.

During my earlier investigations, and for some time afterward, I was, as I am now informed, thus followed and accompanied by one, and sometimes more than one, of the other world; as were others of the party that visited mediums and sat in "circles" with me. And when I again visited mediums in the autumn of 1863, I was followed from one of them by Miss McCauley, who is an average specimen of those surrounding and communicating through the mediums. My friends know little about her, other than that she was born in Ireland, and was a common prostitute in New York. It was at her suggestion that I was directed, through one of the mediums, to sit alone for communications; as she thought she would be able to write with my hand.

But the power of Miss McCauley over my nervous organization was very slight; and never would have become very great had not Mrs. S. arrived. The name first written was obtained from my own mind, although not one I was thinking of at the time. Others were obtained in the same way; but some were given by an individual who had lived in Cleveland; for as soon as Miss McCauley became able to write at all, the lying creatures that surround mediums began to gather around me; although I was not acting as a medium for communications to others. The errors in spelling the names were generally owing to Miss McCauley's ignorance; but the error in attempting to give the name of my sister was from a different cause. I had thought of my sister when Miss McCauley was with me; but, of course, her name was not prominent in my mind; and it seems that all Miss McCauley could make out was the latter portion of the name, forming the somewhat common one—Ella. My sister suggests that one cause for the error may be the fact that her name is a very uncommon one in Ireland. This idea was suggested while writing the above last lines, and I am not prepared to say whether such is the fact, or not; but I cannot at this moment recollect having ever known or heard of an Irish female having the name. Of course, if Miss McCauley had not been an idiot, she would have perceived the first time she wrote *Ella* that it was not the name of my sister.

In the spring of 1864 Miss M. heard of, and visited me. She then gave the names of some of the earlier residents of Cleveland; and, for her aid in this respect, Miss McCauley permitted and assisted her to write; but the power of Miss M. proved to be even less than that of Miss McCauley. The first visit of Mrs. S. to Cleveland was prior to the death of Miss M., and the two girls, of about the same age, then met. They had again met in the other world; and Miss M., after visiting me, brought Mrs. S. At first, Miss McCauley permitted, and assisted Mrs. S. to write, as she had Miss M., and for the same reason; but the power of Mrs. S. became so rapidly developed that Miss McCauley, fearing she would lose the control, soon refused to let her write. This occurred shortly before I left New York for Trenton; and the ungrammatical and coarse communications, purporting to be written by a deceased friend of mine during the last sittings in New York, were all by Miss McCauley. Mrs. S., in increasing her own power, had also increased that of Miss McCauley. But Mrs. S. also believed that if Miss McCauley could be induced to let her write a little longer she would get the control; and she, with Miss M. and Miss McCauley, went with me to Trenton.

One of my visitors at the hotel in New York was a female who had been acquainted with Mr. A., and who saw him there. This female also followed me to Trenton; and it was at her suggestion that the personation of Mr. A. was undertaken. As this personation has no particular connection with the main theme of my narrative, it is unnecessary to explain it further than to say that the object of the female was to annoy Mr. A.; and also that it was a silly scheme, as it assumed that I could be induced to send a letter purporting to be from Mr. A. to his wife, without first having learned through ordinary channels of the death of the former. To carry out this scheme, Miss McCauley was induced to let Mrs. S. write. The latter, to avoid exciting my suspicion that I had been followed from New York, for several days personated only individuals who had lived in the vicinity of Trenton. Then followed the personation of Mr. A.; and when it was found that I would not send the letter, and probably because I would not, the females determined to mortify me by inducing me to inquire as often as possible about the death of Mr. A.; but as the two individuals of whom I inquired must have supposed that I had heard of the death in the ordinary way, I fail to perceive what great mortification I was expected to experience.

The statement which Miss McCauley gave me at Trenton of her former life and present character was a pretty correct one; and as she now wrote in her true character, this increased her power. Mrs. S., perceiving the latter fact, advised me—personating Mr. A.— not to let her write. The one who at this sitting gave her name as Annie Allen was Miss M. She stated that her father was a New-York banker because I had been engaged in that business there. In writing, at this time, Miss M. had to be assisted by Mrs. S. Soon afterward Mrs. S., perceiving that her power was diminished when personating a man, gave her name as Mrs. Arnold. She had heard of North Bend, Ohio, the late residence of General Harrison, but now thought the name was South Bend, and gave the latter as her former residence. Subsequently Mrs. S. sometimes assumed the *alias* of Annie Allen, sometimes that of Mrs. Arnold, for reasons which will appear.

The likeness of Mr. A.'s acquaintance was obtained from my mind; and the individual first mistaken for him was seen in the street by one who informed Mrs. S. Afterward, at my suggestion, Miss M., guided by one who had lived in Trenton, went to the gentleman's hotel, and seeing an elderly person sitting there thought this might be the one, as I had stated that the gentleman was older than the one first taken for him. A *form* is, according to the dictionary, "a long bench or seat;" but Miss M. thought that a plain desk, such as are used in school-houses, and such as the gentleman was sitting at, was called a form.

The electric shocks which I experienced about this time were caused by efforts to remove Miss McCauley : as it was perceived that this might kill me, the attempt was abandoned. The statement that the shocks were caused by Ellen because I would not let her write, was written by Mrs. S. The subsequent choking was by Mrs. S., and she did all the talking at the time. The explanation she gave my friends of this matter was, that by making me believe Ellen was trying to choke me, while she, as Mrs. Arnold, was endeavoring to protect me, she hoped to increase her power. But Mrs. Arnold did not pretend to be doing anything to prevent the choking; she represented, at the time, that she had no power to prevent it; and my friends are convinced that the persecution was solely from malignancy.

As I wish to throw all the light possible upon this subject, I will here state that, although there was no quarrel, or particular enmity, there was not, within my recollection, a very warm friendship existing between the two families of which Mrs. S. and myself were members ; and this accounts for the fact that I know so little about her. Whether this had anything to do with the persecution, or not, I cannot say. It appears that Miss M. assisted in the matter as far as was in her power. My own acquaintance with Mrs. S. was very slight, and I had none at all with Miss M. ; but from the information I have received I infer that if these fallen creatures had previously known nothing about me or the family of which I was a member, they would not then have persecuted me; for, as yet, I had in no way—except in the refusal to send the letter to Mrs. A., about which these two could not have cared much—thwarted their inclinations. But this fiendish malignancy towards one they had formerly known, or rather towards a member of a family which they had known—whatever may have produced it—was undoubtedly the cause of this persecution, and also of the readiness of these two females to enter into the personation of Mr. A.; for if I had been prevailed on to send the letter to Mrs. A., the result would, of course, have been extremely mortifying to me.

The choking, or attempts at choking, were performed by creating what, when they become visible, Spiritualists call "spirit-hands;" in which operation my electricity, or nervous fluid, as it is called, was used; and it was the exhaustion of this fluid that brought on the palpitation of the heart and partial paralysis of the limbs. And it was Mrs. S. who, personating Ellen, said she produced this, and meant to kill me. The power of Miss McCauley had by this time been so far overcome that she could neither write or talk when Mrs. S. endeavored to prevent her.

But the power of Miss McCauley was still so great that, being an idiot, she was an impediment to Mrs. S. and Miss M. The latter two would have had the assistance of others present in removing her if it had been thought prudent to do so; but it was still feared that this might kill me. The two females then conceived the idea of making me believe that Ellen was killed. They now thought of trying to induce me to act as a public medium, and wished first to reduce the power of Miss McCauley as far as possible. They had now learned the operation of my mind, and understood that if I could be made to believe Ellen was killed, her power would be greatly diminished. Of course the effect would be the same if I believed she was removed, which I would have been far more likely to do; but of these two plans, the females naturally chose the most silly one. Mrs. S. believed that my thinking intently of my father for such a length of time would increase her power; but why she thus believed is not very clear, and it had little, if any, effect of the kind. My error as to the effect of this night's operations arose from the fact that up to this time Mrs. S. frequently personated Ellen in speaking; and as she now ceased doing so, I inferred that Ellen's power had been destroyed.

The original intention of the two females in reference to my acting as a public medium, was simply persona-tions and deceptions, as through others. How they expected to induce me to relinquish the business in which I was then engaged, to enter upon that of a medium, which I think cannot be very lucrative, I do not understand. But they knew I could not be induced to act at all as a medium in Trenton, and besides, pre-ferred having me go to New York where visitors would be more numerous.

When I was told in New York the preceding autumn of the suicide of Mr. K., the stock-broker, neither Mrs. S. or Miss M. was with me. But it appears that I had thought of the matter since, when they both were with me; and they received the impression from my mind that Mr. K. would be a man suitable for their purpose. This purpose was to have some one come and personate deceased bankers and brokers, late of New York, and thus induce me to go there and act as a medium. I am told that the two females received from me the impression that Mr. K. was a man who would be likely to do this; and suppose such must be the fact. But the truth is that I would not, at that time, have believed Mr. K. would enter into such a scheme; for I could not then, nor can I now, understand how any man, whether in this world or the other, can feel any interest, or find any amusement in such nonsense. The impression I really had of Mr. K. was, that he was about as honest as the average of stock-brokers—perhaps it would be more correct to say *stock-gamblers*, for he was of the latter class—and that he was not such a man as I would choose for an intimate companion. I think my impression of him was no worse than this; and the impression the two females really received was, not that Mr. K. when in our world would engage in such trifling deceptions, but that he would probably become such a being on passing into their world.

Miss M. therefore went in search of, and found Mr. K. ; and here, as might be expected, there is a discrepancy in the statements. Miss M. asserts that Mr. K., before she brought him to me, agreed to assist in the personations; Mr. K. avers that he entered into no such agreement. It appears to me that the point is not a very important one, inasmuch as Mr. K. did, when he came, personate another individual.

Up to this date there was nothing in my case differing from that of other mediums, except that Mrs. S. and Miss M. are more intellectual than those in control of any other, and the consequent conflict between them and

Miss McCauley. And if the two females had succeeded in their original scheme, there would have occurred nothing new. The truth is, however, that there never was any possibility of their success in this scheme. Neither of them had acquired the power of communicating freely before I became unwell; in fact, it was during my illness that Mrs. S. became able to talk with me. I was not then in a condition to test the identity of individuals, or, in fact, to reason very strongly upon the subject; but even then, the personations appeared so vague and unsatisfactory that I should not have entertained for a moment the idea of serving as a medium for communications to others. Before the arrival of Mr. K., I had become sceptical as to whether any of my friends had communicated with me; and I knew that most, if not all, the communications since my recovery from illness were personations. In order to have induced me to serve as a medium, it would have been absolutely necessary to have brought my friends and permitted them to communicate freely with me; which, of course, would have defeated the scheme of these females.

I very much doubt whether mediums, generally, have as much faith in the genuineness of the communications as their visitors. During my earlier investigations, I once asked a celebrated medium if he had ever, for himself, received a communication purporting to be from a departed friend which he was perfectly satisfied was genuine. He frankly replied that he never had. Yet this man was every day serving as a medium for communications to others, which the recipients were "perfectly satisfied" came from the friends whose names were given. One of the mediums that I visited in the autumn of 1865, for the purpose stated, was Mrs. Under-hill—formerly Mrs. Brown—and I asked her the same question, stating my own convictions. She replied, after some hesitation, that she *thought* she had received such; but did not speak with the confidence of those who had received communications through her; and it was to me evident from her remarks that, while she was honest in the matter, and allowed the recipients to judge for themselves, she had, herself, not much faith in the genuineness of the immense number of messages which had been delivered through her. It is proper to state that she was not at this time, and has not been since her last marriage, a public medium. Her husband, who was present when I made the above inquiry, re-marked, after her reply, that if there had, as yet, been no medium through whom truthful communications could be received, perhaps there would be such a one hereafter. This remark shows very clearly his opinion upon this point; and, although not himself a medium, he must have had opportunities for forming a correct judgment.

But, aside from all this, if I had commenced acting as a public medium, my friends in the other world would soon have learned the fact, and found me; and would have taken the course they did when brought to me.

It here becomes necessary to make a statement which may appear rather egotistical; but the statement is one which I have received, and I cannot avoid giving it if what follows is to be rendered intelligible. There has never lived in our world another individual with whom any of the other world but the most degraded class, could communicate, except on very rare occasions, and then only for a moment. It is a fact that one of our world may in a certain stage of sleep receive, in some way, a communication from a departed friend; or the one of the other world may have succeeded in becoming so perfectly *en rapport* with the one of this while the latter was asleep as to be able to deliver the message, by impression of ideas, by vision, or even by audible words, at the moment of the latter's awaking; but as soon as the individual is fully awake the *rapport* is dissolved, and the power of communication is gone. What is meant is, that there has never lived one with whom communication could be held at any time, or for any length of time, by any of the other world except the degraded and lying class. And it is not meant that there are no others who could be brought into the same condition as myself, but simply that circumstances have not conspired to bring them into this condition. Why one class of the other world has more power in this respect than another, will be explained hereafter so far as I am able; but it cannot be fully explained; like life itself, it must remain a mystery.

One reason why those of the other world will not communicate with their friends in ours through the mediums is, that the devils in control of the latter will not permit all the facts to be given. It is not merely that the friend would be left subject to the receipt of false messages and liable to impositions, but that as he would continue to visit mediums when no friend of the other world was present to prevent, he would soon, perhaps, be in the condition of myself and many others; some devil would become so far *en rapport* that he, or she, could not be removed without injury.

When Mr. K. was brought to me at Trenton, he perceived that almost any one of his world could be placed *en rapport* with me by Mrs. S., so as to be able to communicate direct. He told the two females that it would be useless to try to persuade me to act as a medium in the way they proposed; that my friends must first be placed in communication with me, and the idea of personations be abandoned. He suggested, also, that it would be more interesting to have real communications made through me, than merely to practice personations as was done through other mediums. But one difficulty was, that Mrs. S. and Miss M., although more intelligent, are as great liars as those in control of other mediums.

On learning what relatives I had in his world, Mr. K. proposed that one of my sisters should be placed *en rapport* to remain constantly with me. In this way he thought I might be induced to act as a medium. His idea was that I should serve mostly for communications to wealthy individuals, charging a large fee, so as to make the business a lucrative one. And he wished to be connected with the business as a sort of manager in his world. But here, as Mr. K. had given the females his opinion on one point, they now gave him theirs on another. They told him that I would not have him for manager. The idea then occurred to Mr. K. of getting some one to act as manager who would permit him to be associated. He knew of the death of Mr. H., the late bank president, as it occurred before his own; and appears to have assumed that because Mr. H. was formerly president of the M—— Bank he would be acceptable to me. I know nothing about Mr. H.

further than that he was president of this bank, which would not, of itself, be with me any recommendation for such a position; one of the duties of which would have been, as I understand, to decide who might communicate through me; for, of course, even if I devoted my whole time to the business, but a small proportion of the other world could do so. My friends state that Mr. H. is not a proper person for such a position; and the fact that he entered into the scheme of Mr. K., and concealed the matter from my friends, is sufficient evidence on this point. The truth is that if he had been qualified for the position, Mr. K. would not have attempted to negotiate with him.

Mr. K. found Mr. H. and proposed the scheme, when the latter readily entered into it; but, as the females objected to having him brought to me until an arrangement had been made with my friends, Mr. K. attempted to personate Mr. H. The delay in speaking to my friends about the matter, was owing to the fact that neither Mr. K. or Mr. H. had any valid reasons to offer for being permitted to act as managers; and it was necessary for them to arrange some plan by which they could be of service to me.

It will be recollected that I had heard nothing about Miss Annie Allen since learning definitely that Mr. A. was still living in our world. This name having been used in that attempt at deception, had not since been given. But Mrs. S.—personating the late bank president—now stated that he had engaged Miss Allen to stay with me and prevent deceptions. In the personations of the bank president and others at this time, Mrs. S. did most of the writing and talking; she would not permit Mr. K. to do much of either. And in order to carry out the new scheme, it was necessary that the *aliases* of the two females should be dropped, and their real names given before the arrival of my friends. Mrs. Arnold was now to leave, and in a short time Mrs. S. was to arrive. In the meantime, Miss Allen was to re main with me ; after the arrival of Mrs. S. she too would leave, and Miss M. arrive. Mrs. S. had sometimes conversed under the *alias* of Miss Allen, as well as under that of Mrs. Arnold. As regards the fictitious names, the effect with me was the same as if the females had given their real ones ; I had become acquainted, so to speak, with Mrs. Arnold and Miss Allen ; and it was feared that if both these characters were at once withdrawn Miss McCauley would gain power. There was some cunning in this, but not much wisdom ; for it would have been impossible to have concealed from my friends—especially if my sister had been placed inti mately *en rapport* with me—what had occurred. There appears to have been at this time no definite plan for getting rid of Miss McCauley ; though it was thought they might eventually accomplish this by placing her *en rapport* with some other person.

Mr. H. suggested the idea of having some one of our world associated with me ; the advantage of which I do not perceive ; but the probability is that he thought by having some former acquaintance of his associated with me he would be better able to secure his position as manager. He named David L——, formerly president of one of the largest banks in New York, for this pur pose ; and the object in having a letter written at once to Mr. L, was, probably, to procure his influence with me in favor of Mr. H. as manager; an influence which would have amounted to nothing. I know very little about Mr. L. other than what my invisible friends have told me. On inquiring, I have learned that he was president of the bank they named, but resigned several years prior to my coming to New York, and is now living in Massachusetts. I have not taken the trouble to learn whether he had left New York prior to the time of which I am now writing, or not. The Mr. L. whose name I had seen with the prefix of *Reverend* is Joshua L., editor of a religious newspaper in New York.

Mr. H. gave Mr. K., orally, the substance of the letter to be written Mr. L.; and gave him correctly the first name of the latter. Mr. K. had somehow got the impression that the name of the cashier of the bank was that of the president; and, which is more inexplicable, this error was not corrected at his interview with Mr. H. What seems, if possible, still more strange is, that Mr. K. did not recollect the first name of either cashier or president: and did not, at the interview, inquire for it, although he must have known it would have to be signed to the letter. It must be borne in mind that Mr. K., although when in our world considered about as *sharp* as the average of brokers, is now very stupid. I was slightly acquainted in New York with a Mr. Joseph M. (the surname being that of the former cashier of the bank), who was connected with a Wall street insurance company; and it appears that after the first personation of the late bank president, when the surname M—— only was given, I thought of this person and his name. Mrs. S. thus got the impression that the first name of the late bank president was Joseph. The letter to Mr. L., although partly dictated by Mr. K., was written by Mrs. S. ; but Mr. K. knew what name she signed to the letter, and the affair was so very stupid as scarcely to admit of an intelligible explanation. The error in directing the letter to David A. L——, Mr. L. having no middle name, was, I am informed, by Mr. K. The blunders would appear less strange if these persons had not been engaged in what was to them an important scheme.

Mr. K. was the first visitor who gave his real name. There was no reason for concealing it that I can perceive ; but it seems strange that, having such a scheme in view, he and the females could not at this time avoid useless personations ; that is, personations having no connection with the scheme. It will be recollected that when his name was first given—which was after the first personation of the late bank president—I was told that about forty persons, including Howard, Daboll, Dudley M., and a Mr. T., were present. The only explanation given of this is, that Mr. K. thought it the best mode of accounting for his presence. Why the name of Dudley M. happened to be given, was to me a mystery which is now explained. The person they intended to make me believe present, was Horace M., late president of an Ohio college, and well known for his services in the cause of education. When I spoke of Dudley M. having gone to Europe, the mistake was perceived, but as it could not well be rectified, it was stated that he died in Paris. The name of Daboll was suggested by Miss M., who had studied his Arithmetic ; a work superseded many years since.

During the last six years of my residence in Cleveland I was secretary of a railway company. The banking-house of which Mr. W. was the senior member was the financial agent of the company; and the firm of which Mr. K. was a partner, owing to circumstances not necessary to be mentioned, at that time dealt more largely in the stock of the company than other brokers; owing to which fact I became acquainted with him before I left Cleveland. The gentleman who was president of the company during most of the time that I was con-. nected with it—a very prominent person in Ohio—died in the year 1860.

When I inquired of Mr. K., who was personating the late bank president, if he had met Mr. W. in the other world, he intimated in his reply that he was not aware that the latter had entered it. This appears to have been an aimless falsehood, for Mr. K. was well acquainted with Mr. W., and knew of the latter's death at the time it occurred. But this inquiry suggested to Mr. K. the idea that the association of Mr. W. and the late president of the railway company—especially the latter—in the scheme, would be more likely to meet my approval, and secure my co-operation, than that of the late bank president, whom, as he now perceived, I knew nothing about. He therefore found Mr. W., who readily assented to the proposal, and who subsequently spoke to the late railway president and secured his co-operation. It was assumed by these persons that my relatives in their world, especially my father, would have great influence with me; and they aimed at securing this influence. The late railway president, although not for many years previous to his death a resident of Cleveland, had formerly resided there, and been ac-

quainted with my father. It was therefore decided that
he should call on my father and endeavor to secure his
influence; but the matter was still postponed for the
reason that they had no satisfactory inducement to offer.

The letter to Mr. L. was written before I made the inquiry about Mr. W.; and my visit to New York, when
I called for the answer, was soon after Mr. K. had seen
Mr. W. and made the proposal. When, at this visit, I
made the inquiries and learned that the name of the late
bank president was not M. but H., the two females decided that Mr. K. was too stupid for their purpose, and
that Mr. W. should be brought. Mr. K. then immediately conducted Miss M. to Mr. W., and the latter accompanied her to Trenton the same evening. When,
sitting on the piazza of the hotel at Trenton that evening, I was told by one personating the late bank president that he had been " home " and learned that his name
was H., Mr. W. was present; and although the words
were spoken by Mrs. S., they were suggested by Mr. W.

It was the intention of Mr. W., at this time, not to
give his name until after Mrs. S. and Miss M. had given
theirs, and Mrs. Arnold with Miss Allen had, as would
be represented, left; which would obviate the necessity
of explanation on the part of Mr. W. as to his connection with the latter two. As Mr. H. had been, to a
certain extent, advised of the facts, it was the intention
of Mr. W. that he should be associated in the matter;
and should, when he came, corroborate what I was now
told. It is probable that Mr. W. did not expect to deceive my friends in his world, but did expect that they
might be induced to conceal the facts from me; and this
expectation was based upon his knowledge that it would

be difficult, safely for me, forcibly to remove Mrs. S. and Miss McCauley. But the idea that I could serve for any length of time as a medium for genuine communications, thus learning how distinctly those of the other world recollect the incidents in their former lives, and yet believe that some forget their names, was a very silly one.

But Mr. W., soon after his arrival, told the two females that my friends would be very much opposed to their remaining with me; and he suggested the idea of developing for them another medium. In consequence of this, they decided to postpone giving their real names.

It was thought another medium, with whom Mrs. S. and Miss M. could communicate, might be developed with my assistance; though the attempt would be an experiment. The two females having been with me when I met Miss B. in New York the preceding spring, named her as one who they thought might be made such a medium: one reason for naming her being the fact that her father was at this time in their world, and they, for reasons not necessary to be specified, believed he would co-operate in the matter. Nothing, however, was said to him about it at this time.

As it was doubtful whether another medium with whom she could communicate would or could be developed, Mrs. S., knowing the difficulty there would be in removing her, determined to make an effort to remain with me. The scheme on this point as finally agreed upon was as follows:—If my friends agreed that Mrs. S. should remain with me, I was to be told that my father brought her, and wished to have her remain with me, and that she had not before seen me. If my friends would not consent to this, then an attempt was to be made, provided I would assist, to develop another medium. If another medium was developed, Miss M. was also to be connected with her; but if not, she would be unprovided for, as it was known there would be little difficulty in removing her from me. And if Mr. W. could not arrange to be connected with me, he was to be one of the managers of the other medium.

Of course, if Mrs. S. and Miss M. were to have control of the other medium, individuals of the other world would be no more inclined to communicate with their friends here through this medium than through others; and therefore Mr. W. would have no inducement to be connected with the medium. But, as explained to me, those of the opposite sexes are the greatest electrical affinities —a term which, as here applied, I confess I do not quite understand—and the other medium was to be a female, so that a male of the other world would have the control. It was the intention if Miss B. was made a medium, that her father should be the one having control.

The *alias* Mrs. Arnold had been dropped by Mrs. S. soon after the arrival of Mr. K., for the reason given; but she found that she had not as much power under the *alias* of Miss Allen as she formerly had under that of Mrs. Arnold. I had become acquainted, so to speak, with two distinct females, Mrs. S. as Mrs. Arnold, and Miss M. as Miss Allen; and these two females are not now precisely alike in character, as they were not in our world. As Mrs. S. had concluded not to give me her name at this time, she decided to resume the *alias* of Mrs. Arnold. But at the same time, as she had not lately used that name, and I had the impression that

Mrs. Arnold had left, she apprehended that she might not now have her former power under that *alias*; for these silly females had, from experience, become very knowing as to the effect of my mind.

At the time of Mr. W.'s arrival, I was contemplating the visit to Long Branch; and it was decided, for no very profound reason, so far as I can learn, to take advantage of this visit for the experiment of resuming the *alias* of Mrs. Arnold, and also for giving me the name of Miss M.

The plan was that on leaving for Long Branch I should be told Miss Allen would not accompany me, and Mrs. Arnold would. If it was found that Mrs. S. under the *alias* of Mrs. Arnold retained her former power, or had more power than under the *alias* of Miss Allen, the latter name was not to be further used; I was to be told, at first, that she had probably been unable to find me, and afterward some other reason would be given for her continued absence. If, however, it was found that Mrs. S. had now less power under the *alias* of Mrs. Arnold than under that of Miss Allen, the latter was to be resumed by her. Miss M. had decided to give me her name, representing that she visited me for the first time at Long Branch. She seems to have hoped that, even if Mrs. S. remained with me, I might be induced to assist in developing another medium.

The result of the experiment showed that Mrs. S. had now less power under the *alias* of Mrs. Arnold than under that of Miss Allen. When I thought the latter was not with me, Miss McCauley became able to annoy me by talking. The coarse and vulgar talking on the boat, and during the first two days and nights at Long Branch, was by her. If she had again given her name as Ellen, it would have increased her power; but, being an idiot, she thought she could frighten me more by personating a man. It will be recollected that the previous efforts to frighten me, when the name Ellen was used, were not by her, but by Mrs. S. The *alias* of Miss Allen was resumed by Mrs. S., and ultimately the power of Miss McCauley to talk was overcome; but my walking on the bluff and thinking intently of Miss Allen had little effect, that not being the action of the mind which is most efficient. This occurrence suggested the idea of ceasing, for awhile, oral conversation and writing when they wished to communicate; a resolution not strictly adhered to, however, for the females would talk, though much less than formerly.

The name of Miss M. was given me only once at Long Branch; and then I was merely told by Mrs. S. that she was present; she did not say any thing herself. The name was given me to see what my recollection of her would be; but, as I have said, I could not recollect her at all. At first, I thought it was a sister, who died later; but immediately remembered that the first name of this sister was not Mary, and then recollected having heard of the death of Mary M.

Mr. W. and party, in order to secure the management, intended to be of service to me; and this was to be accomplished by means of communications through me. One plan, and the prominent one, which they had in view, has been partly explained to me; but it is unnecessary to state it. It was neither a very profound nor a silly one, but about such as might have occurred to an individual of our world under similar circumstances. But nothing was to be done, in reference to carrying out this plan, until I went to New York in the autumn; and before I left Long Branch, an event occurred which obliged this party, as was thought, to abandon the idea of being connected with me, and caused Mr. W. to aim at procuring another medium.

As stated in the preceding narrative, there is involved in the affair of the Count and wife a fraud on the British nation. It has been, and is still, the cause of some expense to the nation; how much, I have not taken the trouble to ascertain, but presume that, comparatively speaking, the sum is not very great. Aside from this, so far as concerns the British nation, I do not know that the fraud has had, or will have any injurious effect if it remains undiscovered. But upon this point I have not sufficient information to enable me to decide intelligently. Be this as it may, with Englishmen the expense which the nation has incurred would not be the important item.

Now, although this fraud is not universally known in the other world, it is known to many there; and some Englishmen by birth would like to have the matter rectified. Mr. W. and party, in endeavoring to carry out their plan, had been making certain inquiries, and these inquiries were of such a nature that it became necessary to state their object. It thus became known to several that a medium differing from any hitherto found had been discovered; though not who or where this medium was. This intelligence reached one who had knowledge of the Count's affair, and was by him communicated to the Count, with the suggestion that this might offer means for rectifying the fraud he had committed. The Count on hearing of the matter, and of the inducement which Mr. W. and party intended to offer in order to secure the management, conceived the same incomprehensible desire to be manager; and he thought he could offer an inducement of the same nature as that proposed by Mr. W., which would be a much higher one. He therefore found Mr. W. and made known to him his intention. Here was a difficulty for Mr. W. and party; the Count wished me to go to England and remain there, and to be himself the chief, if not the sole manager. Mr W. thought as the Count did, that the inducement which the latter named would be a greater one than any he could offer; and he knew that the Count would learn who and where I was, and who were my relatives in their world, as soon as the latter were spoken to about the management. Mr. W. and party therefore abandoned their scheme.

But Mr. W. now determined to endeavor to carry out the idea he had formerly suggested of developing with my aid another medium, and to be connected with the latter. I understand that neither Mr. H. or the late railway president had any connection with this new scheme; but the latter was induced to postpone speaking to my friends, and the former never knew them. It was the intention of Mr. W. to have some relative or friend of the person to be made a medium associated with him; and the Count agreed to aid as far as possible.

Mr. B. was then found, and the proposal to have his daughter made a medium submitted to him. There appears to have been no particular reason for selecting

Miss B. for the experiment, or rather for now making the proposal to her father, other than those already given. Mr. B. thought favorably of the proposal; but the difficulty was that his daughter could not be made such a medium as was wanted without my agency; and if developed with my agency, one or both of the two females with me—Mrs. S. and Miss M. —must be placed *en rapport* with her. Of course Mr. W. had to state this fact; and when Mr. B. proposed visiting me to see the females, and converse with me about them, Mr. W., fearing from his remarks that he would then decline the proposition, refused to conduct him to me, or tell him where I was. At this time I was at Long Branch, and the pretended visit of Mr. B. there was merely a personation.

Mr. W. next made the proposition to others of his world, but met with the same difficulty. In these efforts, and in further attempts at negotiation with Mr. B. the time was passed until I went to New York in the autumn. The Count waited for two reasons : first, because, he did not know where I was or who were my friends in his world ; and second, because he wished the two females to leave me, and understood the easiest mode of accomplishing this would be the development of another medium for them.

My name had been given Mr. B., and as he knew where I boarded the preceding winter, and that I would probably be at the same hotel the coming one, he would have found me. Mr. W., therefore, after I returned to New York, concluded to conduct him to me. In October he was brought to my room at the hotel in New York. He was told that he had been personated at Long

Branch, and therefore, either thoughtlessly or foolishly, stated that he had visited me there, as a test of identity. Such an incident as he next gave, and which at the time satisfied me, would not now, unsupported by further evidence, have the same effect; for this incident occurred at a time when, as I am informed, one of the other world was most of the time with me; and if either Mrs. S. or Miss M. had then been with me, and en *rapport*, they could have narrated all that Mr. B. did.

After his visit, Mr. B. consented, or at least partially consented, to the proposition of Mr. W. In partial explanation of this it should be recollected that Mr. B. was to be placed intimately en *rapport* with his daughter, and that it was presumed his power with her would be greater than that of Mrs. S. ; also that, if so desired, Mrs. S. could be removed. The reason Mrs. S. must be placed en *rapport*, in case my friends would not consent that she should remain with me, was, that the necessary communications through me could not be made against her opposition.

As it was deemed necessary to secure the concurrence and influence of my relatives in the other world, the scheme—embracing the proposal of the Count, and making a medium of Miss B.—was then submitted to my father, who assented to letting me decide for myself after I had learned the facts. But on submitting it to my mother and sisters, they, or, at least, my mother and the sister most frequently referred to, made strenuous objections, and said they should endeavor to prevent me from either accepting the proposal of the Count, or assisting in the development of another medium. It seems that to neither of these did the proposition of the

Count seem so visionary and impracticable as it did to me. Its success would mainly depend on the influence which the Count and others of his world might be able to exert through me in case I withheld the knowledge of the former's present character.

My relatives were not informed where I was, and they thought I was not in New York; but as they were now advised of my situation, they would eventually have found me, and therefore it was finally decid d to bring them. Several periods had been named within which I would be "relieved;" the last named would expire on the second Monday in December, and Mr. W. concluded to bring my relatives on that day; first, however, bringing the Count and letting him submit to me his proposition. The Count was brought two days prior to that date. I was told in the morning that he would come at four o'clock in the afternoon, and at the latter hour it was represented that he had just arrived; but, in fact, when I was informed in the morning of the proposed visit he was present, and remained with me all day.

The plan was that if I decided to go to England, Miss B. was to be induced by her father to accompany me, with some lady as companion; and this seems to have suggested to Mr. W. a very silly idea. He named a lady to accompany Miss B., but requested me to suggest her when the Count came as being my own selection. The Count was present at the time, and the idea was to show him that I was not naturally given to deception. But, as I knew that the Count, if placed *en rapport* with me, could read my mind, and thus perceive that the selection was not my own, the device was a very shallow one. The second test as to my honesty made by the Count, was a more reliable one, for at the moment I did not perceive the absurdity of the proposed scheme. But the idea of these liars thus testing my honesty has since appeared to me rather funny.

Why the Count chose to write so much nonsense it would be useless to conjecture; the story he told certainly appeared much worse, both for himself and wife, than the facts. The reason he did not make me, at the first sitting, the proposition submitted to my relatives was, the repugnance evinced towards it by my mother and sister. His first intention on coming to me was, to try to induce me to go to England and remain a few years; but after the first sitting he decided to submit the original proposition, and see how I viewed it. The absurd proposal made at the first sitting that I should go over to act as tutor to a child yet unborn, seems to have been suggested to his crazy brain by the following facts:—His daughter, the legal heiress, is married to a German, and is living in Germany. Her husband's rank and position there are such that he would not go to England to reside; and the Count, with others, thought that one of the daughters' sons would be made the heir, and be educated in England. As for my tutorship, the position would not suit me, and I would not suit the position. The Count must have known at least the latter fact, and I hardly understand what his real idea was, if, indeed, he had any definite one.

But one peculiarity about the lying of these people of the other world is, that they lie when the truth would better serve their purpose. The truth as to the illegitimacy of the children would, for the Count, have appeared better than the falsehood; so would also the real reason for proposing that Miss B. should accompany me to England; and the truth about this tutorship, whatever his idea may have been, would have better served his purpose than the idiotic proposal he made. He must have known, if he knew anything, that these and other falsehoods written by him would have to be contradicted, and the facts given before I went to England; and it seems strange, especially as he knew that he would meet with opposition from some of my relatives, that he should not, at this visit, have tried to avoid letting me know that he was such an inveterate liar. The explanation of the matter must be that he is now almost an idiot.

The Count had an object in writing so much, which was to become as much *en rapport* as possible before my friends were brought. Except Miss M., he was the first that Mrs. S. had endeavored to place intimately *en rapport* with me. She hoped that if the Count was successful she would be permitted to remain with me. The fact that the Count was the first visitor who communicated with me, to any extent, otherwise than as a personator, was one cause, and probably the main one, for my being so strongly impressed that the writer was the person he represented himself to be.

On the second Monday in December, 1864, my relatives were brought; and with them came my acquaintance the late railway president, who until that time had not known where I was. In giving me the narrative up to this date, my friends have been obliged to balance the contradictory statements of liars, and partly guess at the truth; but as the narrative appears to be coherent, I infer that it must be nearly, if not entirely, accurate.

How Mr. W. and his associates expected to explain their statement that I would be "relieved" this day, which meant relieving me of Miss McCauley, is not very clear; but they must have assumed that I was to be kept in ignorance of a portion of the facts. As I understand the matter, the party believed, as my friends did, and appear still to believe, that if I had gone to England, in accordance with the proposition of the Count, accompanied by Mrs. S., I would soon have been relieved of Miss McCauley; and if another medium had been developed, I would have been relieved of Mrs. S. also.

When my friends came, Mrs. S. insisted on an agreement that she might remain with me in case another medium was not developed; and as my friends refused to enter into such an agreement, she would not permit them to communicate with me. The writing purporting to be by my father and mother was, as I supposed, by Mrs. S.

The matter was discussed until I went to bed; then my friends determined to make an attempt to place one or more of my relatives *en rapport* with me. In my normal condition, this could not have been effected; but it was thought that the connection of Mrs. S. with me made it possible. This attempt caused the disturbances during the night.

The result of the night's operations caused my friends to hope that my mother and a sister—the one who was first personated—might soon become so intimately *en rapport* with me that Mrs. S. and Miss McCauley could safely be removed. It appears a little strange that this sister, who died about twenty-six years prior to this time, was a closer affinity—as they term it—than another sister who died only about five years previous; but the former more nearly resembled me in color of the hair and complexion.

Miss M. was at once removed from close proximity to me, so that she was not an interference; and the only reason assigned for not sooner advising me of this fact is, that it was desired to prevent the concentration of my mind on Miss McCauley. Several male friends remained constantly with me, to prevent interference, and also to give their advice to my mother and sister. The Count was permitted to remain for the reason that, having become *en rapport*, he was able, and did, render assistance. Why he chose to remain, I do not clearly understand; he may have believed that I would accept his proposition, but it is probable that he would have remained with me whether he had any definite object in view or not. The explanation of this first night's occurrences given the next day, and purporting to be by the Count, was, of course, by Mrs. S.

Mrs. S. had formerly endeavored to make me believe that my friends visited me; but from the time they really came, it was her policy to make me believe the contrary, and she asserted that they were unable to find me. My sitting and holding my hand for writing did not much aid my mother and sister; that is, holding my hand for this purpose did not, as the power of Mrs. S. in this respect was much greater than theirs. But the *thinking*, while seated at the table, of my mother or sister as being present, did greatly aid them, and therefore Mrs. S. used various expedients to prevent the practice, one of which was the personation of Mr. B.

As the name of Mr. B. and his daughter had been frequently used, and I had therefore frequently thought of them, Mrs. S. had obtained some facts concerning the former from my mind. When she told me in the morning that Mr. B. would be brought in the afternoon of the same day, and that I might test his identity as I pleased, she hoped that my questions would be such as she would be able to answer. But when I wrote the series of questions, she found that she could not answer one of them; and therefore subsequently told me that Mr. B. could not come. Afterward, however, she thought that she had obtained, in another way, answers to the first two questions; and at the sitting which had been arranged—but at which only herself wrote—said that Mr. B. was present.

The first two questions were, as to the number of the building occupied by Mr. B., and the name of his successor. Two of the facts obtained from my mind, both by Mrs. S. and Miss M., were, an approximately correct idea of the location of the building, and of the nature of the business. Miss M., who remained most of the time in my vicinity, and who still hoped that another medium would be developed, on being told by Mrs. S. what the questions were, went in search of some one who could give the answers to these two questions. She found a female who had purchased goods of the class named, at a store which she thought was in the locality described; and this female also thought she recollected the name of the proprietor and the number of the store. These items were given by Miss M. to

Mrs. S., who made of the difficulty in writing an excuse for not answering the other questions.

The idea here occurred to me that, as my friends did not know but Miss M. might procure correct informa· tion, they should either have prevented her from going in search of it, or from communicating to Mrs. S. what she had received. Whether, if communication was less difficult, I should be able fully to comprehend the other world and its inhabitants, I cannot say; but, as it is, I certainly do not. As I am informed, it would not have been impossible to prevent Miss M. from leaving, or from again approaching so near Mrs. S. as to be able to communicate her information. But either course would have been less feasible than with us; and the matter was thought to be of no great importance, as I should soon have been undeceived.

The name of Mr. W. was given for the first time at this sitting. It was given by Mrs. S., who at this time feared that my friends would succeed, and that she would have to leave me; and her object in giving the name was to ascertain if I would be disposed to aid in developing a medium to be under the management of Mr. W. The proposal to give me the name, or title, of the father of the illegitimate children of the Count's wife was also by Mrs. S. Both the Count and Mr. W. were present, but neither was permitted to communi· cate with me.

My discovery, previous to this date, of the influence which Mrs. S., *alias* Miss Allen, was able to exert upon my mind, was owing to the counteracting influence of my mother and sister. I have said that my sensations on the evening after the above sitting were, that a foreign influence was being exerted to induce belief in statements which my judgment pronounced false. But the truth is that the moment Mrs. S. commenced exerting her influence, my mother and sister commenced exerting theirs; and as both opposing influences could not have prevailed at the same instant, my sensations must have deceived me on this point. These influences were only temporary; and, in any event, my judgment would ultimately have pronounced the statements false.

As my mother and sister were gaining power, and Mrs. S. had, as she now thought, failed in her efforts to induce me to discontinue my sittings, she concluded to permit my father to communicate with me; but this conclusion must have been based upon the belief that she could induce him to conceal the facts relative to her. My father was less opposed to the proposition of the Count and the plan for developing another medium than my mother and this sister; or, more properly, he was not, under existing circumstances, at all opposed to either. What purported to be the confession of Annie Morford, was in furtherance of a rather imperfectly defined scheme of Mrs. S. to have her past connection with me concealed. But as she failed to effect any arrangement during the night, in the morning she again asserted that the Count had visited me—which she had contradicted in the confession of the previous evening—and refused to let my father communicate.

Mrs. S. perceived that the only hold she had on my mind for inducing belief in her connection with any scheme, was the fact that I was not entirely convinced the Count had never communicated with me. In asking for three days more of time for the party to make an arrangement, her idea was that she might, in that time, effect one for herself; for there was a difference of opinion with the advisers surroundi g me as to what was the best course under the circumstances. Not being able to effect any arrangement during the three days, she still refused to let any one communicate with me.

When, on the next Sunday evening, I sat for the purpose of learning something from the female who appeared to be opposing the one still calling herself Miss Allen, the dread, or *horror* I experienced was caused by my mother and sister. The one who then wrote as the opposing party was Mrs. S. ; and although the description given did not at all resemble that of Miss Allen or Mrs. Arnold, nor the appearance of Mrs. S. when in our world, yet my mother and sister feared that the writing might increase the power of Mrs. S., and created the dread to make me stop. As I understand the matter, when all three were exerting their power, the writing, considered by itself—or assuming that I did not think of any one as performing it—increased the power of Mrs. S.; or, at least, did not diminish it, nor increase that of my mother and sister. It was the *thinking* of the latter two which increased their power; and even thinking of my father as present did, through the exertion of his will, increase the *rapport* of my mother and sister with me—a mysterious operation which I confess I do not fully understand.

It will be perceived that the belief I arrived at about this time that my friends in the other world might not know of my situation or where I was, would have been correct several months previous; but it is doubtful if visiting other mediums would have apprised them of the facts. When, on my return from Trenton in the succeeding autumn, I did visit other mediums, my friends made little effort to have me learn the truth, knowing that such efforts would be useless.

As stated in the preceding narrative, after visiting these mediums without any result, I decided to endeavor to divert my mind from the subject, and to forget, as far as possible, that invisible beings were with me. This was what Mrs. S. had been aiming at; and my mother and sister, finding that they could not by any ordinary efforts cause me to think of them, commenced extraordinary efforts on the night of the 23d of November, as soon as I went to bed. And as they perceived that their power was very much increased by these efforts, they renewed them every night for a week or more; and, in fact, extraordinary efforts, with occasional relaxations to permit me to sleep more soundly, were continued until my mother had identified herself. The diminution in the apparent effect upon my brain was partly owing to the increase of the power, or *rapport*, of my mother and sister; but partly, also, to the fact that they were obliged to relax their efforts in order that I might rest better at night.

The writing about the first of February (1866), purporting to be by the opposing female, was by Mrs. S. It was extremely difficult for her to write a word at this time, as the power of my mother and sister had much increased, and I did not think of Miss Allen as the writer. Her idea in writing the sentence, "Because they are so much better than you," in reply to my question as to why my friends could not communicate with me, was, of course, to make me believe that all efforts to get communications direct from them would be hopeless; for she perceived that I had a strong impression they were present.

When I sat down on Sunday, May 6, 1866, to endeavor to get a communication from my mother, such power had been gained that she, with the aid of my sister, was able to identify herself, though with great difficulty.

When, subsequently, I undertook the task of procuring sufficient information to enable me to write a book upon the subject, Mrs. S. sometimes assisted, and sometimes opposed. She was told, and believed, that if I gave a correct explanation of the phenomena, the book would gain credence, and the author become known, even if the name was not given. And as the same plan was stated in the former work as in this for the development of another medium of a higher order than the present ones, she believed that I would be solicited by persons of our world to aid in the development of one, with whom she might manage to be connected. Her intention was that the explanatory narrative should be so written as to produce this result. As published, however, it differed very little from the present one.

Mrs. S. would not consent that her name should be given me, and my friends did not think it advisable to give it, fearing that if I was aware of her presence her power would be increased. The name of Miss M. as being that of the one assisting, was given by Mrs. S., apparently without any definite purpose.

In order to secure the assistance of Mrs. S. it was necessary sometimes to permit her to give her own statements; and therefore the explanatory narrative as

first written was far from correct. It was not the intention of my friends to permit its publication in that
form ; and, in fact, while Mrs. S. wished the narrative
to be so written as to produce the development of another medium, my mother and sister were desirous that
it should discourage any such attempt.

When I attempted to have the narrative corrected, I
only endeavored to get corrections of such statements
as appeared to me altogether improbable or incoherent ;
and therefore all the errors were not corrected ; though,
with the exception of the idea that it was physically
impossible to remove the females, the following is the
only one of any importance that was published :

The explanation of the attempt to give the number
of the store lately occupied by Mr. B., and the name of
his successor, was, that having, as was thought, obtained
from my mind a correct idea of the location of the store
and nature of the business, one of the females went down
Broadway and found such a store in what she thought was
the location of that occupied by Mr. B., and read the
name, and, as she thought, the number over the store ;
that the error in writing the name found was owing to
the interference of my friends ; and that the error of
giving the number of the adjoining store was owing to
the facts that this number was placed near the end
of the sign (over the store thought to be the correct
one), while the correct number was partly hidden by the
sign.

The latter facts were obtained from my mind, as I
ascertained them on looking for the number given the
day following the attempt at the personation. At the
time, the explanation did not seem to me improbable ;

but, as now informed, those of the other world cannot distinguish the colors of ours, and therefore cannot read our painted signs or numbers. The explanation first given shows how aimlessly those of the other world will lie; for Mrs. S. could have had no definite object in view in giving such a statement.

CHAPTER IV.

AFTER the completion of the former work, the efforts
of my friends were directed towards the removal of
Miss McCauley; for which purpose special attempts
were made to place my sister intimately *en rapport.*
Mrs. S. was induced at times, and to a certain extent, to
assist, by the assurance that another medium would be
developed. But the difficulty here was, that she knew
my mother and sister would oppose the development
of another medium; and she also knew that if Miss
McCauley was removed, her own removal would be less
difficult. Consequently her co-operation never was
very hearty; and she constantly aimed at increasing,
or, at least, at preventing the diminution of her own
power.

In a short time my sister became able to converse
orally with me, but only by the exertion of the will of
Mrs. S.; and she was obliged to agree to say nothing
that Mrs. S. objected to.

No explanation of further occurrences is required
until we come to those in the spring of 1869. Before
this time, my friends had become convinced that it
would be difficult, if not impossible, to remove Miss

McCauley without the hearty co-operation of Mrs. S. ; and the question was, how to secure this. My mother and sister were still opposed to the development of another medium ; but it was finally decided that the name of Mrs. S. should be given me, and that I should be told the facts relative to her, in order to ascertain how I would feel upon the subject. Of course, I could not agree to any such plan until I understood all the facts bearing upon the case ; and I insisted that Miss McCauley should first be removed, so that communication might be less difficult, and I could get the advice of those upon whose judgment I could place reliance; for I supposed that there must be some such in the other world.

The agreement under which I went to England, it will be recollected, conceded the latter point ; I was first to be relieved of Miss McCauley, and then, after taking the advice of those I thought most competent to give it, to decide whether I would aid in the development of another medium. As I have said in the preceding narrative, I cannot give the reasons advanced why I should go to England before the removal of Miss McCauley, an operation which would require some time. Some of the reasons urged by the Count were frivolous; but the main one, the one upon which I acted, and which had reference solely to my being relieved as soon as possible of the presence of Miss McCauley and Mrs. S., was, as I am now informed, a valid one.

Until I came to this point in the narrative, I had supposed that the Count, in this scheme, deceived all my friends ; and it has been to me a mystery why, such being the fact, he was permitted to remain with me.

But I now learn that such was not the fact. It appears that my fruitless voyage to England was the result of, what I consider, a childish scheme formed by some of my professed friends—persons of more sense when in our world than this scheme indicates.

At this time my mother and sister were so much *en rapport* with me that nothing could be done without their co-operation; and, although they were anxious that the two females should be removed, they would not consent to the only practicable plan for accomplishing this, namely, the development of another medium.* How Mrs. S. was induced to believe that I would aid in this after the removal of Miss McCauley, I do not quite understand, but it seems that she did so believe. My mother and sister, however, consented to advise me to go to England under the agreement entered into, because they believed that I would not aid in the matter; and they intended to exert their influence to prevent my doing so. The Count, it seems, had no desire to make known the fraud he had committed, unless by doing so he could become connected with a medium; and he also thought it doubtful whether I would aid in developing another; besides, it was far from certain that one could be developed through whom he could communicate.

Under these circumstances, the scheme was formed to induce me to go to England. My male friends understood that the Count would not carry out his part of the plan agreed upon unless his original proposition was

---

* It will, of course, be understood that I do not state this matter precisely as given me by my sister, but state the facts, so far as given, in my own language.

accepted by me; but they deemed it advisable, under the circumstances, that it should be accepted; and believed that if I went to England, my mother and sister, rather than have me return disappointed, would cease their opposition, or, at least, would permit all the facts bearing upon the case to be stated, and let me decide for myself.

If the Count's proposition had been accepted by me, Mrs. S. would, probably, have assisted in the removal of Miss McCauley, for the same reason that she would have done so under the agreement entered into; that part of the plan would not have been changed. And if, after the removal of Miss McCauley, I declined to aid in the development of another medium, the removal of Mrs. S. could have been effected; though if she stopped talking, and did not in any way annoy me, it would have been a matter of indifference to me whether she was removed or not.

The result of the scheme was about such as might have been expected. When my mother and sister, after I had sailed for England, were informed that the Count would not carry out his part of the plan agreed upon unless his original proposition was accepted, and perceived how they had been entrapped into advising me to go under false pretences, they were, of course, very indignant; and my mother, especially, had such a repugnance to this proposal that she was inclined to prevent, if possible, any communication with the parties I went over to visit.

But Mrs. S. still wished to bring about such a meeting, hoping that if this was effected something would be agreed upon. When I sat down in London for the letter

to be written, as agreed upon, Mrs. S., finding that the
Count would not write or dictate one, attempted at each
sitting to write one herself which I would believe
genuine and send, hoping that this would lead to an
interview; though she could have had no definite idea
as to any result. As she failed at the first sitting to
imitate the Count's style, at the second she told
me his mother-in-law would write, thinking she might
thus succeed in deceiving me. These attempts were, of
course, very childish. Even if there had been no interference, she could not have written a letter which would
have deceived me; if I had been deceived, my mother
or sister could have undeceived me before the letter was
sent; and even if it had been sent, as neither the Count
or the mother-in-law would have been identified, it
would have received no attention.

Of course all efforts to effect an arrangement did not
cease when I left London; and when, in Paris, Mrs. S.
stated that the letter would be written at some point in
my travels, she hoped it would be done. The object in
telling me this was to prevent me from making any arrangement to sail from a French port for home. If the
letter had been written, I should have retained it until I
returned to England; but my mother, fearing the Count
might conclude to write, and that I would at once mail
the letter, made extraordinary efforts in the following
night to give me the brief communication stated in the
preceding narrative.

The suspicions of my mother and sister were so aroused
by the discovery of the scheme described, that, as I
understand the matter, it would have been difficult to
have carried out the plan agreed upon, even if the Count

had consented to assist. The course taken by my
mother and sister was, as concerns me, a very strange
one; and I find it difficult to understand the change
individuals undergo on passing into the other world.
The whole matter should, of course, have been submitted
for my decision. If I had known all the facts, I should,
probably, have accepted the proposition of, the Count;
although under ordinary circumstances I would not have
done so. I have stated that Mr. W. and party thought
it an inducement with which they could not hope to
compete successfully; but it did not appear to me so
very attractive. I still think it was a visionary and impracticable scheme; but if I had entered into it, whether
it failed or not, it would not have interfered with the
plan upon which I went over.

The explanation of the difficulty given by my sister
after I had engaged my passage home was not a full one,
and therefore did not make the matter clear to me. It
appears, however, that while my mother's main objection to the proposition of the Count was the association
in our world proposed, that of my sister had reference
more particularly to my serving as a medium for the
Count and his friends. The truth appears to be that
the objections of my sister to my serving as a medium
for this party, or developing another for them, were of
a religious, or, more correctly, sectarian character; for
there are different religious views in the other world as
in ours, and she feared that false doctrines would be
promulgated.

At the sitting when my sister gave the explanation
referred to, the Count stated that his story about the
illegitimacy of his wife's children was a fiction; for he

feared that I would return so indignant at his deception
that I would make the facts known if I continued to
believe them. It would, of course, have been very silly
to have stated these facts, even if there was any incen
tive for doing so, as no one would have believed me.

The fact that my male friends, or professed friends,
connived at the deception of the Count, explains why
he was not removed, as my mother and sister had not
power to remove him ; but why he should have desired
to remain with me I cannot understand.

I have not attempted to learn what discussions took
place after my return from England, but it was finally
decided to attempt the removal of Miss McCauley ; and
I was then, for the first time, told my true situation.
It was thought the co-operation of Mrs. S. would be had,
as there appeared to be no other way of getting another
medium developed, or of inducing me to act as such,
than this removal.

On the night of January 26 (1870), the operation was
commenced, but suspended when the sinking of my
pulse was perceived. On after consultation, it was
thought the operation might safely have been performed,
and it was decided to make another trial. The second
experiment was carried farther than the first; and, for
a moment, there were apprehensions that it had been
carried too far. It was the Count who said, " You
are going, sir," and he thought, or said he did, that I
was dying. I recovered so quickly, however, that it
was still thought the operation might have been completed; and some of the party advised that another trial
should be made. I was then told that the removal of
the two females (it will be recollected that at this time

I thought there were two besides Mrs. S.) had been effected, and that Mrs. S. was the one still opposing my
friends.

It appears that in consequence of the effect of the
first trial, my imagination, or thinking during this second one of what the result might be, had such an injurious effect that it was deemed advisable to take this
course. The trouble, so far as I could judge at the
time, was in the action of my heart; and it was the unavoidable direction of my mind to the action of this organ which increased the difficulty. By telling me that
the removal of Miss McCauley, the most dangerous one,
had been effected, and that the removal of Mrs. S. would
affect only my head, it was hoped to avoid this injurious operation of my mind. It was also thought the
effect on my mind, and consequently its injurious action, would be less in daylight than in darkness; and it
was therefore decided to make the next attempt in the
morning.

All these directions were given by persons who had
been physicians in our world; and the conversation
with me was by the Count. In order that my mother
or sister should talk with me, certain changes were necessary which during an operation of this kind could not
safely be made; the Count therefore was chosen to do
the necessary talking.

But during the night preceding the morning fixed
upon for the third trial, it was decided to postpone it.
The only explanation of the Count's statement in the
morning that Mrs. S. was removed, and that, consequently, I was relieved of all three of the females, is,
that as I had been told her removal would have little

effect upon me, no plausible reason could be given for the postponement: and he thought I could be made to believe that I was relieved until Miss McCauley would be removed, which he supposed could soon be effected. I think it would have been impossible to have made me believe this for any length of time, even if Mrs. S. had been willing that I should believe it, for I should soon have perceived there was at least one opposing my mother and sister. But Mrs. S. feared that if I continued to believe for any considerable length of time that she was removed, her *rapport* would be lessened; and she therefore commenced talking almost immediately after the Count told me she was removed.

It was believed by the party, including the physicians, that the removal of Miss McCauley could be effected within less than one year from that time; and therefore my mother, when I subsequently made the inquiry, named that period.

The assertions subsequently made that I would be " relieved " before the close of the year 1870 were, with the exception of that made on the last day of the year, by Mrs. S.; though my friends hoped such would be the fact. The operation was postponed from time to time until the last day of the year 1870 had arrived; then, as the assertions of Mrs. S. had not been contradicted, and I had consequently formed the hope of being relieved before the close of the year, it was decided to make the attempt during the coming night. The intention at this time was, to make the experiment while I was asleep, and if that appeared to be an unfavorable time, to postpone the operation until I awoke in the morning.

In the afternoon of December 31st my sister informed me that it was intended to make the removal during the coming night; and told me to recollect that she would be unable again to speak to me until after the operation had been performed. This admonition was partly in consequence of what the Count had spoken during the last attempt. His assertion that I was "going," or dying, was injudicious; and my sister did not know what he or Mrs. S. might say to me during the coming operation.

I am unable to give an explanation of the course of Mrs. S. which will appear a rational one; for it was as variable as that of a vicious child. It will be understood that it was the exertion of her will that was required, not any physical effort. Her will was favorably exerted during the former attempts; but since that time her course had been inconstant and unreliable; which is one reason why a third attempt was not earlier made. She promised her assistance on this occasion; but at the last moment insisted that an agreement should be entered into, either that she might remain with me, or that another medium should be developed. My mother and sister would concede neither of these points, and therefore the operation was again necessarily postponed. At the moment of my awaking in the morning, my sister succeeded in telling me that the removal had not been effected; but the subsequent talking was by Mrs. S. The latter, personating my sister, attempted to make me believe the removal had been made, and that she was the one now acting in opposition to my mother and sister—an idea which she probably got from the Count's former statement to the same effect—hoping some ar-

rangement would be made, and that the removal of
Miss McCauley would be effected without my learning
she had caused the postponement. Failing in this, the
Count said the removal was an impossibility.

What the Count really believed was, probably, that
the removal could not be effected without the co-operation of Mrs. S.; and the statement was made for the
purpose of preparing me for receiving some kind of a
proposal. Of course, the efforts made subsequent to
my return from England, had tended to confirm my
male friends in the opinion that the Count's proposition
should have been accepted; and the latter now hoped
it would be.

But my mother and sister would yield nothing; they
would not even consent that the matter should be left
to my decision. Mrs. S. was therefore told by my male
friends that if she did not assist, the next move would
be her removal. She then promised her assistance;
but it was deemed advisable that, before again attempting the operation, my mother and sister should, if possible, gain such control that the removal could be effected with safety, even if at the time Mrs. S. did not
assist. It was still hoped this might be done within
the period first named by my mother; that is, some of
the male advisers so thought, others did not.

The course of Mrs. S. was subsequently about the
same as before; she, ostensibly at least, aided my mother
and sister, but constantly aimed at increasing her own
power. The extraordinary efforts of my mother and
sister, after the expiration of the year first named, were
the cause of the annoyances I suffered at night; and
when the former in the night said, "Bear it one month

longer," it was her intention that if at the expiration of that period they were unable to remove Miss McCauley, the efforts should cease. The efforts did then cease for awhile, and negotiations were entered into.

The plan then agreed upon was somewhat of a compromise with Mrs. S. ; but, as it was soon abandoned, it is not necessary to give a full explanation. It involved the attempt to place the mother-in-law of the Count intimately *en rapport* with me. This was found to be impracticable; the Duchess—her late title—and myself are not, as they term it, *affinities.*

My mother and sister then renewed their former efforts; but, so far as I can learn, without any reasonable prospect of success. The efforts to place the Duchess *en rapport* with me caused me little annoyance, because, not being measures tending to the immediate removal of Miss McCauley, they were less violent; but when my mother and sister renewed their former efforts, the disturbances at night were renewed.

They did not acquire such control that the removal of Miss McCauley could safely be effected without the assistance of Mrs. S. at the time of the operation. But my mother, apparently without any good reason, again believed in the promise of Mrs. S. that her assistance would be given ; and therefore, near the close of the year 1871, told me I would soon be relieved.

The last night of this year was not definitely decided upon, as had been that of the former year, as the time for performing the operation ; for most of my friends had no confidence in the promises of Mrs. S. But the latter assured me when I went to bed on this night, that Miss McCauley would be removed during the night;

and as it was thought possible this might be done, her assertion was not contradicted.

As I understand the matter, what was wanted was the exertion of the will of Mrs. S. to place my sister more intimately *en rapport* with me at the moment when the connection between Miss McCauley and myself was severed; and, as I have already stated, the difficulty in securing this was, that Mrs. S. knew, or believed, that after Miss McCauley was removed, her own removal could be accomplished with little difficulty. Although Mrs. S. did not at this time positively refuse to lend her assistance, it was perceived that it could not be relied on, and therefore no attempt at removal was made. My mother then insisted that all efforts should cease; and in the morning, at the moment of my awaking, told me that it was impossible to relieve me. Her reason for telling me this was that there was a difference of opinion on this point between her and my sister. The latter was unwilling to relinquish the undertaking; and my mother thought if I believed, as she did, that my sister was causing me useless annoyances, she would cease her efforts.

But it was finally decided to attempt the removal of Mrs. S.; for if she would not assist, she was an impediment. For this purpose, my mother again co-operated. Mrs. S. was removed, though only for a brief interval, in the night of January 14th, which caused the piercing pain in my head. She was again removed on the night of the 18th of the same month, soon after I had retired; but in the morning, as there was no abatement of the intense pain, she was returned. Her return alleviated the pain, but did not entirely remove it. She was again removed on the night of the 24th of the same month, soon after I went to bed; and in the morning was again returned for the same reason as before. This ended these experiments.

As the pain was less the third night than the second, it is probable that if there had been no other difficulty, the operations might have been continued until the removal was made final. But such a state of debility was produced by the temporary removals that it was thought advisable to proceed no further.

The removal of Mrs. S. operated very differently from that of Miss McCauley. The immediate effect of the removal of the former was merely intense pain in my head; no effect appeared to be produced upon the action of my heart; and the ultimate result was extreme nausea, loss of appetite, and debility. The attempts to remove Miss McCauley produced, in the first instance, faintness; in the second, violent palpitation of the heart; and it was feared immediate death would be the result of actual removal. It thus appears that the connection of Miss McCauley was at that time of a more vital nature than that of Mrs. S. has ever been; and the reason stated is that she was the first to become *en rapport*. But as Miss McCauley had, even then, much less control of my nervous organization than Mrs. S., not being able to write with my hand or converse orally with me when the latter opposed, it is a matter which I cannot understand. It appears, however, to be understood by, at least, some of those of the other world with me; for when the Count, at the time of the attempts to remove Miss McCauley, told me that the removal of Mrs. S.

would affect only my head, not the action of my heart, it was known that such would be the effect.

Such as I have stated, was the dangerous connection of Miss McCauley with me at the time referred to. Since that time, in consequence of the efforts of my mother and sister, aided by others, her *rapport* has been greatly lessened. Since the removals of Mrs. S., Miss McCauley has been repeatedly removed while I was asleep, without causing anything more than a slight degree of faintness when I awoke, and which in a few minutes passed away.

But I have insisted that all efforts tending to disturb my sleep shall cease. If my friends can remove the two females without causing me further annoyance at night, I shall, of course, be pleased to have it done. But I would not consent again to suffer such disturbances at night as I have passed through, if I could be sure that by so doing I would be relieved of the presence of the females. My former anxiety for the removal of Miss McCauley, and which occasioned the trip to England, was partly owing to the impression that she had power to produce these annoyances. This was stated as the fact by Mrs. S.; and the truth appears to be that my friends, in order to induce me to bear them patiently, have partly concealed from me the facts. The disturbances, since the arrival of my mother and sister, have been owing almost wholly to their efforts to obtain control. As I have now learned that the connection of Miss McCauley is no longer of a dangerous nature, and that she is unable to disturb my sleep, provided my mother and sister cease their efforts, I have requested that this should be done; for as I do not wish to serve as a medium for

communications to others, I care but little how many
devils remain near me so long as I am not in any way
annoyed by them. As stated, previous to the commencement of the violent efforts of my mother and sister,
I had almost forgotten the presence of invisible beings;
and I hope that soon after the completion of this work,
such will again be the case.

It will be perceived that the reason why I have
suffered such annoyances, while other mediums have
suffered none, is, that almost from the commencement
of my experience there has been a contest for the control; first, between Mrs. S. and Miss McCauley, and
subsequently between my mother and sister on the one
part, and the two former on the other, though these two
have not acted in concert. It is true that Mrs. S. did,
for several nights, annoy me by her infantile attempts
at choking; but this would not have occurred, probably,
had she been an entire stranger: and from the time the
idea occurred to her of having me act as a medium, she
caused me no annoyance until my friends arrived and
attempted to remove her. I state this in reply to the
frequent assertions of Spiritualists that the "spirits"
who communicate through mediums, and produce the
physical phenomena, must be benevolent ones because
they do no harm. These "spirits" very closely resemble certain animals of our world; they do no harm so
long as they are not irritated.

So far as has reference merely to the presence of invisible beings with me, my situation does not differ, as
I am informed, from that of thousands, or hundreds of
thousands, who have no knowledge or suspicion of the
fact. And when I consider the strange desire of those

of the other world to learn what is passing in ours—
which desire can be gratified only by becoming *en rapport* with one of us—also, that with every visitor to a
medium who has received answers to questions not made
known to the medium, one of the other world must have
been to a certain extent *en rapport*, I have no hesitation
in believing the statement.

Although I have stated only such facts in reference
to the individuals of the other world who have communicated with me as were necessary to make the narrative intelligible, some of my acquaintances, should
they read this work, will know who two of the male
persons designated by initials are; and it is possible that
it may at least be suspected who is designated by the
title of Count.   For this reason, I wish to avoid making
the course taken by these individuals appear any worse
than it really has been.   All that I have stated in reference to them is, as I am now informed and believe,
strictly accurate; and no valid excuse is, or can be given
for the deceptions practiced.   But as my mother and
sister have evinced such an unconquerable aversion to
their propositions, and as I have stated that the objections, especially of the latter, were of a religious nature,
it may be inferred by some that these persons were
engaged in some very unholy scheme; and it is upon
this point that I think it proper to state my opinion,
based upon all the facts which I can learn.

First, then, as to the proposition of the Count, towards
which—considered without reference to my serving as a
medium—my mother, especially, evinced such a repugnance.   If it was proper to state the proposition, this
matter could be made very clear.   It was, as I have said,

in my judgment a visionary scheme; but that is here of no consequence, as the Count believed it practicable. The aversion of my mother to the proposition would have been the same if she had still been in our world. It is a matter in reference to which her present position gives her no peculiar facilities for forming a correct judgment; therefore her opinion is of no more value now than if she was still a resident of our world; and it was a proposition of such a nature that in deciding upon it men would not, as a rule, take the advice of females. And, further, it was a proposition in reference to which the inclinations of different individuals would vary. I presume that nine individuals out of every ten whose pecuniary circumstances were no better than my own, would gladly have accepted such a proposal. This, I think, is sufficient in reference to that matter.

It is proper to state, however, that since the trip to England, the Count has remained with me and retained his *rapport* at the request of my male friends; and that, having received in our world a university education, he has rendered some service in giving the theories presented in this work. Nevertheless, I am confident that I have not at all misstated the character of the Count. In the spring of 1869, to induce me to go to England, he did tell the most egregious lies as to what great things he would accomplish for me; lies which were utterly useless because I did not believe them, and also because a prospect of getting rid of the two females was sufficient inducement. In short, the Count is unquestionably an incorrigible liar. His idea, in reference to the trip to England was, that if I was first relieved of Miss Mc-Cauley, I would not accept his original proposition; but

that, in my depressed state of mind, if I found it was
my only chance of getting rid of her, I would accept it—
which is about the truth. But, as I have said, my
mother and sister—very unreasonably on their part—
refused to permit the proposition to be fairly submitted
to me; and their suspicions were so excited that the
plan upon which I went over could not have been carried out. I still think that if the matter has been fully
explained to me, this scheme, concurred in by my male
friends, for inducing me to go to England under false
pretences, was a childish one; but it is probable that,
under the circumstances, the retention of the Count *en
rapport* with me was a judicious measure.

Now, in reference to the plan for placing a medium
under the charge of one or more of this party. To this
scheme, although both my mother and sister objected,
the objections of the latter appear to have been the
strongest; and. it is a matter in reference to which her
present position *might* enable her to judge more correctly than I can. My sister believed, and still does,
that great evil would be done in our world by the pro-
mulgation of false doctrines through a medium placed
under the control of such persons. It is possible that
if communication was less difficult, so that my sister
could state fully her views, and the views of others who
agree with her upon this point, my opinion might be
changed; but my present opinion is that we can decide
as accurately in this matter as those of the other world;
assuming that I have received and given a correct idea
of the characters of these persons.

Now, while I do not believe that much good would
be done, I cannot perceive how any great amount of

evil could be wrought. The truth is, unless I am greatly mistaken, these individuals have no particular doctrines which they wish to promulgate; their desire is, solely, for communication with our world. As the communications would be genuine, and not personations, they would do some good by making known the deceptions practiced through other mediums; and many of the female visitors to these mediums can poorly afford to pay the fees charged for delivering short and silly communications from personators of their deceased friends.

In short, although I should have wanted a little more information before deciding, and do not now feel inclined to have anything to do with such an undertaking, yet I think that if at the time the proposal was made I had understood this matter as I now do, I should have been willing to assist in placing Mr. B. *en rapport* with his daughter—provided, of course, that the latter, after learning all the facts, desired it—and let him choose his associates. But the scheme, so far as Mr. B. was concerned, was necessarily abandoned some time since, for the reason that his daughter was married; and, owing to the opposition of my mother and sister, no definite arrangement of the kind was made with another person. It was thought that my aid would be more effectual if the individual of the other world was a former acquaintance than if he was one whom I had never seen. But the undertaking would have been an experiment; and it is doubtful whether Mr. B., or any individual of his class, could become so intimately *en rapport* with one of our world, through such a process, as to be able to communicate.

I have thus stated my opinion of the schemes of these individuals; there was, in my judgment, nothing either unholy or righteous, malevolent or benevolent, connected with them. But why they, and others of their world, are so extremely desirous of communication with ours, is a matter which I cannot yet fully understand. Of course, the explanation, so far as it goes, is, that our world is to them more attractive than their own. Further than this, I should be unable, with my limited information respecting the other world, to throw much light upon the subject, and it is one somewhat foreign to the main object of this work.

CHAPTER V.

MODERN SPIRITUALISM.

As this work is written under the impression that the writer is the first individual of our world who has been able to obtain any truth respecting the other, and as such has been stated to be the fact, I propose in this chapter to give extracts from the writings of modern "seers" and Spiritualists sufficient to show that there is no agreement whatever between their revelations and the communications I have received. I devote a chapter to this purpose because to most persons it will seem almost impossible that there should have existed for the last twenty years constant means for communication between the other world and ours, and yet no truth have been received by the latter from the former. This fact can only be explained by the statement that those of the other world able to communicate through the mediums are not only all liars, but also excessively stupid; so stupid that they lie when the truth would better serve their purpose, at least with intelligent people.

The "seers" really see nothing which they pretend to describe, and I only copy from their writings because their revelations are believed by Spiritualists, and confirmed through the mediums; and because the theories of Spiritualists, so far as they have any, can thus be stated more conveniently than by copying disconnected communications given through mediums. I had intended to give extracts from the writings of Swedenborg, but find that it would be impossible within the limits of a single chapter to give a correct idea of them. A correct *understanding* of them I could not give within any limits, for I am unable to understand them myself, or, more properly, I interpret them as being the writings of a learned lunatic. It will be sufficient to state that the theories of Spiritualists are based upon the writings of Swedenborg; for the theories are formed by the Spiritualists, and merely confirmed by the "spirits," so called. The latter will confirm any theory, no matter what, if it is only false. This I know from my own experience. And the diversity of theories held by Spiritualists is, in a great measure, owing to this cause— namely, that the writings of Swedenborg are differently understood, consequently different beliefs are formed, and all these beliefs being entirely false, are all confirmed by the so-called spirits.

Of course the fact that the doctrines of all Spiritualists entirely differ from those I have received is not the slightest evidence that the former are erroneous. My only aim in giving these extracts is to show that there is a radical difference; that upon no single point is there any agreement; and, especially, that in the fundamental doctrines regarding the change in a human being called death, and the location or boundary of the world into which he then enters, the doctrines differ so greatly as to be utterly irreconcilable.

Those who are familiar with the writings of Spiritualists may as well omit reading this chapter, for it is tedious stuff. I confess that I have myself had patience to read only so far as seemed necessary for the purpose stated.

I will first give extracts from a lecture by Hon. J. W. Edmonds, published under the title "What is Death?"

"So, too, in the case of a brother-in-law, who died after a lingering illness, and of advanced age. I saw who attended his dying moments. I visited him frequently during his illness, and, at his request, I detailed to him what I had then learned as to the life after death. One night, when sleeping in my own home, I was awakened out of a sound sleep about midnight, and saw his spirit standing by my bedside. He told me that he had been up there with his sister-in-law, who had been dead some months, and he had found it to be just as I had told him. I supposed he was then dead, but I found the next morning that he was not, that he had that morning revived from the unconsciousness that had been stealing over him, and told his wife that he had been in the spirit-world; that he had there met some friends, whom he named; that he had found it to be as I had told him; that he knew where he was going; that he was very happy, and wished her not to be distressed at his death, for it was all well with him."

"As I understand it, man is a trinity, consisting—1st, of the animal body, which is possessed of attributes which he shares in common with the whole animal creation; 2d, of the soul, which has its intellect and its affections, proper to itself; and 3d, of what I may call, for want of a better phrase, his electrical body, which connects the soul with the animal body, and which at death leaves the body and passes into the spirit-world with the soul, and there constitutes its form or tenement. As the three united constitute the mortal man on earth, so the soul and the electrical body together constitute the spirit in its existence beyond the grave."

"The next consideration is, what happens immediately after death? The first thing, as I understand it, is the formation of the spirit-body . . . . The formation of the spirit-body has been beheld by me on two occasions, and once, if I recollect aright, it was described by Mr. Davis as having been seen by him. That was in the case of a man who was crushed by a falling bank of earth. When we die, the mortal body decays — passes back to the dust from which it is said to come. But the other two parts of the trinity which I have mentioned—the electrical body and the soul—together pass into the other world. The spirit forms its body there. At the moment, or immediately after death, it passes out of the corpse in the shape of a pale smoke-like flame, and hovers directly over it, an unformed, unshapen cloud for awhile, but gradually assuming the human form. When the process is through, and the electrical body has thus passed from the mortal, and is hovering about it, it assumes the precise form of the corpse it leaves behind. And here you see two persons, the dead body of the person lying on the bed, and the electrical body hovering over it, and both inanimate.

"I beheld in one instance the spirit-body forming directly over the body of the man that lay dead, and when thus formed, I was struck with the marvelous resemblance to the earthly form of the individual who had thus died, represented in the cloud-body first formed. It lay there perfect in form, but there was no animation; suddenly it started into new life. I understood then what it was—it was the soul entering that spirit-body that was its tenement for the other life.

"The next step after the formation of the spirit-body is the awakening to consciousness in the spirit life. With some this is a long time coming; with others it takes but a single instant, varying in different persons between these two extremes, and is produced partly by physical causes, but chiefly by our moral condition.

"I can best illustrate the proposition by telling some incidents that have enabled me to come to something like a correct conclusion upon this subject; whether right or wrong judge you upon your own examination. I say, in some instances it is long before consciousness returns. Once, at a circle, I was visited by the spirit of a young girl—this was, I think, in the month of March —she was the grand-daughter of an English nobleman; she had died in London when dancing at a party. When she awakened to consciousness she was with us. She thought she had been carried into the green-house, and that she was there when peaking to us. She heard our voices, and talked with us under that impression, and she was wonderfully surprised when we told her she was not in London, but in America.

"She was surprised to find that we were not savages, as she had always thought the Americans were, and in the course of my inquiries I found she had never been awakened to consciousness from the moment that she fell and expired until that moment. Then the inquiry was how long that unconsciousness had continued. She could not measure the time, but she remembered one of the feasts of the Church which occurred just before her death, and we knowing when that was, were thus enabled to know that she had been in this state of unconsciousness from the previous November until March. During these four months she had known nothing; she supposed that she had merely fainted in the ball-room, and was then recovering her consciousness in the greenhouse immediately adjoining."

"I had a friend who died here a few years ago, a most good-natured, honest, noble-hearted fellow, but rather indolent. He was brought on one occasion after his death to my house by some spirit friends who desired to rouse him from this state of semi-torpor in which he was involved. He had heard it all his life long preached about the last judgment day, so when he arrived there and began to awaken, he settled down into a state of dreamy composure and waited to hear the last trump. He determined he would not stir, and ought not to stir until the trump had sounded. He was brought to my house by those friends in order to see if they could fully awaken him ; and when told by those friends that he was then in my presence, he said it was all nonsense, and sank again into his half-unconscious condition, and refused to be disturbed."

It must be assumed that the process is the same, whether the "spirit body" leaves the "mortal body" before or after death. The spirit of the brother-in-law of Judge Edmonds must then, according to the latter's theory, have passed through the following process :—First, the electrical body passed out of the mortal body, and hovered for a while over it, "an unformed, unshapen cloud ; " gradually it assumed the human form ;

but, since it had no life of any kind, what caused this is not easily understood. Second, the soul passed from the mortal body, and entered the electrical body; and yet, the man was not dead! Third, the spirit must have procured clothing, for the spirits are never seen naked by the seers; this point the Judge has entirely overlooked. Fourth, after going "up there," and conversing with the sister-in-law, and then visiting the Judge, the above process was reversed: that is, the spirit returned to the mortal body, unclothed itself, the soul left it and entered the mortal body, the spirit body became an unformed, unshapen cloud, and then itself entered the mortal body!

I have copied two of the incidents given by Judge Edmonds as showing that in some cases a state of unconsciousness exists for a long time after death, mainly for the purpose of exhibiting the credulity of Spiritualists. It may be thought by some that if all those of the other world able to communicate through mediums were as stupid as I have intimated, they could not have deceived so many persons apparently cautious upon other subjects. Now, Judge Edmonds is a lawyer accustomed to the cross-examination of witnesses; and yet, when communications from the other world are received by him, he manifests almost childish credulity. If any one of our world told him that the grand-daughter of an English nobleman thought Americans were all savages, he would consider the individual a very ignorant person. Again, if this spirit was not only unconscious, but unable to see where it was, how could it find its way from London to Judge Edmonds? The success of the "spirits" in deceiving people of our world is owing to the fact that the latter do not criticise these communications as they do those of our world. The anecdote of the *rather* indolent friend of the Judge is, if possible, more absurd than that of the grand-daughter of an English nobleman.

I will next give a few extracts from a lecture by Andrew Jackson Davis upon "Death and the After-Life:"

"Man is a triple organization. This fact is established in two ways—(1) by the concurrent observations of all seers, sensitives and mediums, and (2) by the phenomenal developments of individual men and women. Man's external body is a casing composed of the aggregate refinements of the grossest substances. We will name the physical body iron, merely to give it a just classification and position, in relation to mind and spirit. Next, we find that there is an intermediate organization—which Paul called the spiritual body—composed of still finer substances, the ultimation of the coarser elements which make up the corporeal or iron organization. The combination of the finer substances composing the intermediate or spiritual body, being so white and shining, may be called the silver organization. The inmost, or inside of this silvery body (which interior Paul definitely said nothing about), is the immortal golden image."

" We call the inmost spirit—signifying the finest, the super-essential portion of man's nature, composed of all impersonal principles, which flow from. the Deific centre of this glorious universe, taking a permanent residence within the spiritual body, which they fill and exalt, just as the elements of the spiritual body live within this corporeal or iron organization, which is composed of mineral, vegetable, and animal atoms and vitalities.

"And now, having disposed of these general considerations, I will tell you what *I have seen.* I will not give descriptions of phenomena from my supposition or imagination. I suppose that I need not repeat that I have had the periscopic and clairvoyant ability to see through man's iron coating for the past fifteen years; neither need I again remark that, within the last twelve years, the result of the exercise of this faculty has come to be to me an education. I have stood by the side of many death-beds; but a description of manifestations in one case will suffice for the whole."

I omit his description of the passage of the spiritual body from the "corporeal" one, as it does not essentially differ from that of Judge Edmonds.

"The fine life-thread continues attached to the old brain. The next thing is the withdrawal of the electric principle. When this thread snaps the spiritual body is free! and prepared to accompany its guardians to the Summer-Land."

"The clairvoyant sees the newly-arisen spiritual body move off toward a thread of magnetic light which has penetrated the room. There is a golden shaft of celestial light touching this spiritual body near its head. That delicate chain of love-light is sent from above as a guiding power. The spiritual being is asleep, like a just-born happy babe; the eyes are closed, and there seems to be no consciousness of existence. It is an unconscious slumber. In many cases this sleep is long; in others not at all. The love-thread now draws the new-born baby to the outside door. A thought-shaft descends upon some one who is busy about the body. This person is all at once "impressed" to open the door of the dwelling, and to leave it open for a few moments, or some other door of egress is opened; and the spiritual body is silently removed from the house. The thread of celestial attraction gathers about, and draws it obliquely through the forty-five miles of air."

"At the battle of Fort Donelson I saw a soldier instantly killed by a cannon-ball. One arm was thrown over the high trees; a part of his brain went a great distance; other fragments were scattered about in the open field; his limbs and fingers flew among the dead and dying. Now, what of this man's spiritual body? I have seen similar things many times—not deaths by cannon-balls, but analogous deaths by sudden accidents or explosions. Of this person whose body was so utterly annihilated at Fort Donelson, I saw that all the particles streamed up and met together in the air. The atmosphere was filled with these golden particles—emanations from the dead—over the whole battle-field. About three-quarters of a mile above the smoke of the battle-field, above all the 'clouds that lowered' upon the hills and forests of black discord, there was visible a beautiful accumulation from the fingers and toes, and heart, and brain, of that suddenly killed soldier. There stood the new spiritual body three-quarters of mile above all the discord and din and havoc of the furious battle! And the bodies of many others were coming up from other directions at the same time; so that from half a mile to three and five miles in the clear, tranquil air, I could see spiritual organisms forming and departing thence in all directions.

"Individuality usually returns, in cases of sudden death, after a few days in the homes of the Summer-Land. They are usually guided to some Brotherhood, to some Hospital, or to some open-armed Pavilion, and there they are watched and tenderly cared for, as are all who arrive from lower worlds. When the time approaches for the spirit's awakening, then celestial music, or some gentle manipulation, or the murmuring melody of distant streams, or something like breathing passes made over the sleeping one, causes 'sensation' to return, and thus the new comer is introduced to the Summer-Land." –

Judge Edmonds professes to believe Davis to be a seer, and I suppose the latter believes the former to be one; but there is not much coherence in their statements. The spirit of Judge Edmonds's brother-in-law went "up there"—which I suppose means the Summer-Land—without the "life-thread" being snapped, or the door being opened. If it is necessary that some one of our world release the spirit before it can go to the Summer-Land, thousands of spirits must have had a tedious time of waiting for this to be done. I presume that Judge Edmonds really believes that he sees what he professes to describe; but it is quite certain that Davis does not. Davis knew nothing about the battle of Fort Donelson until he read the account in the newspapers; and therefore he could not even have imagined that he saw what he pretends to describe.

I cannot get from these lectures of Davis and Judge Edmonds any definite idea of the "Summer-Land." The volume containing the above lecture by Davis contains also one by him on "Scenes in the Summer-Land," but the boundary is not defined. The following is the nearest approach to a definite description given in the lecture:

"The spiritual world is made from life-points sent out from the chemical coalitions of the planets. . . . . The Summer-Land is the comprehensive sphere. Astronomically speaking, the earth is on one side of that vast galaxy of suns and planets termed the 'milky way,' and directly across this great physical belt of stars we find the sublime repose of the Summer-Land; and this is but the receptacle of the immortal inhabitants who ascend from the different planets that belong to our solar system. These planets all have celestial rivers which lead from them toward the heavenly shores. As each organ in the human body holds its physical relation to the brain by means of nerves and blood-rivers, so these different planets in the physical universe hold a currental, magnetic, and electrical relation to the Summer-Land, which corresponds to the brain."

Judge Edmonds, also, evidently believes that the Summer-Land is the abode of spirits from other planets, as well as from the earth. In his lecture he says that his wife, when she died, was met " by spirits from other planets, with whom she passed away from earth."

In a work by Robert Hare, late Professor of Chemistry in the University of Pennsylvania, entitled " Experimental Investigations of Spirit Manifestations," I find a more definite description of the spirit world. The following, Prof. Hare states to be a communication received

by him from his father, in the spirit world, through Mrs.
Gourley, a writing-medium:

"The spirit world lies between sixty and one hundred
and twenty miles from the terrestrial surface; the whole
intermediate space, including that immediately over the
earth, the habitation of mortals, is divided into seven
concentric regions called spheres. The region next the
earth, the primary scene of man's existence, is known as
the first or rudimental sphere. The remaining six may
be distinguished as the spiritual spheres. The six spiritual spheres are concentric zones, or circles of exceedingly refined matter, encompassing the earth like belts
or girdles. The distance of each. from the other is
regulated by fixed laws."

If I understand this, the nearest zone, or belt—called
a *sphere*—is sixty miles distant from the surface of the
earth, and the farthest, one hundred and twenty miles.
This differs *a little* from the statement of Davis that the
Summer-Land stretches across the milky-way; but
Spiritualists are not at all staggered by trifling differences
like this. The seventh sphere, according to Prof. Hare,
is the highest region attained by any one from our planet;
but beyond this are the "Supernal Heavens," inhabited
by spirits from other planets, who, from some unex-
plained cause, are superior to those from the earth.

"Having spoken of the angels of the 'Supernal
Heavens,' I will explain what is meant by this designation. They are those pure and comparatively exalted
beings who, having advanced beyond the highest sphere
of the planet to which they belonged, and attained a
very high state of moral and intellectual development,
have been admitted into that great and illimitable sphere

of progression which lies outside of all other spheres, and in which the greatest conceivable degree of harmony reigns. It is composed of one grand harmonial society, whose members are privileged to go wheresoever they will through the boundless empire of space. They are principally from the planets Jupiter and Saturn, and hold a much more distinguished rank in the intellectual, moral, and social system than the inhabitants of earth. I have not learned that any spirit from our planet has yet reached the Supernal Heaven."

The belief that the spirit, or spiritual body, can leave temporarily the physical body, is generally, if not universally, held by Spiritualists. I have already given Judge Edmonds' views upon this point. I am informed by acquaintances of the Judge that, according to his statement, his own spirit frequently leaves his physical body, and visits the spirit world; and the spirit of his daughter is represented as doing the same. Mr. B. Coleman, a prominent English Spiritualist, has written a book entitled "Spiritualism in America," in which, after speaking of the case of Miss Edmonds, he says that he is acquainted with a lady whose spirit one night left her body, visited a friend, awoke him by a box on the ear, and repeated to him a verse of Keats.

The principal organ of the Spiritualists in the United States is a newspaper published in Boston, Mass., called the *Banner of Light*. This paper has attached to it a medium, a Mrs. Conant; and nearly a page of the paper has, for a number of years, been filled with communications purporting to be received from the spirit world through her. The following is part of an editorial article referring to Mrs. Conant, taken from this paper:

"When she is sick a constant spirit friend of hers takes possession of her organism and holds control for a time, in order to relieve the *tired* spirit that owns the tabernacle of clay. This fact is patent to us and others who have personally known the medium for years. It is a scientific fact. There is no illusion about it; no psychological hypothesis to be considered. Her spirit roams at will through space, while another spirit has charge of the body. She is sometimes absent for hours. Lately she visited a circle in Dresden, and wrote through the hand of the medium there these words :—'America greets Germany. Mrs. J. H. Conant, of the *Banner of Light.*' Subsequently the *spirit* of the German medium paid his compliments to us, through the body of Mrs. Conant. He said that as the little medium he was then controlling had manifested through his organism in Germany, he could do no less than return the compliment, and added, 'Germany greets America.'"

But it appears that the spirit of Mrs. Conant is sometimes obliged unwillingly to leave her body. In one communication, the spirit making it states that it obtained control by surrounding her with an atmosphere not in harmony with her spirit, which, therefore, left her body, thus giving the spirit then communicating an opportunity to enter and take possession. And this spirit, in reply to a question upon that point, stated that it could, if it chose, retain possession of her body, to the exclusion of the original spirit; adding, that there was danger of evil spirits performing such operations. Another communication states that a spirit can enter a dead body, and cause it to rise, walk, and speak.

I will next give the most explicit explanations I have

been able to find of rapping and table-moving ; of other phenomena I have been unable to find any explanations whatever. The following, purporting to be explanations by the spirits, is from Prof. Hare's work :

"The raps are produced by *voluntary* discharges of the vitalized spiritual electricity from the spirit, coming in contact with the animal electricity emanating from the medium. These discharges we can direct at will to any particular locality, thereby producing sounds or concussions.

" The question being often asked, ' *How do you move solid substances ?* ' I would partly answer it by asking, How does a magnet attract and raise from their resting places certain bodies within whose sphere it is brought? How does a man move his body and direct it whithersoever it goeth? How does God, the Almighty cause of all causes, move and keep in perpetual motion the immense systems which revolve in space, and maintain each in its due relative position? I answer, By the magnetism of a *positive* will.

" We, in common with you and all animals, possess an infinitesimal portion of this power, varying in degree in different classes and in different individuals. When you raise your arm, as in the act of lifting or moving a body, you direct, by the force of your will-power, galvanic currents on the muscles required to perform the function. The muscles acting as levers, through the stimulus of the subtile element, act and react on the more solid parts, the bones, and thus is the object laid hold of and moved, and still *you* do not come into direct contact with the object. Now, this is called a *very simple* operation, and so it would appear, but who understands it? Although advanced spirits are much more conversant with the forces operating in nature than the most intellectually developed man in the form, still they do not, nor can they ever, as long as eternity rolls on, understand the hidden sphere of cause. The operation of the will it is impossible to understand. Now, as I have said, we are not possessed of physical bodies; still we can make the imponderable elements subserve our purpose by acting as bones, nerves, and muscles."

If the spirit had simply explained the last sentence, and stated *how* the imponderable elements were made to act as "bones, nerves, and muscles," there would be some sense in the extract; as it is, I can perceive none. The "spirits" are not asked to explain "the hidden sphere of cause," nor "the operation of the will;" but simply to state how they use the imponderable elements, if they are used, in moving a table; just as, for example, one familiar with the electric telegraph, where an imponderable element is used, would explain its operations. However, the "spirits" probably had little, if any, agency in this communication; it was the product of the medium's own brain. These impressible and writing mediums sometimes give communications from the other world; but as frequently—especially when they are lengthy—the communications are their own productions. I copy this as being, apparently, the most explicit explanation of table-moving the Professor was able to obtain. He does not, himself, appear to think it very clear, since it does not account for the necessity of the presence of a medium. He says:

"The only explanation of which I can conceive is, that spirits, by volition, can deprive bodies of *vis iner-*

tiæ, and move bodies, as they do themselves, by their
will. But the necessity of the presence of a medium
to the display of this power, granting its existence, is a
mystery."

Not much common sense is to be looked for in a man
who—in common with many Spiritualists—is prepared
to believe that spirits can move a table, as they do themselves, by volition ; still, it does appear very strange
that the Professor should not have known the spirits
could explain this "mystery" if they were disposed to
do so.

In another work by Davis, I find what purport to be
explanations of table-moving and rapping. Table-
moving is illustrated by an engraving representing a
group of spirits above the clouds, and over the dwelling
in which a circle is seated around a table. A line is
drawn from the group of spirits to the table, representing a "thread of magnetism" proceeding from the former to the latter.

" There is always a supermundane circle *corresponding* to the structure and conditions of the circle on earth.
And each guardian mind of the *spiritual group* contrib-
utes its proportion of magnetic emanation, to form a
line of communication, just as each person in the *terrestrial group* lends his or her mental and physical influence to *mediumize* the table. Thus there is an earthly
terminus and there is a spiritual terminus to the *fine
thread of magnetism*, which perforating and passing
through all intervening substances, accomplishes the
wonders herein described.

" The above engraving is designed expressly to illustrate the process of table-moving, as accomplished on

principles already explained. Elevated above the cloud-region is seen the spirit-circle in telegraphic correspond-ence with the mundane party in the lower story of the dwelling. The influence from the upper circle is seen passing down through the roof and floors to the surface of the table, where it imperceptibly radiates and emits invisible rays in every direction, and fills the *substance* of the table as water saturates a sponge. This is a true copy from nature. The descending line, it may be re-marked, proceeds in an *oblique* direction, in order to exert a leverage influence on the substance to be moved. But when the 'sounds' are desired to be produced, this line descends almost perpendicularly, as will be here-after shown. The diameter of this magnetic current, which is fine and very strong, as I have frequently seen, varies in size from that of a knitting-needle to a child's little finger."

Evidently, Prof. Hare's informants knew nothing about this sort of an arrangement. And I can perceive no necessity for it if, as Davis states, the spirits cannot enter or leave a room while the openings are closed. If that was the fact, they could move a table precisely as we do.

The mode of producing the "raps" was shown to Davis by a boy, who visited him in company with an Italian gentleman. These visitors from the spirit world, by the way, were unable to enter Davis' room until he opened the door. Davis requested the boy to show him how the raps were produced :

"Immediately he drew near the table, and raised himself about two feet above its level. Still the gentle-man held his left hand. His right hand being at liberty, he moved it rapidly in several directions for a few minutes; then brought it in a calm, firm manner, at a right angle with the surface of the table. The beautiful spontaneous grace accompanying these gestures made the exhibition exceedingly entertaining. His hand had not been in this posture more than three minutes, remaining fixed as by the strongest effort of Will, *when I saw a current of amber softness pass down from the middle finger to the table, on which slight concussions were instantly pro luced.* This phenomenon was very beautiful. But I saw how difficult it was to make them loud, or rapidly, as he and I desired. The concussions were caused by the fine current, proceeding from the hand of the spirit, directed by the will-power, *coming in sudden contact with the electricity which reposed, like latent heat, in the interstices of the board*—in the spaces between the particles composing the top and standard of the table."

Without entering into any further criticism upon it, I will merely state, that if I have received correct information, beyond the fact that these phenomena are produced by beings of another world, once inhabitants of ours, there is no truth, nor even an approximation to the truth, in all that I have copied into this chapter. There is no spiritual body in man, and therefore none to leave the physical body, either before or at the death of the latter; and man is no more a spirit after the death of the present body than before. The inhabitants of the other world—those producing these phenomena—have no more power to leave this globe than we have; and they know no more about the inhabitants of other planets, if there are such than we do. The explanations of table-moving and rapping are equally far from the truth.

It is asserted by some Spiritualists that the writings of Mr. Davis contain matter of a scientific and philosophical nature, which an uneducated man like him would be incompetent to write if it were not dictated by an intelligence higher than his own. I have read very little of his writings; but the following theory of the tides, taken from "Nature's Divine Revelations," which is, I believe, called one of his greatest works, will give an idea both of his science and logic:

"The theories that have been presented to the world concerning the phenomenon of tides, have generally been very incorrect. It has been supposed by a conspicuous astronomer that tides were produced by the law of *attraction*—by the action of the moon upon the earth. This cannot be true, for attraction is not an established principle, especially beyond the atmosphere of any body or substance. To show plainly the impossibility of this being the cause of tides, I will present some of the chief considerations which have an important bearing upon the subject.

"If the moon has any attractive influence upon the earth (more than what consists in the natural relation existing between the two bodies), why, when the moon is in conjunction with the sun, does not the water become *more elevated* on the side of the earth next to these bodies, as might naturally be expected if such attraction existed? Also, substances upon that side of the earth would not then weigh near so much as when the moon was otherwise situated. Also, when the moon is on the opposite side of the earth, and the earth sustains a posi-

tion between it and the sun, why is not the elevation of
the water *equal* at all positions of the earth? For if the
sun and moon exert an equal influence, the result should
be equal heights of water all over the earth.

"It is a well-ascertained truth in astronomy, and in
the principles of mechanics, that a body rotating like the
earth on its axis, has the tendency to throw off substances
in the direction in which it revolves. As the earth revolves from west to east, and at the present time once
in twenty-four hours, it must of necessity produce two
elevations of water, especially as the water surrounds
the whole globe. Every twelve hours the water would
be elevated at the extreme east and extreme west, or, in
other words, at given antipodes of the earth. The elevation of water once in twelve hours is a result of the
centrifugal tendency that the globe creates in one-half
of its period of rotation—corresponding tides being thus
produced on the opposite sides of the earth."

This work, Davis says, was written while he was in
a "superior state." Now, let the philosophers either
prove that the moon has an attractive influence upon
the earth, "more than what consists in the natural relation existing between the two bodies," or accept this
centrifugal theory. Seriously, the fact that individuals
can be found who will cite the writings of Andrew
Jackson Davis as evidence that he must be inspired by
an intelligence higher than his own, sufficiently explains
the spread of Modern Spiritualism.

CHAPTER VI.

I HAVE before me a series of lectures on Sound by Prof. J. Tyndall;* and from the position occupied by the lecturer, as well as from the fact, stated in his preface, that the proof-sheets have been examined by his friends, I feel warranted in concluding that the theory of sound now generally held by scientific men is by the Professor correctly stated. In my examination of the theory, I will, therefore, confine myself to a brief review of this work.

From the following it will be perceived that Prof. Tyndall thinks all our sensations are to be accounted for upon the theory of motion:

" We have the strongest reasons for believing that what the nerves convey to the brain is in all cases *motion*. It is the motion excited by sugar in the nerves of taste which, transmitted to the brain, produces the sensation of sweetness, while bitterness is the result of the motion produced by aloes. It is the motion excited in the olfactory nerves by the effluvium of a rose,

* "SOUND. A course of eight lectures delivered at the Royal Institution of Great Britain by John Tyndall, LL.D., F.R.S., Professor of Natural Philosophy in the Royal Institution and in the Royal School of Mines. London : Longmans, Green & Co., 1867."

which announces itself in the brain as the odor of the rose. It is the motion imparted by the sunbeams to the optic nerve which, when it reaches the brain, awakes the consciousness of light; while a similar motion imparted to other nerves resolves itself into heat in the same wonderful organ." Pp. 1, 2.

The following is given as an imperfect illustration of the mode in which sound is conveyed through the air:

"The process may be rudely represented by the propagation of motion through a row of glass balls, such as are employed in the game of *solitaire*. I place these balls along a groove thus,* each of them touching its neighbors. Taking one of them in my hand, I urge it against the end of the row. The motion thus imparted to the first ball is delivered up to the second, the motion of the second is delivered up to the third, the motion of the third is imparted to the fourth; each ball, after having given up its motion, returning itself to rest. The last ball only of the row flies away. Thus is sound conveyed from particle to particle through the air. The particles which fill the cavity of the ear are finally driven against the *tympanic membrane*, which is stretched across the passage leading to the brain. This membrane, which closes the "drum" of the ear, is thrown into vibration, its motion is transmitted to the ends of the auditory nerve, and afterward along the nerve to the brain, where the vibrations are translated into sound." Pp. 3, 4.

If this experiment with the glass balls was a correct illustration of the theory, I should have nothing to say

---

* The work is illustrated by engravings, which I have not thought it necessary to copy.

against this portion of it; that is, the mode in which it supposes sound to be conveyed through the air. But the truth is, it is no illustration at all of the wave theory. This theory assumes that the particles of matter are separated by an "elastic force," which Prof. Tyndall compares to a "spiral spring;" and sound is supposed to be conveyed by condensations and rarefactions of the conducting medium.

"You ought, in short, to be able to seize the conception that a sonorous wave consists of two portions, in the one of which the air is more dense, and in the other of which it is less dense than usual. A condensation and a rarefaction, then, are the two constituents of a wave of sound." P. 5.

If the reader will suppose the glass balls to be separated by spiral springs, and a series of condensations and rarefactions to be propagated through the string, he will have a correct idea of what is meant by sound-waves. The waves generated by a man's organs of speech in common conversation are said to be from eight to twelve feet, those of a woman from two to four feet in length. That such waves are propagated, the Professor undertakes to demonstrate by the following experiment :—Placing a tin tube, fifteen feet in length and terminating at one end in a small opening, in a horizontal position, with the small opening near a lighted candle, he places a piece of burning paper in the other end, then, by clapping two books together close to the latter extinguishes the candle, and, because no smoke from the burning paper is ejected from the end next the candle, he claims that the candle is extinguished by a sound-wave, and not by a puff of air.

"To show you that it is a *pulse* and not a *puff* of air, I fill one end of the tube with the smoke of brown paper. On clapping the books together no trace of this smoke is ejected from the other end. The pulse has passed through both smoke and air without carrying either of them along with it." P. 12.

This is inexcusably silly. The books, when clapped together as represented in the engraving, forced a quantity of air into the large opening of the tube; this air forced an equal quantity out of the end next the candle; and it requires but a small quantity of air, when forced out of a small opening near a lighted candle, to extinguish the flame. No smoke would be ejected from the opening next the candle—provided the experiment was made immediately upon the burning paper being placed in the other end—until nearly the whole fifteen feet of air was expelled. I find by repeating the experiment (except that I place my mouth at one end instead of the books) with a tube only about *one-fourth* the length of the Professor's, rudely formed from a piece of paper I happen to have in my room, that I can by a "puff" blow out the gas—partially turned down—without forcing any smoke out of the end of the tube next it.

I repeat, such nonsense in what purports to be a scientific lecture is inexcusable; because, as the trial would have been so very easy, the Professor, before claiming that such an experiment demonstrated the truth of his theory, should have ascertained whether a "puff" would not extinguish the candle without forcing smoke through the tube; though, really, it seems to me that an "LL. D., F. R. S.," and "Professor of Natural

Philosophy in the Royal Institution and in the Royal School of Mines," should be able to understand so simple a phenomenon without any trial. The following was, according to the Professor, a tremendous sound-wave:

"The most striking example of this inflection of a sonorous wave that I have ever seen, was exhibited at Erith after the tremendous explosion of a powder magazine which occurred there in 1864. The village of Erith was some miles distant from the magazine, but in nearly all cases the windows were shattered; and it was noticeable that the windows turned away from the origin of the explosion suffered almost as much as those which faced it. Lead sashes were employed in Erith church, and these being in some degree flexible, enabled the windows to yield to pressure without much fracture of the glass. Every window in the church, front and back, was bent *inwards*. In fact, as the sound-wave reached the church it separated right and left, and, for a moment, the edifice was clasped by a girdle of intensely compressed air, which forced all its windows inwards. After compression, the air within the church no doubt dilated, and tended to restore the windows to their first condition. The bending in of the windows, however, produced but a small condensation of the whole mass of air within the church; the force of recoil was therefore feeble in comparison with the force of impact, and insufficient to undo what the latter had accomplished." P. 23.

The theory assumes that the condensation would be succeeded by an equal degree of rarefaction; and if such had been the fact, the windows would have been forced, not merely back to their original position, but outward. But I copy the paragraph mainly for the purpose of letting the reader fully understand what, in the opinion of Prof. Tyndall, constitutes a sound-wave.

The Professor's definition of *pitch*, namely, that it depends upon the rapidity, or rate of vibration of the sounding body, is, I presume, correct; but his explanation of the difference in the *quality* of sound appears to me less satisfactory. It is comprised in the following paragraph:

" Finally, with regard to the vibrations of a wire, the experiments of Dr. Young, who was the first to employ optical methods in such experiments, must be mentioned. He allowed a sheet of sunlight to cross a pianoforte wire, and obtained thus a brilliant dot. Striking the wire, he caused it to vibrate, the dot described a luminous line like that produced by the whirling of a burning coal in the air, and the form of this line revealed the character of the vibration. It was rendered manifest by these experiments that the oscillations of the wire were not confined to a single plane, but that it described in its vibrations curves of greater or less complexity. Superposed upon the vibration of the whole string were partial vibrations, which revealed themselves as loops and sinuosities. . . . . The form of the sonorous wave is affected by these superposed vibrations, and thus they influence the clang-tint or quality of the sound." Pp. 123, 124.

This is excessively absurd. What possible effect can the *form* of the wave have upon the quality of the sound? Besides, that infinitesimal portion of the wave which enters the small and irregular opening called the outer ear, must always be of the form of this opening, in other words, always of the same form.

Without occupying more space with Prof. Tyndall's explanations of any particular phenomenon, I will state my objection to the whole theory. I hold it to be impossible that sound is propagated by a series of condensations and rarefactions, such as the theory supposes, for the reason that all sounds, however much they may vary in intensity, travel with the same velocity; at least, there is no appreciable difference in the velocity. Prof. Tyndall says nothing about this, but it is a known fact, ascertained by experiment; and is stated in most works on the subject. It is also a fact which cannot be reconciled to this theory that the velocity of sound does not diminish as the distance from the sounding body increases; it continues the same to any distance at which it is perceptible. To make my objection understood, I will copy further from Prof. Tyndall's lectures:

" The wave-length is found by dividing the velocity of sound per second by the number of vibrations executed by the sounding body in a second. Thus a tuning-fork which vibrates 256 times in a second produces in air of 15° C., where the velocity is 1.120 feet a second, waves four feet four inches long. While two other forks vibrating respectively 320 and 384 times a second, generate waves three feet six inches and two feet eleven inches long." P. 84.

It will be perceived that the theory assumes the waves to be, at any distance, of the same length as at the starting point. This, in fact, appears to be a necessary assumption, since the sound continues to travel with the same velocity. It is also a necessary assumption from the latter fact, that the waves are propagated with the same rapidity as at the start; that is, that the same number are formed in a given time. In one place Prof. Tyndall calls the condensations and rarefactions *pulses*, and this is a more correct definition than the word waves. Now, if the pulses continue, at any distance from the sounding body, to be propagated of the same length, and with the same rapidity as at the starting point, the loudness, or intensity of the sound must continue the same. This can need no argument, for the pulses would continue precisely the same in every respect. But the *fact* is, that the intensity of sound diminishes as the distance increases. Prof. Tyndall states the law as being that, the intensity of the sound varies inversely as the square of the distance. It is impossible to reconcile the theory, on this point, with the facts.

Again: It will also be perceived from the last quotation that the theory accounts for the fact that sounds of different intensity travel with the same velocity, by assuming that the frequency of the pulses, or the number formed in a second, varies accordingly. Thus Tyndall, having ascertained the distance which sound travels in a second, and the number of vibrations which different tuning-forks execute in the same time, divides the former by the latter; thus showing that if the amplitude, or length of the waves—which, according to this theory, determines the intensity of the sound—created by one fork is greater than that of those created by another, the number of waves created by the latter in a given time is proportionally greater; and, therefore, the rapidity with which the sound is propagated is in each case the same. The fallacy of this mode of reasoning will be perceived by observing the vibrations of a single fork.

"When I first excite the tuning-fork the sound issues from it with maximum loudness, becoming gradually feebler as the fork continues to vibrate. I, being close to the fork, can notice at the same time that the amplitude or space through which the prongs oscillate becomes less and less. But within the limits here employed the most expert ear in this assembly can detect no change in the pitch of the note. The lowering of the intensity of a note does not, therefore, imply a lowering of its pitch. In fact, though the amplitude changes, the rate of vibration remains the same." Pp. 58, 59.

In this case, then, the rate of vibration does not increase as the amplitude diminishes. Now, when the amplitude of vibration has become reduced to one-half its maximum, the pulses have become reduced one-half in length; and as the pulses continue to be propagated at the same rate—the same number per second—as when their length was at its maximum, the rate at which the sound travels must be reduced to one-half its maximum. But the *fact* is, that so long as the sound continues to be audible it travels with the same velocity as when the fork commenced its vibrations. It is utterly impossible to reconcile this theory with the fact that all sounds travel with the same velocity.

As to the mode in which the motion is transmitted from the tympanic membrane to the brain, Prof. Tyndall speaks less positively than in reference to other parts of the theory. The following are, he says, the views now entertained by the most eminent authorities upon this point:

" In the organ of hearing in man we have first of all the external orifice of the ear, which is closed at the bottom by the circular tympanic membrane. Behind that membrane is the cavity called the drum of the ear, this cavity being separated from the space between it and the brain by a bony partition, in which there are two orifices, the one round and the other oval. These orifices are also closed by fine membranes. Across the cavity of the drum stretches a series of four little bones; the first, called the *hammer*, is attached to the tympanic membrane; the second, called the *anvil*, is connected by a joint with the hammer; a third little round bone connects the anvil with the *stirrup-bone*, which has its oval base planted against the membrane of the oval orifice above referred to. The base of the stirrup-bone abuts against this membrane, almost covering it, and leaving but a narrow rim of the membrane surrounding the bone. Behind the bony partition, and between it and the brain, we have the extraordinary organ called the *labyrinth*, which is filled with water, and over the living membrane of which the terminal fibres of the auditory nerve are distributed. When the tympanic membrane receives a shock, that shock is transmitted through the series of bones above referred to, and is concentrated on the membrane against which the base of the stirrup-bone is planted. That membrane transfers the shock to the water of the labyrinth, which, in its turn, transfers it to the nerves.

" The transmission, however, is not direct. At a certain place within the labyrinth exceedingly fine elastic

bristles, terminating in sharp points, grow up between
the terminal nerve fibres. These bristles, discovered by
Max Schultze, are eminently calculated to sympathize
with those vibrations of the water which correspond to
their proper periods. Thrown thus into vibration, the
bristles stir the nerve fibres which lie between their roots
and excite audition. At another place in the labyrinth
we have little crystalline particles called *otolithes*—the
Hörsteine of the Germans—embedded among the nervous filaments, and which, when they vibrate, exert an
intermittent pressure upon the adjacent nerve fibres,
thus exciting audition. The otolithes probably subserve a different purpose from that fulfilled by the
bristles of Schultze. They are fitted, by their weight,
to accept and prolong the vibrations of evanescent
sounds, which might otherwise escape attention. The
bristles of Schultze, on the contrary, because of their
lightness, would instantly yield up an evanescent motion,
while they are eminently fitted for the transmission of
continuous vibrations. Finally, there is in the labyrinth
a wonderful organ, discovered by the Marchese Corti,
which is to all appearance a musical instrument, with
its chords so stretched as to accept vibrations of different periods, and transmit them to the nerve filaments
which traverse the organ. Within the ears of men, and
without their knowledge or contrivance, this lute of
3,000 strings has existed for ages, accepting the music
of the outer world, and rendering it fit for reception by
the brain. Each musical tremor which falls upon this
organ selects from its tensioned fibres the one appro-
priate to its own pitch, and throws that fibre into uni-
sonant vibration. And thus, no matter how complicated

the motion of the external air may be, those microscopic strings can analyze it and reveal the constituents of which it is composed." Pp. 323–325.

The theory which I have received, so far as regards the conveyance of sound from the sounding body to the outer ear, may be very briefly stated. The mode of conveyance was precisely illustrated by Prof. Tyndall with the row of glass balls. It is by a shock communicated from particle to particle, and not by a series of condensations and rarefactions. The vibrating body does *move*—not simply *condense*—a mass of air; but this mass soon comes to rest, while the shock travels on. Now, I shall not undertake to prove, because I presume it will not be disputed, that if the particles touch each other, as in the case of the glass balls, a shock travels with the same rapidity whether it is more or less violent; at least, there can be no appreciable difference. And, which is merely stating the same fact, it travels at the same rate whatever the distance may be from the point of origin.

It is unnecessary for me to apply this theory to the solution of the various phenomena of sound, as the explanation would in most cases be the same as that given in the wave theory; the assumed origin of the sound being in each theory the same. I will, however, copy from Prof. Tyndall's work the account of one more experiment, made to demonstrate the wave theory. I hope to be able to make it understood without copying the engraving. He has a number of jars, of small diameters and various lengths, and by holding a vibrating tuning-fork over the mouths of different jars, so that the vibrations are in a line with the axis of the jar, ascertains that when the fork is held over one jar there is sound, when held over a jar of different length no sound is heard. In the following the letter *a* designates the position of the prong when farthest from the mouth of the jar, and *b* the position when nearest the mouth :

"Our next question is, what is the length of the column of air which most powerfully resounds to this fork? By measurement* with a two-foot rule I find it to be thirteen inches. But the length of the wave emitted by the fork is fifty-two inches ; hence *the length of the column of air which resounds to the fork is equal to one-fourth of the length of the wave produced by the fork.* This rule is general, and might be illustrated by any other of the forks instead of this one.

" Figure, then, to your minds the prong, vibrating between the limits *a* and *b*, placed over its resonant jar. In the time required by the prong to move from *a* to *b*, the condensation which it produces runs down to the bottom of the jar, is there reflected, and as the distance to the bottom and back is twenty-six inches, the reflected wave will reach the prong at the moment when it is on the point of returning from *b* to *a*. The rarefaction of the wave is produced by the retreat of the prong from *b* to *a*. This rarefaction will also run to the bottom of the jar and back, overtaking the prong just as it reaches the limit *a*, of its excursion. It is plain from this analysis, that the vibrations of the fork are perfectly synchronous with the vibrations of the aërial column ; and in virtue of this synchronism the motion accumulates in the jar,

* Of the jar.

spreads abroad in the room, and produces this vast augmentation of the sound."   Pp. 174, 175.

By the wave fifty-two inches in length is meant the condensation and rarefaction produced by one vibration; the condensation is one-half of this, or twenty-six inches. Perhaps the absurdity of Tyndall's idea will be more readily apparent to the reader by supposing the vibrating body to be a piston working in the top of a cylinder.   The piston in moving from *a* to *b* would, according to Tyndall, produce a condensation twenty-six inches in length if the cylinder was long enough; but because the cylinder is only thirteen inches in length, the condensation runs to the bottom of the cylinder, is there reflected, and runs up to the top.   Now, what sense is there in the idea of the condensation running to the bottom and back again?   It seems to me to indicate a strangely muddled condition of the Professor's intellect.   If the condensation would be twenty-six inches in length provided the cylinder was of sufficient length, then, if the cylinder is only one-half that length, the degree of condensation produced will be twice as great. That is all that would occur: there would be no running down and back, or reflection in the case.   And the proper length of jar for that tuning-fork would be twenty-six inches.   At least, if a shorter jar gave more sound, it could only be because the air became more condensed; and, therefore, a still shorter jar, one less than thirteen inches in length, would give still greater sound.   It appears, however, that Tyndall found thirteen inches to be the proper length.

Suppose, now, a column of the glass balls, touching each other, to extend from the bottom to the top of the jar, and that the prong of the tuning-fork when at b strikes the top of the column. Suppose, also, that the shock thus communicated to the top ball would, if the column was of sufficient length, travel twenty-six inches while the prong was moving from b to a; then it would, of course, travel to the bottom of the jar, be there reflected, and again reach the top in the same time.

So far, this new theory is simple enough; but the mode in which it supposes sound to be transmitted to the brain is more difficult of comprehension. The difficulty is in comprehending the functions of the inner ear; and this difficulty is equally great upon any theory. The following description, taken from Dalton's *Physiology*, is, I think, as intelligible as any I could give without copying engravings :

" All the vibrations which are received by the *membrana tympani*, are transmitted by the chain of bones to the membrane of the *foramen ovale*. Behind the membrane of the foramen ovale lies the *labyrinth* or *internal ear*. This consists of a complicated cavity, excavated in the petrous portion of the temporal bone, and comprising an ovoid central portion, the *vestibule*, a double spiral canal, the *cochlea*, and three *semicircular canals*, all communicating by means of the common vestibule. All parts of this cavity contain a watery fluid termed the *perilymph*. The vestibule and semicircular canals also contain closed membranous sacs, suspended in the fluid of the perilymph, which reproduce exactly the form of the bony cavities themselves, and communicate with each other in a similar way. These sacs are filled with another watery fluid, the *endolymph ;* and the terminal filaments of the auditory nerve are distributed upon the membranous sac of the vestibule and upon the ampullæ, or membranous dilatations, at the commencement of the three semicircular canals. The remaining portion of the auditory nerve is distributed upon the septum between the two spiral canals of the cochlea."

It is certainly difficult to imagine that this complicated organ serves merely for the transmission of motion; it does not appear to be at all adapted to that purpose. Owing to the difficulty in communicating, I can only give, in my own language, the idea I have received; and the reader must decide for himself which theory appears the most probable.

A shock, or jar, whether communicated to a living or an inanimate body, always developes electricity. The internal ear is an organ peculiarly adapted to the sudden development and discharge of electricity by percussion; so that the slightest shock received by it causes a sensible discharge. Each shock communicated to the "membrane of the foramen ovale," and consequently to the "labyrinth," causes an electric discharge which is conveyed by the auditory nerve to the brain. The sensation of sound, then, according to this theory, is produced by a rapid succession of electric shocks, transmitted through the auditory nerve to the brain.

The *pitch* of a note depends, as Prof. Tyndall states, upon the rapidity of vibration ; that is, upon the rapidity with which the electric shocks are received. And the *quality*, or that by which we distinguish the music of one instrument from that of another, is determined by the fact stated by the Professor, namely, the minute vibrations. But as there is no wave, there is no " form " in the case. Each minute vibration produces a distinct shock; and it is the order of succession of the shocks of different intensity which determines the quality.

CHAPTER VII.

PROFESSOR TYNDALL has published, under the title of "Heat considered as a Mode of Motion," a series of lectures delivered in the Royal Institution. Having already noticed one work by Prof. Tyndall, I should have preferred here reviewing one by some other author, but have been unable to find such. The assertion that heat is simply a mode of motion, is made frequently enough; but if any other work upon the theory than the above has been published, it has not fallen under my notice. And, in fact, this work contains very little matter purporting to prove, or demonstrate, that heat is motion. The following extracts—which I hope will be understood without the engravings—are all from the third lecture, the only one in which the Professor makes any special attempt to prove his theory :

"Suppose I have a quantity of air contained in a very tall cylinder, A B, the transverse section of which is one square inch in area. Let the top A of the cylinder be open to the air, and let P be a piston, which, for rea-sons to be explained immediately, I will suppose to weigh two pounds one ounce, and which moves air-tight and without friction, up or down in the cylinder. At the commencement of the experiment, let the piston be at the point P of the cylinder, and let the height of the cylinder from its bottom B to the point P be 273 inches, the air underneath the piston being at a temperature of 0° C. Then, on heating the air from 0° to 1° C. the piston will rise one inch; it will now stand at 274 inches above the bottom. If the temperature be raised two degrees, the piston will stand at 275, if raised three degrees it will stand at 276, if raised ten degrees it will stand at 283, if one hundred degrees it will stand at 373 inches above the bottom; finally, if. the temperature were raised to 273° C., it is quite manifest 273 inches would be added to the height of the column, or, in other words, by heating the air to 273° C., *its volume would be doubled.*

" It is evident that the gas in this experiment executes work. In expanding from P upwards, it has to overcome the downward pressure of the atmosphere, which amounts to fifteen pounds on every square inch, and also the weight of the piston itself, which is two pounds one ounce. Hence, the section of the cylinder being one square inch in area, in expanding from P to P′ the work done by the gas is equivalent to the raising a weight of seventeen pounds one ounce, or 273 ounces, to a height of 273 inches. It is just the same as what it would accomplish if the air above P were entirely abolished, and a piston weighing seventeen pounds one ounce were placed at P.

" Let us now alter our mode of experiment, and instead of allowing our gas to expand when heated, let us oppose its expansion by augmenting the pressure upon it. In other words, let us keep *its volume constant* while it is being heated. Suppose, as before, the initial temperature of the gas to be 0° C., the pressure upon it, including the weight of the piston P, being, as formerly, 273 ounces. Let us warm the gas from 0° C. to 1° C. ; what weight must we add to P in order to keep its volume constant? Exactly one ounce. But we have supposed the gas, at the commencement, to be under a pressure of 273 ounces, and the pressure it sustains is the measure of its elastic force ; hence, by being heated one degree, the elastic force of the gas has augmented by $\frac{1}{273}$ of what it possessed at 0°. If we warm it 2°, two ounces must be added. And if we raise its temperature 273°, we should have to add 273 ounces ; that is, we should have to *double the original pressure* to keep the volume constant.

"It is simply for the sake of clearness, and to avoid fractions in our reflections, that I have supposed the gas to be under the original pressure of 273 ounces. No matter what its pressure may be, the addition of 1° C. to its temperature produces an augmentation of $\frac{1}{273}$ of the elastic force which the gas possesses at the freezing temperature ; and by raising its temperature 273°, while its volume is kept constant, its elastic force is doubled. Let us now compare this experiment with the last one. *There* we heated a certain amount of gas from 0° to 273°, and doubled its volume by so doing, the double volume being attained while the gas lifted a weight of 273 ounces to a height of 273 inches. *Here* we heat the same amount of gas from 0° to 273°, but we do not permit it to lift any weight. We keep its volume constant. The quantity of matter heated in both cases is the same ; the *temperature* to which it is heated is in both cases the same ; but are the *absolute quantities* of heat imparted in both cases the same? By no means. Supposing that to raise the temperature of the gas, whose *volume* is kept constant, 273°, ten grains of combustible matter are necessary; then to raise the temperature of the gas whose *pressure* is kept constant an equal number of degrees, would require the consumption of fourteen and one-quarter grains of the same combustible matter. *The heat produced by the consump tion of the additional four and one-quarter grains, in the latter case, is entirely consumed in lifting the weight."*

The deduction, stated in the closing sentence, is all that I have any occasion to notice. This is about as silly as that from the experiment with the tin tube in the lecture on sound. If there had been no weight whatever upon the gas in the latter case, or if the piston had been raised by some external force, and the gas permitted to expand without lifting an ounce, then to raise the temperature to 273° would have required precisely the same additional amount of combustible matter over that required in the former case. The cause of this is that the *capacity for heat* of the gas is increased by expansion; a fact almost as well known, and as long known, as any phenomenon connected with heat.

"Let us now check our conclusions regarding the influence which the performance of work has on the quantity of heat communicated to the gas. Is it possible to allow a gas to expand without performing work? This question is answered by the following important experiment, which was first made by Gay Lussac. I have here two copper vessels, A, B, of the same size, one of which, A, is exhausted, and the other, B, filled with air. I turn the cock C; the air rushes out of B into A, until the same pressure exists in both vessels. Now the air, in driving its own particles out of B, performs work, and experiments which we have already made inform us, that the residue of air which remains in B must be chilled. The particles of air enter A with a certain velocity, to generate which the heat of the air in B has been sacrificed; but they immediately strike against the interior surface of A, their motion of translation is annihilated, and the exact quantity of heat lost by B appears in A. Mix the contents of A and B together, and you have air of the original temperature. There is no work performed, and there is no heat lost."

This is called an important experiment. Now, the idea which most persons have of an experiment is, that it is performed to ascertain or demonstrate something; this did nothing of the kind. It was not even shown that the air rushed out of B into A; though I think we may assume that such would be the fact, because this has been demonstrated by other experiments. But the succeeding idiotic statements of the Professor were not confirmed by merely turning "the cock C," which appears to be all that was done. He says the heat lost by B appears in A; but he made no attempt to show that such was the fact. And what could the man have meant by such a statement, or by the statement that if the contents of the two vessels were mixed together the air would be of the original temperature? The truth evidently is, that the Professor had somehow got the idea in his muddled brain that this was a "scientific" theory, but had no clear conception, or definite idea of what he was talking about. To perceive any sense in the paragraph, it would be necessary to assume that the

air in A became actually warmer than before the expansion occurred. But every one of ordinary education
knows that the air in both vessels would become alike
cooled; and, therefore, that if mixed together, no change
of temperature would occur. If the contents of both
vessels were again *condensed* into one, the air would return to its original temperature. But to assume that
the Professor meant *condense* when he said *mix* would
be to assume that he does not understand the English
language; besides, this would make the paragraph utterly meaningless. No heat was "lost" in this case,
and none is lost by air which performs "work." If in
the latter case the air was condensed to its original volume, it would regain its original temperature; assuming, of course, that no heat was subtracted by contact
with colder surfaces.

"Mr. Joule made this experiment by compressing
twenty-two atmospheres of air into one of his vessels,
while the other was exhausted. On surrounding both
vessels by water, kept properly agitated, no augmentation of temperature was observed in the water, when the
gas was allowed to stream from one vessel into the
other."

I can readily believe that. Instead of the temperature of the water being augmented, it would, of course,
be decreased by the operation. The air would be cooled
by the expansion, and would then extract heat from the
water; assuming that the air and water were at the same
temperature before the expansion occurred. I know
nothing about Mr. Joule, but is it possible that there is,
or has recently been, living in England, another philos-
opher besides Tyndall who would make an experiment

to ascertain whether the expansion of air surrounded by
water *heated* the water? I had supposed that every one
of ordinary information knew that the expansion of air
cooled it, and that it would extract heat from any body
warmer than itself placed in contact with it.

I suppose Tyndall's idea must have been this: In
this experiment the air performed no work, consequently
it lost no heat; and the fact that the water gained no
heat proves that the air lost none. No theory of heat
with which I am familiar, assumes that the air would
lose heat in such a case. The *caloric* theory, as it is
called, does not; it simply assumes that the heat becomes less sensible, and that if the air was condensed
to its original volume it would be as warm as before.
In the illustration of the cylinder, where the expanding
air lifted a weight, it performed "work." In this case
heat was added to the air. But let us suppose a body
of compressed air in the lower portion of the cylinder.
The air would, by expansion, lift a weight to the top
of the cylinder without any heat being added to it;
though, of course, a less weight than if heat was added.
According to Tyndall's theory, if the cylinder in this
case was surrounded with water of the temperature of
the air before it commenced expanding, the water would
gain heat, because the air performs work, and therefore
loses heat. But the well-known *fact* is, that the water
would lose heat, instead of gaining. Tyndall admits
that in such a case the air would become cooled; and
every one knows that if two bodies of unequal temperature are placed in contact the colder will extract heat
from the warmer until both become of the same temperature.

But look at the incoherency of the Professor's ideas, viewed upon his own theory. The heat of a body according to his theory, is simply motion of the particles of the body. By losing heat, must be meant, that the particles lose their motion, or that their motion becomes less violent. Tyndall's idea, then, must be that air in lifting a weight loses heat because the pressure of the weight upon the particles reduces their motion. Now, can any sane man imagine how the reduction of the motion of the particles of the air by the pressure of the weight would increase the motion of the particles of the water surrounding the air? If the theory assumed that when two bodies of unequal temperature are placed in contact, the warmer body will gain heat from the colder one, then it might be assumed that the water in such a case would gain heat, but not otherwise.

"In like manner, supposing the top of the cylinder* to be closed, and the half above the piston a perfect vacuum; and suppose the air in the lower half to be heated 273°, its volume being kept constant. If the pressure were removed the air would expand and fill the cylinder; the lower portion of the column would thereby be chilled, but the upper portion would be heated, and mixing both portions together, we should have the whole column at a temperature of 273°. In this case we raise the temperature of the gas from 0° to 273°, and afterwards allow it to double its volume; the state of the gas at the commencement, and at the end, is the same as when the gas expands against a constant pressure, or lifts a constant weight; but the absolute quantity of

* Referring to former illustration.

heat in the latter case is 1 421 times that employed in the former, the difference being due to the fact that the gas, in the one case, performs mechanical work, and in the other not."

This, again, is positively idiotic. The Professor here states plainly, that when a column of air expands, the upper portion becomes warmer, so that, although the lower portion is chilled, the mean temperature remains the same. My readers, at least those who are *not* professors of natural philosophy, must know that the whole column would be cooled, and cooled in the same degree. And it makes not the slightest difference whether the air does, or does not, lift a weight; the degree of refrigeration produced by the expansion is in each case precisely the same; and it would require, in each case, precisely the same amount of heat to raise the temperature of the expanded air to any given point.

"We are taught by this experiment that mere rarefaction is not of itself sufficient to produce a lowering of the mean temperature of a mass of air. It was, and is still, a current notion, that the mere expansion of a gas produced refrigeration, no matter how that expansion was effected. The coldness of the higher atmospheric regions was accounted for by reference to the expansion of the air. It was thought that what we have called the 'capacity for heat' was greater in the case of the rarefied than of the unrarefied gas. But the refrigeration which accompanies expansion is, in reality, due to the consumption of heat in the performance of work by the expanding gas. Where no work is performed there is no absolute refrigeration."

This is another of the Professor's "experiments."

In this case he did not even do as much as in the "important exp riment," where "the cock C" was turned; at least I infer it was. How "we are taught" anything by an experiment, where no experiment is performed, I fail to perceive. Speaking for myself, I do not feel as though I had been "taught" much. If the Professor had permitted a column of air to expand, as supposed, tested with a thermometer the temperature of the air before expansion, and that of the upper portion of the column after expansion, this would have been an experiment; and this would have shown him that the upper portion was cooled by the expansion, for this kind of an experiment has been often made. It is, and I hope will continue to be, with all but a few crack-brained professors like this one, "a current notion" that expansion produces refrigeration, whether "work" is performed or not.

And look again at the incoherency of the Professor. The upper portion of the atmosphere, according to him, becomes cooled by expansion, while the upper portion of air in a cylinder becomes heated from the same cause. For all the air in the cylinder performs precisely the same kind of "work" that the upper portion of the atmosphere does.

As I have already stated, if heat is simply a motion of the particles of a body, and expansion does not produce refrigeration unless a weight is lifted, then it must be that the pressure upon the particles impedes their motion, and brings them to a state of rest, or of less violent motion. No meaning or coherence can be perceived in the theory unless this is the assumption. But if this were true, then the greater the weight, or pressure, the more rapid would be the refrigeration. A weight which a column of air could not lift would bring the particles to a state of rest sooner than one which it could lift. In other words, if a column of heated air was prevented from expanding, it would, according to this theory, cool more rapidly than if expansion was permitted, whether it lifted a weight or not.

The preceding twaddle is followed by this exhortation, which closes the lecture :—" All this needs reflection to arrive at clearness, but every effort of this kind which you make will render your subsequent efforts easier, and should you fail, at present, to gain clearness of comprehension, I repeat my recommendation of patience. Do not quit this portion of the subject without an effort to comprehend it—wrestle with it for a time, but do not despair if you fail to arrive at clearness."

Wrestle with it ! One might as profitably " wrestle " with Andrew Jackson Davis' theory of the tides, which I have given at the close of the fifth chapter.

Professor Tyndall is one of those wonderfully " scientific " men, who know, without examination, that all the phenomena called by some spiritual, are mere jugglery. Or, perhaps they will visit a medium once or twice, and then explain the "whole thing;" while to common people, like myself, after the most careful and cautious examination, the phenomena remain a profound mystery.

In a work by Prof. Tyndall, entitled " Fragments of Science for Unscientific People," there is an article under the heading of "Science and the Spirits"— Science being represented by Tyndall—giving an account of a *séance* where an attempt was made to investigate the subject by, as stated, "a scientific man," namely, Tyndall. I have here given all the "science" there is in the article; why it was published, since it does not give a particle of information, no one but "a scientific man," like Tyndall—and *just* such an one—can perceive. However, Tyndall got under the table to see how the raps were made; and he states that he arose from under that table with a despair for humanity, such as he never felt before. Here the Professor leaves us in the dark ; as to what caused such great depression he does not give the slightest hint; it is enough that "a scientific man" arose from under that table with despair for humanity. This leads me to the repetition of a remark which I have read several times, namely, that this is a melancholy and despairing world ! Prof. Tyndall despairs because "unscientific people" will believe the evidence of their senses against the assertions of "scientific men" like himself; while the reflection that such humbugs are considered scientific men has upon my mind an equally depressing effect.

CHAPTER VIII.

In the *Encyclopedia Metropolitana*, I find the following definitions of the *corpuscular* and *undulatory* theories of light, by Sir J. F. W. Herschel :

" *The Newtonian, or Corpuscular Theory.*

" Postula 1. That light consists of particles of matter possessed of inertia and endowed with attractive and repulsive forces, and projected or emitted from all luminous bodies with nearly the same velocity, about 200,000 miles per second.

" 2. That these particles differ from each other in the intensity of the attractive and repulsive forces which reside in them, and in their relations to the other bodies of the material world, and also in their actual masses, or inertia.

" 3. That these particles, impinging on the retina, stimulate it and excite vision. The particles whose inertia is greatest producing the sensation of red, those of least inertia of violet, and those in which it is intermediate the intermediate colors.

" 4. That the molecules of material bodies, and those of light, exert a mutual action on each other, which consists in attraction and repulsion, according to some law or function of the distance between them ; that this law is such as to admit, perhaps, of several alternations, or changes from repulsive to attractive force; but that when the distance is below a certain very small limit it is always attractive up to actual contact; and that be-yond this limit resides at least one sphere of repulsion. This repulsive sphere is that which causes the reflexion of light at the external surfaces of dense media ; and the interior attraction that which produces the refraction and interior reflexion of light.

" 5. That the forces have different absolute values, or intensities, not only for all different material bodies, but for every different species of the luminous molecules, being of a nature analogous to chemical affinities, or electric attractions, and that hence arises the different refrangibility of the rays of light.

" 6. That the motion of a particle of light under the influence of these forces and its own velocity is regulated by the same mechanical laws which govern the motions of ordinary matter, and that therefore each particle de-scribes a trajectory capable of strict calculation so soon as the forces which act on it are assigned.

" 7. That the distance between the molecules of material bodies is exceedingly small in comparison with the extent of their spheres of attraction and repulsion on the particles of light.   And

" 8. That the forces which produce the reflexion and refraction of light are, nevertheless, absolutely insensible at all measurable or appreciable distances from the molecules which exert them.

" 9. That every luminous molecule, during the whole of its progress through space, is continually passing through certain periodically recurring states, called by Newton fits of easy reflexion and easy transmission, in virtue of which (from whatever cause arising, whether from a rotation of the molecules on their axes, and the consequent alternate presentation of attractive and repulsive poles, or from any other conceivable cause) they are more disposed, when in the former states or phases of their periods, to obey the impulse of the repulsive or reflective forces of the molecules of a medium; and when in the latter, of the attractive."

This theory has now, I believe, no advocates; and I copy these definitions merely for the purpose of letting the reader perceive wherein it agrees with, and wherein it differs from, that which I have received.

" The Undulatory Theory.

"1. That an excessively rare, subtle and elastic medium, or *ether*, fills all space, and pervades all material bodies, occupying the intervals between their molecules; and either by passing freely among them, or by its extreme rarity, offering no resistance to the motion of the earth, the planets or comets in their orbits appreciable by the most delicate astronomical observations; and having inertia but not gravity.

"2. That the molecules of the ether are susceptible of being set in motion by the agitation of the particles of ponderable matter; and that when any one is thus set in motion it communicates a similar motion to those adjacent to it, and thus the motion is propagated farther and farther in all directions, according to the same mechanical laws which regulate the propagation of undulations in other elastic media, as air, water or solids, according to their respective constitutions.

" 3. That in the interior of refracting media the ether exists in a state of less elasticity, compared with its density, than in vacuo; *i. e.*, in space empty of all other matter; and that the more refractive the medium, the less, relatively speaking, is the elasticity of the ether in its interior.

" 4. That vibrations communicated to the ether in free space are propagated through refractive media by means of the ether in their interior, but with a velocity corresponding to its inferior degree of elasticity.

" 5. That when regular vibratory motions of a proper kind are propagated through the ether, and passing through our eyes, reach and agitate the nerves of the retina, they produce in us the sensation of light, in a manner having a more or less close analogy to that in which the vibrations of the air affect the auditory nerves with that of sound.

" 6. That as in the doctrine of sound, the frequency of the aërial pulses, or the number of excursions to and fro, from the point of rest, made by each molecule of the air, determines the pitch or note, so, in the theory of light, the frequency of the pulses, or number of impulses made on our nerves in a given time by the ethereal molecules next in contact with them, determines the *color* of the light; and that as the absolute extent of the motion to and fro of the particles of air determines the loudness of the sound, so the *amplitude* or extent of the excursions of the ethereal molecules from their points of rest determines the *brightness* or intensity of the light."

After stating the doctrine that, "supposing the elastic medium uniform and homogeneous, all motions of whatever kind are propagated through it in all directions with one and the same uniform velocity," Herschel makes the following comment:

"Now, here arises, *in limine*, a great difficulty; and it must not be dissembled that it is impossible not to look at it as a most formidable objection to the undulatory doctrine. It will be shown presently that the deviation of light by refraction is a consequence of the difference of its velocities within and without the refracting medium, and that when these velocities are given the amount of deviation is also given. Hence it would appear to follow unavoidably, that rays of all colors must be in all cases equally refracted; and that, therefore, there could exist no such phenomenon as dispersion. Dr. Young has attempted to gloss over this difficulty, by calling in to his assistance the vibrations of the ponderable matter of the refracting medium itself, as modifying the velocity of the ethereal undulations within it, and that differently according to their frequency, and thus producing a difference in the velocity of propagation of the different colors; but to us it appears with more ingenuity than success. We hold it better to state it at once in its broadest terms, and call on the reader to suspend his condemnation of the doctrine for what it *apparently* will not explain, till he has become acquainted with the immense variety and complication of the phenomena which it will. The fact is, that neither the corpuscular nor the undulatory, nor any other system which has yet been devised, will furnish that complete and satisfactory explanation of all the phenomena of light which is desirable."

In a more recent work I find it stated as a compara-tively modern discovery, that the velocity of propaga-tion varies with the length of the wave, being greatest for the longer ones, and least for the shorter; and this discovery, the writer thought, removed the objection stated by Herschel. Whether this reputed discovery has been fully confirmed, or supposed to have been, or not, I am unable to state. Of course there could be no truth in it if Herschel's doctrine that, in a homogeneous medium, all motions are propagated with equal velocity, was correct; but it appears to me certain that upon this point Herschel was entirely, and unaccountably, mis-taken.

The explanation given by Herschel of the fact that light transmitted through a prism exhibits colors—the *prismatic spectrum*—while that transmitted through a plate of glass having parallel sides does not, appears to me unsatisfactory. The explanation is, in brief, that in the latter case, the light, which is decomposed by the first surface, is recomposed by the second surface. Each undulation suffers the same degree of refraction by the second surface as by the first, and in the oppo-site direction, therefore, on leaving the second surface the undulations are propagated parallel to each other, and the light is thus recomposed. Now, if the colors are separated by the first surface, if the red waves are refracted to one side of the beam of light, and the violet to the other side, they must remain separated on leaving the second surface, although they proceed parallel to each other. But it is said *all* the colors are not transposed, or separated, by the first surface. Then they are not all separated by a prism. The degree of separation, or decomposition, effected by a prism would be greater than that effected by a plate of glass having parallel sides ; and, therefore, in the former case the colors would be more distinct; but the fact that in the latter case the light appears *entirely colorless* is not explained by this theory.

Sir David Brewster, in his *Treatise on Optics*, gives the same explanation as Herschel, of the effect of the two surfaces of a plate of glass having parallel sides; and demonstrates the theory, as he thinks, by the following experiment:

"The refraction and re-union of the rays in this experiment may be well exhibited by placing a thick plate of oil of cassia between two parallel plates of glass, and making a narrow beam of the sun's light fall upon it very obliquely. The spectrum formed by the action of the first surface will be distinctly visible, and the re-union of the colors by the second will be equally distinct. We may, therefore, consider the action of a plate of parallel glass on the sun's rays passing obliquely through it, that is, its property of transmitting them colorless, as a sufficient proof of the recomposition of light."

This is rather loose language for a scientific treatise. No re-union of the rays by the second surface can be perceived ; all that can properly be said is, that the light which passes through the parallel sides appears colorless. But how could Sir David perceive the spectrum formed, as he thought, by the first surface ? There is no possibility of perceiving the action of the first surface; for the light which enters the eye must pass through two surfaces. I presume that Sir David, in viewing the spectrum, let the beam of light fall upon the side of the plate, and viewed the first surface through the top, or edge, of the plate. The light which entered his eyes, had, therefore, passed through what was practically a *prism;* and the experiment demonstrated nothing, except that light passed through a prism exhibits colors while that passed through parallel surfaces does not.*

I cannot, of course, within the limits of a single chapter, undertake a general examination of this theory; but will notice what is, I believe, considered one of its strongest evidences, and state what I think the most valid objections. The ethereal undulations have been compared to those of a stretched cord : and an assemblage of stretched cords through which undulations in all planes, and of different lengths, are propagated, will give an idea of what is meant in this theory by a ray of light. The discovery, as is thought, of the interference of light, is considered one of the strongest evidences of the truth of the theory ; and this reputed discovery appears to be a deduction from an experiment by Dr. Young. The following is from Herschel's Treatise :

" Dr. Young passed a sunbeam through a hole made

* When the above was written, I thought the phenomena referred to could not be explained upon the undulatory theory. I should still think so if there was no other explanation than that given by Herschel and Brewster, and therefore have not cancelled the criticism. But the theory I have since received explains the refraction in each case in the same way. The explanation of the fact that no colors are distinguished in the case of the parallel sides is, however, entirely different.

with a fine needle in thick paper, and brought into the
diverging beam a slip of card one-thirtieth of an inch
in breadth, and observed its shadow on a white screen at
different distances. The shadow was divided by parallel
bands, but the central line was always white. That
these bands originated in the interference of the light
passing on both sides of the card Dr. Young demonstrated by simply intercepting the light passing on one
side by a screen, leaving the rays on the other side to
pass freely. In this arrangement, all the fringes which
had before existed in the shadow disappeared."

The following is Herschel's explanation of interference:
"If two waves arrive at once at the same molecule of
the ether, that molecule will receive at once both the
motions it would have had in virtue of each separately,
and its resultant motion will, therefore, be the diagonal
of a parallelogram whose sides are the separate ones. If,
therefore, the two component motions agree in direction
or very nearly so, the resultant will be very nearly equal
to their sum, and in the same direction. If they very
nearly oppose each other, then to their difference. Suppose, now, two vibratory motions consisting of a series
of successive undulations in an elastic medium, all
similar and equal to each other, and indefinitely repeated, to arrive at the same point from the same original
centre of vibration, but by different routes (owing to the
interposition of obstacles or other causes) exactly, or
very nearly in the same final direction; and suppose,
also, that owing either to a difference in the lengths of
the routes, or to a difference in the velocities with which
they are traversed, the time occupied by a wave in
arriving by the first route (A) is less than that of its

arriving by the other (B). It is clear, then, that any ethereal molecule placed in any point common to the two routes A B will begin to vibrate in virtue of the undulations propagated along A before the moment when the first wave propagated along B reached it. Up, then, to this moment its motions will be the same as if the waves along B had no existence. But after this moment its motions will be very nearly the sum or difference of the motions it would have separately in virtue of the two undulations each subsisting alone, and the more nearly, the more nearly the two routes of arrival agree in their final direction. Now, it may happen that the difference in the lengths of the routes, or the difference of velocities is such, that the waves propagated along B shall reach the intersection exactly one-half an undulation behind the others, *i. e.*, later by exactly half the time of a wave running over a space equal to a complete undulation. In that case, the molecule which in virtue of the vibrations propagated along A would (at any future instant) be in one phase of its excursions from its point of rest, would in virtue of that propagated along B, if subsisting alone, be at the same instant in exactly the opposite phase, *i. e.*, moving with equal velocity in the contrary direction. Hence, when both systems of vibration co-exist the motions will constantly destroy each other, and the molecule will remain at rest. The same will hold good if the difference of routes or velocities be such, that the vibrations propagated along B shall reach the intersection of the routes exactly $\frac{3}{2}$, $\frac{5}{2}$, $\frac{7}{2}$, etc., of a complete period of undulations after those propagated along A."

This is all clear enough with one exception. I am

unable to perceive what difference it can make, as to
interference, whether the two series of un.lulations do, or
do not, proceed from the same original centre of vibration and nearly agree in their final direction. Other
writers take the same view of this point as Herschel;
but it seems to me a strange hallucination. Suppose
undulations propagated along two cords which cross
each other, can it make any difference, as to the interference of the undulations, what the angle of intersection
is? If the cords crossed at right angles, and the vibrations at the point of intersection were opposed, one being
downward and the other upward, they would destroy
each other just as certainly as if the cords were nearly
parallel. It is the direction of each force operating
upon the molecule, in the case supposed, which determines the result, not the direction of each wave.

Herschel illustrates the matter by supposing a wave
formed in a reservoir to be divided by entering two
canals which unite at some distance from the reservoir.
If the difference in the lengths of the canals is such,
that at the point of junction the elevation of the water
in one will coincide with the depression in the other,
there will be smooth water in the joint canal. The
objection to this is, that it is not an illustration of the
phenomena under consideration. A parallel case would
be to suppose a thousand waves, originated by a thousand independent impulses, proceeding by a thousand
canals into one common canal. The *number* of waves
which conflict and coincide would be the same whether
the canals were of the same, or of different lengths.

The point to be ascertained is, how the insertion of
the slip of card, in Dr. Young's experiment, produced

sensible interference, when otherwise there would have been none. Granting Herschel's views to be correct, how does the slip of card produce interference? The only attempt at a definite explanation of this point that I have seen is in a work by Jonathan Pereira on *Polarized Light*. Pereira's theory is, that a portion of the waves are reflected, or caused to diverge from their original course by the slip of card; these intersect waves which continue their original course; and when at the point of intersection the vibrations of the two waves conflict, there will be mutual destruction, and a dark spot will be the result.

Now, Pereira, in another place, says that "any sensible portion of light must contain an infinity of rays;" here he assumes the undulations to be of such magnitude that the destruction of two will produce a dark spot. Again, as the undulations proceed in straight lines from the sun to the screen, they must intersect without the insertion of the card; in fact, the undulations reflected by the card would, if they had continued their original course, have intersected other undulations. Why, then, are not the dark lines observed without the insertion of the card? Finally, if Pereira's theory was correct, the insertion of a wider slip would have the same effect; but it is quite certain that if a slip of any considerable width was inserted no such phenomena would be observed. If any advocate of the undulatory theory has given a clear and sensible explanation of this experiment, cited as one of the strongest proofs of the theory, I have been unable to find it.

One of the principal objections advanced against this

theory is, that it does not account for the effect of light upon vegetation, or for its various chemical effects. In a work by Robert Hunt, F.R.S., entitled *Researches on Light in its Chemical Relations*, I find, among others of similar import, the following statements:

"Those rays which give the most light—the yellow and the orange rays—will not produce change of color in the chloride of silver.

"Those rays which have the least illuminating power —the blue and violet—produce the greatest change, and in an exceedingly short space of time.

"The rays which pass through certain yellow glasses have no effect on chloride of silver.

"The rays which pass through very dark blue glasses rapidly change the color.

"The yellow glasses obstruct scarcely any light; the blue glasses may be so dark as to admit of the permeation of a very small quantity."

Mr. Hunt thinks that the undulatory theory does not account for the results of his experiments. And is it conceivable that while one undulation will rapidly effect a certain chemical change, another undulation will not produce it at all?

Sir David Brewster, in his *Treatise on Optics*, makes the following remarks upon this point:

"The colors of vegetable life and those of various kinds of solids arise, we are persuaded, from a specific attraction which the particles of these bodies exercise over the differently colored rays of light. It is by the light of the sun that the colored juices of plants are elaborated, that the colors of bodies are changed, and that many chemical combinations and decompositions are effected. It is not easy to allow that such effects can be produced by the mere vibration of an ethereal m - dium ; and we are forced, by this class of facts, to reason as if light was material. When a portion of light enters a body, and is never again seen, we are entitled to say that it is detained by some power exerted over the light by the particles of the body. That it is attracted by the particles seems extremely probable, and that it enters into combination with them, and produces various chemical and physical effects, cannot well be doubted ; and without knowing the manner in which this combination takes place, we may say that the light is *absorbed*, which is an accurate expression of the fact."

But what appears to me the greatest, and indeed an unanswerable objection to the undulatory theory, has never, so far as my reading has extended, been advanced. It is to be found in the fact that the intensity of light is inversely as the square of the distance from the luminous body. This has been definitely ascertained by experiments with photometers.

The undulations, as I have already stated, are compared to those running through a stretched cord. These, that is, the vibrations to each side of a straight line, become less and less as they recede from the point of origin; and as it is the extent, or amplitude, of these vibrations which determines the intensity of the light, the intensity of the light must diminish from this cause as the distance increases. " Thus," Herschel says, " while the intensity of light, like that of sound, diminishes as the distance from its origin increases, its velocity remains invariable."

Herschel is here speaking with reference to this theory; and the idea conveyed is, that the undulations continue of the same *length*, and are performed in the same time as at the commencement, but the extent of the vibrations transversely diminishes as the distance increases. He states the law as being that the vibrations are "inversely as the distance;" and, by a chain of reasoning which I think it unnecessary to copy, arrives at the conclusion that the intensity of effect produced upon the retina by each undulation is *inversely as the square of the distance;* "and thus," he says, "the observed law of the diminution of light is reconciled to the undulatory doctrine."

That is, according to Herschel's statement here, the diminution in intensity of *each undulation* accounts for all the diminution that occurs. In a preceding portion of his Treatise, Herschel makes the following statement:

"If light be a material emanation, a something scattered in minute particles in all directions, it is obvious that the same quantity which is diffused over the surface of a sphere concentric with the luminous points, if it continue its course will successively be diffused over larger and larger concentric spherical surfaces; and that its intensity, or the number of rays which fall on a given space, in each will be inversely as the whole surfaces over which it is diffused; that is, inversely as the squares of their radii, or of their distances from the source of light."

And thus the observed law of the diminution of light is also reconciled to the corpuscular doctrine. That is, according to this Treatise, if the corpuscular theory is

the correct one, the diffusion of light accounts for all
the diminution of intensity which occurs ; if the undulatory is the correct one, the diminution in intensity of
each undulation accounts for all that occurs, and consequently no diminution can occur from diffusion.   Such
philosophy is worthy of being propounded by the scientific Tyndall.   To me " it is obvious " that the rate of
diffusion, and consequently the diminution of intensity
from this cause, must be precisely the same whether
light be a material emanation or ethereal undulations.

The same work (*Enc. Metropolitana*) contains a *Treatise
on Optics*, by Peter Barlow, F.R.S., from which I
copy the following, written, it will be perceived, without reference to any particular theory of light :

"In a free medium, the force and intensity of light
which propagates itself in rays emanating from the same
point, or which concur in the same point, are inversely
as the squares of the distances from that point.

"For the deviations from each other of two rays of
light which proceed from the same point are always
proportional to their distances from that point (since
those deviations form parallel bases of isosceles triangles,
of which the two rays are the sides).   Suppose, therefore, that having intercepted a certain number of rays
by a plane posited at a certain distance from the radiant
point, we remove this plane to a double distance, then
to a triple, to a quadruple distance, and so on : the
deviations of the rays from each other will be as the
numbers 1, 2, 3, 4, etc., and each dimension of the base
of each luminous pyramid which is thus formed in
succession will be in the same ratio.   Consequently, the
surface of those bases will be as the numbers 1, 4, 9, 16,

etc. So that the same number of rays are found distributed successively over surfaces which are respectively
as the squares of the distances from the radiant point,
or point of concourse, and, therefore, the intensity of
light that they excite will diminish in the same proportion."

Perhaps the matter will be as readily understood
from the simple statement that the surfaces of spheres
of different diameters are as the squares of their radii.

Here, then, is a *fact*, namely, the diffusion of light,
which fully accounts for all the diminution of intensity
that occurs, supposing—with reference to the undulatory
theory—each undulation to retain its original intensity.
Now, whether Herschel's doctrine, that the intensity in
effect of each undulation is inversely as the square of
the distance, is, or is not correct, is a point of little importance.   As the undulations are supposed to be
propagated by the inertia of the ethereal molecules, we
know that the vibrations would become less and less as
they recede from the point of origin; and the facts do
not admit of the supposition that any diminution in the
intensity of light occurs from such a cause.

Before leaving this subject, I wish to notice a doctrine
enunciated by Herschel in this Treatise on Light which
has no very important bearing here, but has in any
theory of sound.   After defining the undulatory theory,
he says :

" The application of these postulates to the explanation of the phenomena of light, presumes an acquiantance
with the theory of the propagation of motion through
elastic media.   This we shall assume, referring to our

article on sound for the demonstration of all the properties
and laws of motion so propagated as we shall have occasion to employ. One of the principal of these is,
that supposing the elastic medium uniform and homogeneous, all motions of whatever kind are propagated
through it in all directions with one and the same
uniform velocity, a velocity depending solely on the
elasticity of the medium as compared with its inertia,
and bearing no relation to the greatness or smallness,
regularity or irregularity of the original disturbance.
Thus, while the intensity of light, like that of sound,
diminishes as the distance from its origin increases, its
velocity remains invariable, and thus, too, as sounds of
every pitch, so light of every color travels with one
and the same velocity, either in vacuo, or in a homogeneous medium."

His Treatise on Sound is contained in the same work,
but it is unnecessary to notice it further than to say that
he assumes the wave theory of sound to be correct, and
attempts to show why all sounds are propagated with the
same velocity. The doctrine is especially absurd when
applied to the wave theory of sound; because in this
case the motions or pulses are in the direction in which
the sound is traveling; and if the reader will turn to
the chapter on this subject, and read my remarks on this
point, he will, I think, perceive that the doctrine is
equivalent to saying that if a man takes ten steps per
second of one foot each, he travels as fast as a man who
takes the same number per second of two feet each.

CHAPTER IX.

THE theory of electricity which I have received, so far as relates to the explanation of most electrical phenomena, is not new; yet it does differ somewhat from any heretofore held in our world; and it is necessary briefly to state it, in order that the theory of light, which is entirely new, may be understood.

The theory, if it can properly be called such, that electricity is simply motion of the particles of a body, requires no notice, as its advocates, so far as I am informed, have never attempted to apply it to the solution of a single phenomenon. Two theories, properly such, have been advanced to account for the phenomena of electricity. One theory assumes the existence of two fluids, one *vitreous*, or *positive*, the other *resinous*, or *negative;* that vitreous repels vitreous, and resinous repels resinous, while vitreous and resinous attract each other. The other theory assumes the existence of a single fluid; the vitreous, or positive electrical condition of a body being due to the fact that it holds an excess, over its natural quantity of electricity; and the resinous, or negative state, to the fact that the body is deficient in electricity, or holds less than its natural quantity. I believe the theory of two fluids has been received with most favor; but so far as my knowledge of electricity extends, either theory would equally well account for the phenomena.

This theory assumes that the conditions known as positive and negative are owing to excess and deficiency of electricity; that so far the single-fluid theory is correct. But it also assumes that there are almost innumerable varieties of electricity; that, for example, the electricity developed, or set free, by the decomposition of bodies, varies with the chemical properties of the bodies; and that electricity, like what is called ponderable matter, undergoes changes by decomposition and recomposition. It assigns to electricity a far more important position than has heretofore been given it; affirming that all we know of matter is through electricity; and that if a body, say a stone, could be deprived of electricity, to us it would have no existence; we could neither see it or feel it. These are the only new ideas I have to advance regarding electricity; the explanation of most electrical phenomena would be the same by this as by the single-fluid theory.

Heat is simply one form, or state, of electricity. Electricity, as I have said, undergoes changes, and one of the most important of these changes is into the state known as heat. Thus, for example, if the wire attached to a galvanic battery has capacity sufficient to convey the electricity as rapidly as developed, the electricity will pass along the surface of the wire, undergoing no change. But if the conducting power of the wire is not sufficient, if the electricity becomes *crowded* upon it, a portion of the electricity will undergo a change, passing into the state known as heat. The idea I have received is, that the primary development in the decomposition and re-composition of any body, is electricity, and not heat; but the electricity is instantly converted into heat if it becomes crowded, or condensed to a certain degree. In other words, it is assumed that the production of heat, whether by decomposition, recomposition, or friction, is due to the fact that a quantity of electricity is set free which is converted into heat. There are many chemical changes by which bodies become condensed, and heat becomes *sensible* in the same way as if the bodies were condensed by physical force; this is not, strictly speaking, a *production* of heat. Heat is also reconverted into electricity, though this change is generally less manifest to us.

The expansion of a body by heat is in consequence of the same law that causes two bodies charged with an excess of electricity upon the surface to repel each other. Heat, to a certain extent, retains this repelling property. It would seem, at first, that, such being the fact, two heated bodies should repel each other. It is assumed that the repelling power of heat is very slight, and operates only at an inappreciable distance.

I do not know that a better explanation of the fact that the capacity for heat of a body is increased by expansion, can be given than this, namely, that the heat is also expanded, and therefore it requires an additional amount to bring it to its former state of condensation. The expansion and contraction of matter, like matter itself, is, I think, a mystery. The doctrine that in expansion the ultimate atoms become farther removed from each other, appears to me very unsatisfactory. Neither do I understand the connection between heat and what we call matter. But we know that when a body is expanded, the heat which it contains follows the particles of the body, and, therefore, must also be expanded.

One fact occurs to me which seems to require explanation. A resinous body, when rubbed upon another, say a piece of cloth, loses, according to this theory, electricity; and yet it is a fact that it becomes warmer. It does part with electricity; that is, electricity which remains such; but the friction sets free electricity more rapidly than it is conveyed away; a portion, therefore, becomes converted into heat, and this penetrates the resinous body.

CHAPTER X.

LIGHT consists of particles of matter emitted from self-luminous bodies, of uniform shape, but possessing different chemical and magnetic properties. These particles, entering the eye, are absorbed by the retina, and, undergoing chemical decomposition, cause currents of electricity to flow along the optic nerve to the brain, thus exciting vision; the different colors being due to the different chemical properties of the particles. For convenience, I will hereafter designate the particles by the colors which they produce.

There exists between these particles and ordinary matter an attractive force, varying with the colors of the particles.

There is also a resisting force, varying in different bodies for all particles, and in the same body for particles of different colors.

A chemical affinity also exists between the particles and most bodies of ordinary matter, varying with the colors; and which, with reference to the latter point, is inversely as the resistance to penetration; that is, if the resistance of the body to penetration is greater for the red particles than for other colors, then the chemical affinity is greater for other colors than for red.

As the shape of the particles is, in this theory, a matter of importance, I give longitudinal sections perpendicular to the longest and shortest diameters, and a tranverse section through the middle.

These must be considered as only approximately correct. If the reader will imagine a cylinder, having hemispherical ends, partially flattened, the flattening process commencing at one extreme end and terminating at the other, he will have a sufficiently correct idea of the shape. The form is supposed to be due to the fact that the particles have been forced through an enveloping substance ; a point relative to which I have not attempted to get a definite idea. In their flight, the axes of the particles are parallel to the line of direction. I will attempt to apply the theory to the solution of some of the most prominent phenomena.

Refraction, and the prismatic spectrum.—Here the theory does not, I believe, differ from the Newtonian. When a ray of light falls obliquely upon a glass surface, the particles which penetrate the glass are, in consequence of the attractive force, drawn aside from their former course ; and as this force varies with the color— being greatest for violet, least for red, and intermediate for the intermediate colors of the spectrum—the refraction of each color varies accordingly. If the glass is a prism, each color, on leaving the second surface, will again be refracted in the same direction and to the same extent as by the first surface, and, consequently, the colors will continue to diverge. If the sides of the glass are parallel, each color, on leaving the second surface, will be refracted to the same extent as by the first surface, but in the opposite direction ; consequently, the colors proceed from the second surface parallel to each other, and the whole ray of light resumes a course parallel to its original one. The ray appears white in the latter case, not because the light is recomposed by the second surface, as Herschel and Brewster state, but because it has not been sufficiently decomposed for the eye to distinguish the colors.   In order that the eye may distinguish colors, they must strike the retina at points sufficiently far apart. If a number of fine lines of different colors are drawn on a surface close to and parallel to each other, the effect upon the eye, at a very short distance, is the same as if the colors were first mixed and then placed upon the surface. A glass, the sides of which are not parallel, may be so thin that the colors, on leaving it, are less separated than on leaving a thicker glass of parallel sides; but in the former case the colors continue to diverge, and consequently strike the retina more completely separated than in the latter case. As, in the case of a glass having parallel sides, the colors continue to diverge until they leave the second surface, if a ray of light could be passed through a glass of sufficient thickness, so that the colors would be sufficiently separated on reaching the second surface, they would be distinguished; but in a plate of such thickness the ray would be to such an extent absorbed and diffused that the effect could not be observed.

One point it may be proper to explain, though it is fully explained in that part of Herschel's Treatise relating to the Newtonian theory. When I speak of the surfaces of the refracting medium, I mean what to us appears to be such. It is not meant that the whole refraction occurs at a mathematical point; but when the particles of light have entered the medium to an appreciable distance, the attraction on all sides is equal, and consequently they are no longer drawn aside in any direction. The attractive force must be considered with reference to each particle of light, and these are so minute that at any appreciable distance the attraction of the medium is not felt.

Colors of bodies.—In a body which appears either white or black, the resistance to penetration is the same for all colors, but greater in the former body than in the latter. In a body which appears colored, red for example, the resistance to red is greater than to other colors. It is not assumed, however, that all the red particles are reflected, or that all those of other colors penetrate the body; but solely that a larger proportion of red than of other colors is reflected. The facility of penetration, in any case, depends not only upon the color of the particle, but also, as in the case of ordinary matter, upon the angle at which it strikes the surface of the body, and upon the extent of surface which the particle presents at the point of contact. Thus it may occur that, although the resistance of a body to a red particle is greater than to a green one, the former will penetrate while the latter is reflected.

The opaqueness of bodies is owing, generally, to the fact that the affinity existing between the body and the particles which enter it is such that the latter are absorbed, undergoing chemical decomposition. In some cases, however, such, for example, as a mass of pulverized white glass, the opaqueness is owing to the fact that there are so many surfaces inclined in all planes, that the particles fail to penetrate them. In the case of a colored transparent body, say a plate of green glass, a larger proportion of green than of other colors is reflected; but, of the particles which penetrate the plate, a larger proportion of other colors than of green is absorbed—in consequence of the law that the affinity is inversely as the resistance—so that the transmitted light also appears green.

Polarization.—This word was, as I understand, originally adopted in the Newtonian theory, where it has some appropriateness; it has none in the undulatory theory, or in this, but I must continue to use it. The polarization of light, according to this theory, is in consequence of the law governing ordinary matter that, when several bodies impinge upon another, the resistance to penetration by each, other things being equal, varies with the form, at the point of contact, of the impinging body; that is, a sharp-pointed body will penetrate more readily than a blunt one. If the reader has a correct idea of the form of the particles of light, he will understand that their points have what may be termed flat and sharp sides; and that, consequently, when they strike a surface obliquely, the power of penetration varies with the side brought in contact.

A ray of light consists of particles whose axes are parallel to the line of direction, and whose longest and shortest diameters are in all directions perpendicular to this line. When a ray falls obliquely upon a plate of glass, those particles which strike most favorably for penetration, that is, upon their sharp sides, will penetrate the glass; those which strike upon their flat sides will be reflected. The reflected ray, then, will consist of particles whose corresponding diameters are very nearly in the same plane. If now, a second reflector is placed in the same plane with the first, the particles will also strike it upon their flat sides, and be again reflected; if the second reflector is so placed as to reflect in the same direction as the first, the particles will strike it on the same side; if it is so placed as to reflect in the opposite direction, the particles will strike on the opposite side. If the second reflector is placed in a plane perpendicular to the first, the particles will strike on their sharp sides, and penetrate it. For convenience, I use the word *plane* here as generally used by writers upon this subject; strictly speaking, the reflectors are in neither case in the same plane.

Light is more perfectly polarized by reflection at a certain angle than at others. For common glass this angle is said to be 56° 45'. The explanation of this fact is that, as the angle is diminished the reflection of *all* particles becomes facilitated; when the angle is increased, the reverse is the fact, but as the particles strike more nearly vertical the difference in their power of penetration becomes less (when precisely vertical there is, of course, no difference), and the consequence, in either case, is, that the reflected ray consists of particles whose corresponding diameters are less uniformly in the same plane.

Sir David Brewster states, in explanation of certain phenomena, that light is reflected by both the first and second surfaces of a transparent body. This is not possible upon any conceivable theory of light. If the second surface is not placed in contact with another body, there is no second reflection; if it is so placed, the second reflection is not from the second surface of the first body, but from the first surface of the second body. Sir David applies his theory to the solution of the following phenomena :

Let a beam of light fall at an angle between 80° and 90° upon a plate of glass; "a portion of it will be reflected at its two surfaces, and the refracted beam a is found to contain a small portion of polarized light. If this beam a again falls upon a second plate, No. 2, parallel to the first, it will suffer two reflections ; and the refracted pencil b will contain more polarized light than a. In like manner, by transmitting it through the plates Nos. 3, 4, 5, and 6, the last refracted pencil, b, will be found to consist entirely, so far as the eye can judge, of polarized light. But, what is very interesting, the beam f is not polarized in the plane of refraction or reflection, but in a plane at right angles to it."

There is nothing in the above going to show that light was reflected at both surfaces of the plates ; nor has Sir David shown any facts which support his view. In this experiment the beam of light falls upon the plates at a great angle ; in such a case, as I have said, the difference in the particles as to the power of penetration is slight ; still, as the beam does not fall perpendicularly, there is, upon the whole, a difference, and the beam consequently becomes more and more polarized by every *first* surface upon which it falls. As to the fact that the transmitted beam is polarized in a plane at right angles to the plane of reflection, that is always the case. According to this theory, it is because the longest diameters of the particles which penetrate the plate are in a plane at right angles to it ; consequently, in order that these particles might strike a reflector on their flat sides and be reflected, the reflector would have to be placed in a plane at right angles to that in which the penetrated plates are, and this is what Sir David meant.

For polarization by transmission, a plate of *tourmaline* is generally used. I presume that its resistance to penetration is greater than that of common glass; consequently, a beam of light transmitted through it is more perfectly polarized, or *sifted*, than one transmitted through glass. This, however, does not explain one fact, namely, that a beam which falls upon a plate of tourmaline *perpendicularly* is polarized by transmission. As, for this purpose, the plate must be cut in a certain direction from the crystallized mass, it is evident that some peculiarity of crystallization is the cause of the phenomenon. It is here assumed, that the surface of the plate on which the light falls consists of minute surfaces inclined in one plane; so that although considered as a whole, the beam falls perpendicularly upon the surface, the particles really fall obliquely upon surfaces.

Double refraction and polarization.—There are certain crystals which have the peculiar property of dividing a transmitted beam of light into two rays, and these two rays are found at their emergence-to be polarized in two planes which are at right angles to each other. The crystal most used for this experiment is *Iceland spar*, and the light must be made to pass through it in certain directions, with reference to its crystallization.

Here, again, it is evident that a peculiarity of crystalization is the cause of the phenomena. It is here assumed, that the surface of the crystal upon which the light falls consists of minute surfaces inclined in two planes which are at right angles to each other. Let us first consider the effect of the surfaces inclined in one plane. Of the particles which strike these surfaces, those whose longest diameters are in a plane at right angles to the plane in which the surfaces are inclined —in other words, those which strike on their edges— will penetrate the crystal; the others will be reflected. Those which penetrate will be refracted. The same will occur to those particles which fall upon the surfaces inclined in the opposite plane; and those which penetrate will be refracted in a direction at right angles to that in which the former are refracted. The transmitted light is therefore divided into two rays; and the corresponding diameters of the particles constituting the two rays are in two planes which are at right angles to each other.

I think the explanations I have given will enable any one who has made the subject a study, to understand how the theory should be applied in the solution of most phenomena. According to this theory, there can be no appreciable interference of light; but I would not attempt a definite explanation of Dr. Young's experiment without further facts. One fact absolutely necessary is this: When the light passing on one side of the card was shut off from the screen, did the bright and dark lines disappear because the dark ones became brighter, or because the bright ones became darker? It is a known fact that light passing near the surface of a body is attracted, and drawn out of its course; and the bright *central* line, in this experiment, can only be accounted for upon the supposition that the light passing upon each side of the card was so far drawn out of its original course as to meet upon the screen. Interference, supposing it to occur, would not explain why there was a bright line where if the card had been wider there would have been a shadow. Without hazarding, definitely, a theory upon so meagre a statement, I would suggest the following as being perhaps the correct explanation :

The attractive force of a card upon light passing near its surface is of the same nature as that of a plate of glass upon light passing through it; some colors are more attracted than others, and, of course, are affected by the attractive force at a greater distance. Although the slip of card was very thin, its appreciable force upon the particles of light—for reasons stated when speaking of refraction—was the same as if it had been of greater width. Now, I presume that, the slip of card being so thin, the particles passing on each side near it, not only met, but crossed each other beyond it; and that the lines differing in brightness were due to the fact that at certain points on the screen a larger number of particles met, or there was a greater concourse, than at others; the amount of light being too small to make the colors distinguishable. This explanation assumes that the lines disappeared when the light passing on one side was intercepted, because the bright lines became darker.

It will be perceived that these new theories assume all our sensations to be of an electrical nature. *Taste* and *smell*, which differ but little, are the results of chemical changes which cause currents of electricity to flow through the nerves to the brain. *Touch* is the result of the development by friction of electricity, which is also conveyed to the brain.

CHAPTER XI.

IN speaking of another world, I will, for convenience, use the definite article, without intending to imply that there is but one world besides our own. And it is my intention in this work to say no more about the other world than appears to be absolutely necessary in order to make the phenomena I have attempted to explain understood; for the truth is, I have not myself a very clear conception of it.

It seems to me somewhat strange that, while most writers in treating of matter admit that we are entirely unable to comprehend it, they yet assume, or appear to, that there is no state or condition of matter not cognizable by our senses. The other world, like our own, is constituted of *matter*; that is to say—since we do not at all comprehend matter—the word is as applicable to the other world as to our own. And it is not attenuated matter which in other respects is the same as that of our world; but matter which in its most condensed form, and in its normal condition, is not in any way cognizable by us. In the next chapter I shall have occasion to state that this matter may be made perceptible by our senses of sight and touch; yet in this condition it is no more condensed, or solid, than when entirely imperceptible by us. From the information I now have, I assume that there may be innumerable other states or conditions of matter not cognizable either by us or the inhabitants of this other world.

The other world is constituted of matter which permeates that of our world; and it is, in form and dimensions, the counterpart of our world. The diameters and circumferences of each world are the same and coincident; the mountains, oceans, and rivers of our world are reproduced in the other. When we build a house, we build double; for the walls, floors, and all parts of the building are permeated by the matter of the other world. This fact is due to the attractive force which the matter of our world exerts upon that of the other.

The converse, however, is not true; all the forms of the other world have not their counterparts in matter of ours: and for the reason that the attractive force exerted by the matter of the other world upon that of ours is less than that which the particles of the latter exert upon each other. The attractive force may be compared to that of capillary attraction; and while matter of the other world suffers this attraction by bodies of our world, matter of the latter does not suffer it by bodies of the former. For example, the desk at which I am writing contains a precise duplicate in the matter of the other world. Were I to move this desk, it would carry with it the duplicate; but were the invisible beings with me to remove the latter, it would not stir the former; and my desk would immediately be again permeated by the, to me, invisible matter. This matter is not entirely devoid of gravity; and yet, compared with solids and liquids of our world, it is nearly so.

It may be a little difficult to understand how such

matter can be a solid to the inhabitants of the other world, as the earth is to us; that is, how they walk and live upon the surface of their world, as we do upon that of ours. Such, however, I am informed is the fact; and, bearing in mind that the bodies of these inhabitants are also nearly devoid of gravity. I think a little reflection will show that it is not an impossibility. There is, however, a difference in the two cases. For example, my room constitutes also a room to the invisible beings with me: and the invisible floor which permeates mine bears their weight. Yet they can pass through this floor, or through their walls, without much difficulty; though in doing so, they would have to make an opening, as I would to pass through mine. As the matter constituting their floor and walls is held in its position solely by the attraction of mine, it is not difficult to understand that they can pass through either with little difficulty; and that—their bodies being nearly devoid of gravity—such a floor may bear their weight.

It will be understood, from what I have said, that the inhabitants of the other world have no more power to leave this globe and visit other "spheres" than we have; they are held here by the same laws that hold us.

My informants decline giving me the details regarding death, or our birth into another world; and I confess that I am not anxious to have such information. An indefinite statement of the subject, then, as to details, must suffice.

There is no such thing as a spiritual body in man; in this respect, there is no difference between a human being and a brute. All animate, as well as inanimate matter of our world is permeated by the matter of the other. Our bodies and brains, therefore, are permeated by the matter of the other world. When the body dies, the vital principle, as it has been called—and I can think of no better term—organizes from this matter permeating the brain a new body; and owing to the nature of this matter, the development, or growth of the new body, is very rapid.

I admit that this is a *very* indefinite statement of the subject; but I think most persons will agree with me that, if it is at all accurate, more definite information is not desirable. Aside from the unpleasant nature of the subject, there is another reason for withholding definite information. The truth is, that the second birth is an operation of nature which, like the first, may be, and sometimes is, frustrated. There are unavoidable accidents which prevent the second birth taking place upon the death of the present body; and which, therefore, so far as those of the other world have any knowledge, terminate the individual's existence. Knowledge of the details would, therefore, in some cases, give surviving relatives and friends of the deceased useless pain. Interference with the second birth, except from accidents, may be avoided by observing the following simple rule: Let the corpse be placed in the earth or in a vault, without mutilation or embalmment, to undergo the ordinary processes of nature; let nothing be done to interfere with or obstruct these processes. How far it may be prudent, in certain cases where it is desirable to do so, to depart from this rule, I cannot undertake to define.

It would seem that the second birth creates a new

being; and why there exists any identity between the individual that died and the one that is born, is a great mystery. But it is also a mystery, though perhaps not so great a one, why an individual retains his identity from childhood to old age. I can only state—and this I do upon my own knowledge—that those of the other world have a very distinct recollection of their life in ours, and therefore must retain their identity.

There is here another mystery, or, at least, a fact not easily accounted for. As the bodies of brutes are also permeated by the matter of the other world, the question naturally arises, Why does not a second birth take place upon the death of a brute? The mystery of birth is unsolved by those of the other world, as by ourselves, and therefore I cannot answer this question. A partial explanation, however, may be found in the facts that the phenomenon is of an electrical nature, and that the vital electricity, or nervous fluid of a human being, differs from that of a brute.

It does not follow that because an individual retains his identity, or has a consciousness of past existence, on entering the other world, he must necessarily possess the same characteristics which he had here. There is a great change at death; and in most cases for the worse. Owing to some law which I do not fully understand, the intellect becomes, in most cases, weaker; and vicious propensities are enormously developed. The development of the propensity for lying is especially marvelous; I am sensible that after all I have said, and may hereafter say upon this subject, I shall fail to give the reader a correct appreciation of it. The fact that so many of the other world lie when there is no inducement for lying, can only be accounted for by bearing in mind that while this propensity is increased the intellect is enfeebled. I am not here writing solely about those belonging to the lowest, or most vicious class in our world; a very large proportion of those belonging to the most respectable classes, and who pass for individuals of common integrity and sense, will become lying fools on passing into the other world.

This, again, is somewhat of a mystery. It must be that a great change occurs at death; for the males who have communicated with me had not, when they first visited me, been in the other world long enough to have so far changed in character from any conceivable cause existing there; or to have become so enfeebled in intellect from lack of its proper use. It occurred to me that the fact that these men had been so recently born into the other world—that they were so young, dating from their second birth—might account for their lack of wisdom, though hardly for their propensity for lying. But on inquiring about this, I am told that they have now, probably, about as much wisdom as they ever will have; and the fact that Mrs. S. and Miss M. are still so childish seems to confirm this statement.

Those of the other world have, as compared with ourselves, but little physical strength. They have no need of such strength as we possess. In the explanatory narrative I have stated that Mrs. S. attempted to choke me, but was unable to do so. The latter fact was owing to her physical weakness. The effort was, as it appeared to me at the time, like that of a child of our world. Spiritualists tell of the marvelous feats of strength performed by the spirits; but I have never witnessed anything of the kind myself which could not have been done by a child of our world ten years of age. It is true, however, that they occasionally perform actions requiring considerable physical strength; but on such occasions there are several engaged in the performance.

The senses of sight and hearing are the same in those of the other world as in ourselves; and all bodies which give light to us, give light also to them. As this seems to require an attempt at explanation, the following theory—and it must be considered as only a theory—has been given me: The sun, and all other bodies which are visible or luminous to us, are permeated by matter resembling that of the world connected with our own; and the particles of light which render objects visible to us carry with them a counterpart, or duplicate, in this matter. This counterpart is arrested, absorbed, and reflected by matter of the other world, precisely as the particle which gives light to us is by matter of our world. If, then, in its flight, a particle of light meets a body constituted solely of matter of the other world, the counterpart is either absorbed or reflected by this body; the particle which gives light to us is not, in any way, appreciably affected by it. If the particle first meets a body of our world, and is reflected, the counterpart is also reflected; if absorbed, the counterpart may be absorbed, and may be reflected; the matter of the other world permeating the body determines this point.

It will be perceived that, according to this theory, all

bodies which are visible to us must be visible to those of the other world, provided that no body of their world intercepts their light; but that they cannot perceive the colors of bodies of our world, nor whether a body is, to us, black or white. Whether the theory of light is correct or not, such, I am informed, is the fact.

The sounds of our world are, if loud enough, audible to those of the other; for a shock communicated to our atmosphere produces a shock in theirs. But the minute shocks produced by us in speaking, are not reproduced in their atmosphere with sufficient distinctness to enable them to understand what is said. When we speak with sufficient loudness, those of the other world near us hear a sound, and that is all; they do not understand what is spoken. This fact partly explains the intense desire of many of the other world to be *en rapport* with one of this. They see us, mingle with us, yet cannot understand what is said; and have, therefore, but an imperfect knowledge of what is going on in our world; a world much more attractive to them than their own.

It may, by some, be thought very strange that, if the other world is such as I have described, the personations and deceptions practiced through mediums are not prevented by the better class. But those who would be disposed to prevent the deceptions if it were possible, are so few in number, comparatively speaking, that they have not the power to do so.

In the last chapter of this work I shall give narratives written by a well-known gentleman residing in New York, of apparitions witnessed by him, purporting, and believed by the gentleman, to be the apparitions of his deceased wife and Dr. Franklin. It appears to me sufficiently evident from the gentleman's own narratives that the apparitions and communications were rather weak deceptions; and that no man of common sense should have been deceived by them. Nevertheless, the gentleman was, for several years, thus deceived; and, as I am informed, his wife was advised of the fact, and would, had it been in her power, have prevented the deceptions. But a large number of the other world were engaged in these deceptions; and the wife, unassisted, or with such assistance as she could procure, had not the power to prevent them.

If, of every one hundred persons of the other world, only one is disposed to prevent such deceptions, while ten are disposed to assist in them, it is evident that the one cannot prevent the ten from practicing them. Now, Mr. W. and the Count are representatives of a class which is far from being the lowest one of the other world. They would not, as I am informed, feel any interest in such deceptions as those referred to in the preceding paragraph, or those practiced through common mediums. Yet they would not lend their assistance in preventing them. They profess to believe that the communications through mediums have, upon the whole, done more good than harm; as they have satisfied, beyond all doubt, many, anxious for such assurance, that death will not terminate their existence. But, aside from this, they say that those disposed to practice the deceptions are so numerous that it would be impossible to prevent them.

There is one comforting fact connected with this matter; the vicious of the other world have, as compared

with those of ours, but little power to injure others.
This is a subject of which I have only a partial conception, and I do not think it necessary to attempt an explanation.

What I have, for convenience, called *the* other world,
may more properly be designated as man's second stage
of existence. The inhabitants of this other world die a
second time ; and those now living there have no *actual
knowledge* of any world beyond, or of any future state
of existence. If they continue to exist after the second
death, the second change must, I infer, be greater than
the first ; for, while a large proportion of the population
of our world has always believed in the visits of ghosts
and spirits who manifest their presence—a belief which
I now assume to have been founded to a certain extent
on facts—those of this other world have no such belief.
If the inhabitants of a world beyond theirs visit them,
they are unable to communicate, or in any way manifest
their presence.

Of course, under such circumstances, beliefs regarding
a future existence vary in the other world, as in ours ;
and it would be aside from the scope of this work to
give mere theories upon such a subject. Inasmuch,
however, as I have stated that in some cases there is no
second birth, and that in such a case those of the other
world have no knowledge of the individual's continued
existence—from which it might be inferred that they
believe his existence is terminated—I think it proper to
state that this is not the *universal* belief of those of the
other world. My sister, for example, still believes that
all human beings are immortal ; and that the souls of

those who died without the formation of a second body continue to exist. In short, I cannot perceive that her views regarding a future, or an eternal existence, have at all changed since she left our world; except, of course, as regards this second life in the body. Her views, I am informed, coincide with those of a considerable class of her world.

There is another beli f which, as I have entered upon the subject, I will barely state. It is that there is a third birth, analogous to the second; and that, as the death of the body in our world terminates the existence of brutes, so death of the body in the second world terminates the existence of the larger proportion of its inhabitants; only the comparatively few fitted for a future existence being born into another world.

The question at once arises, Where is this other world? It may be merely another counterpart of our own. But according to the view I now have of matter, there may be no such thing in the universe as empty space; for, unless I am entirely and deliberately deceived, what to us appears such, or only occupied by the atmosphere, is to other beings more solid than the earth upon which we tread. It must be confessed, however, that, assuming I have received correct information, immortality for any of the human race is not demonstrated.

That a birth, such as has been rather vaguely described, should take place upon the death of the body, appeared to me, as it will to the reader, a breach in the uniformity of the operations of the laws of nature. Upon indicating this, I was given a theory which, although it has no direct bearing upon my subject, I will briefly state. It is mainly a deduction from phenomena witnessed at the death of a human being of our world by those of the other; and I understand it to be the theory generally held by those of the other world most competent to form one upon the subject.

The theory is, that the advance in our world from the lowest to the highest forms of animal life, or the origin of species, has not been by natural, or ordinary generation, but by births occurring in a manner analogous to that of man into another world.

It is assumed that owing to the great and successive changes which the earth and its atmosphere have undergone, there have been periods in its history when the conditions for such births were favorable, and when, as now, they were unfavorable; and that during the favorable periods—that is, favorable in the cases of certain species—when an animal died, a birth of a different species took place from its body, or, in the case of an animal having a brain, from the brain.

If the account given me of man's birth into another world is correct, this theory has, at least, some plausibility; and as the theory of light given me exhibits considerable ingenuity, I presume this would also if the details were given. But I have not attempted to get a full statement of the theory, as to give it here would occupy too much space; and, besides, it is not within the scope of this work.

CHAPTER XII.

THE phenomena designated by some as spiritual, or the performances of spirits, may be divided into two classes; one class being performed by action upon, or through, the nervous system of the so-called medium; the other, by using the electricity of the medium to effect changes in matter. The former class may be designated as mental, the latter as physical phenomena, speaking with reference to the beings of the other world. I will first notice the former class.

For the production of the phenomena, there must either exist naturally, or be created, a certain degree of *affinity* between an individual of the other world and the medium. This affinity, so far as it can be understood, consists in a certain degree of similarity, or a similarity in a certain respect, in the electricity of the two individuals. All the sensations received by the brain, and all the operations of the will, are of an electrical nature; and in order that one of the other world may act upon, or control the nervous organization of one of ours, there must exist, in a certain respect, an affinity in the electricity of the two individuals. By the electricity, I mean here what is sometimes called vital electricity, sometimes nervous fluid; it is simply one form or state of electricity. For convenience, I will designate it as vital electricity.

The common electricity of the other world differs from that of our world; and the vital electricities of the two worlds also differ. The vital electricity of a human being differs from that of a lower animal; and that of an intellectual man differs from that of an unintellectual man, whether in our world or the other. Now, it is a fact which I cannot explain, that the very lowest class of the other world, the most unintellectual and stupid beings, are the nearest affinities to people of our world. An intellectual person of the other world cannot control the nervous organization of either an intellectual or unintellectual person of our world; that is, when the latter is in his normal condition. Mediums, as a class, are not very intellectual; but, generally, they are not as stupid as the beings who communicate through them. I have given of the communications of the Count enough to show that he is not *excessively* intellectual; but in my normal condition he could not communicate with me at all; nor could he with any other person of our world; for this purpose he is too intellectual. This explains why all the communications which have been received from the other world are so excessively stupid.

Miss McCauley, who, if in our world, would be considered an idiot, and treated as such, is an average specimen of those who communicate through mediums. When I sat in my room for the purpose of receiving communications, she had not sufficient power to move my hand when at rest, and her power to guide it was almost imperceptible. Since that time an instrument has come into use called *Planchette.* It is a small triangular, or heart-shaped board, mounted on wheels and carrying a pencil, on which the medium places his hand.

The only purpose this instrument serves is, to enable the one of the other world to move more easily the hand of the medium—which carries the board with it—than when it rests on the paper. The cause for my hand moving backward, or from right to left, was, that the muscles which move the right arm from right to left are more powerful than those which move it in the con trary direction; and, at first, the will of Miss McCauley had not entire control of the electric currents which moved the arm.

Practice in writing, that is, in the control of my arm, increased the *rapport* of Miss McCauley; but I should probably never have become much of a medium had not Mrs. S. visited me. Why the degree of blood-relationship existing between us should make Mrs. S. an affinity in the respect here indicated, is a mystery; especially as neither my mother or sister were able to communicate with me in my normal condition. Whether if Mrs. S. had been present when I first sat for communications she would have been able to control my arm, or not, my informants do not feel certain. But when Miss McCauley had placed her to a certain degree *en rapport*, her power rapidly increased. The increase of power was owing to a change in the electricity of each of us, by which the two electricities became assimilated. It may, to some, seem strange that any change of this kind can be produced without injuring a person's health. But when two individuals of our world are closely associated, say a man and his wife, such changes, as I am informed, occur without perceptibly injuring the health of either. So long as the individual of the other world remains with the medium, the latter's health, I think, does not suffer from the mere connection; though, of course, the one of the other world may injure the medium; and the use of his, or her, electricity for the production of physical phenomena is always injurious. But there is danger to the one of our world in violently severing the connection if it has become very intimate.

Mrs. S., soon after becoming able to write with facility, became able to communicate by simply moving my hand as in the act of writing; no legible characters being formed. The operation was merely an impression produced by her mind on mine, aided by the movement of my hand as in the act of writing the words. Subsequently, when receiving communications by writing, I sometimes knew what word would be written as soon as it was commenced, sometimes I knew in advance what the whole sentence would be; at other times I had no idea what the word would be until it was completed.

Finally, I became able to hear Mrs. S., and others of her world, speak; and to me the sensation is precisely the same as hearing one of our world, except that I am unable to distinguish so clearly a difference in the voices of different individuals. In fact, I cannot perceive any difference in the voices of the several females who have conversed with me; but I can generally, if not always, recognize the voice of the Count, the only male of the other world who has conversed orally with me. I am informed that the phenomenon is not the same as when one of our world speaks to me. In the latter case, as I have said, the sensation of sound is produced by a succession of electric shocks conveyed to the brain. When one of the other world speaks, the sensation of sound is produced by electric shocks, but the discharge is *from* the brain. In order that I may hear one of the other world, the *rapport* must, at the time, be *very* intimate. The minute and rapid movements of the organs of speech in speaking, produce corresponding vacuums of electricity in the brain of the speaker; and, the *rapport* being so intimate, these vacuums produce corresponding shocks, by discharges, in my brain. But the very minute shocks, which determine the quality of sound, are not so distinctly experienced as when one of our world speaks; therefore I cannot so clearly distinguish voices. It is a very remarkable fact that I never fail to understand what is spoken; but this is in a great degree owing to the *impression* produced on my mind by that of the speaker.

As one of the other world, sufficiently *en rapport* with one of ours, may communicate by *impression*—that is, without writing or speaking—so the former may receive from the latter communications in the same way. And owing to the greater sensitiveness to impression of the one of the other world, he may be able to know what passes in the mind of one of our world, when the *rapport* is not sufficient to enable him to communicate in any way. This cannot be fully explained, for the reason that it is utterly impossible to understand the connection of mind with matter; but the primary operation—that which produces the mental impression, or conveys the knowledge —is of an electrical nature. Visitors to mediums are generally requested to write the names of friends from whom they wish communications. The operation brings the names into distinctness in the mind of the visitor, and thus enables. one of the other world with the medium to read them. Generally, also, it can be perceived which of the individuals whose names are written the visitor would prefer hearing from; and some-times certain facts, such as the appearance of the individual, and even an incident connected with him, can be learned from the visitor's mind. Of course there is, in this respect, a great difference in visitors; therefore some receive satisfactory "tests," while others do not. And many who receive the satisfactory tests through mediums are constantly accompanied, without their knowledge, by one of the other world, who thus has an opportunity of learning, at different times, incidents to be given as tests of identity.

Hallucinations of vision are also produced by those of the other world; the mental image being formed in the brain, and reproduced, by impression in the brain of one of our world; the latter, perhaps, claiming to be a "seer." When a person experiences an ordinary hallucination, unless deranged, he generally knows that it is an hallucination, and nothing more; but when produced by one of the other world, the power which enables the latter to produce it enables him also to influence the judgment of the one experiencing the hallucination, and to make him believe that he really sees what is presented to his mental vision. In explanation of the phenomena, I will relate two incidents occurring in my own experience.

When my mother first succeeded in identifying her-self, one of the written communications, given as tests of identity, was partly illegible, and I could not read it. I could only make out that she had accidentally broken something which she had purchased the same day.

Now, although I had requested that the incidents given should not be matters of importance, but trifling ones, such as would not be likely to have made any impression on my mind at the time, yet I thought it must have been something valuable that was broken. After trying for some time to recollect what it could be, and endeavoring, ineffectually, to have the communication perfected, I saw, apparently two or three feet distant from and on a level with my eyes, a familiar teapot, one that had been in the possession of our family as long as I could recollect. As I now saw it, it was broken; but I knew it was not broken on the day it was bought; and, in fact, I was sure that the last time I saw it—though I could not recollect when that was—it was perfectly whole. While thinking what connection this could have with the communication, I saw another teapot, entirely different in form and color from the familiar one, but broken precisely as the latter appeared; and I then recollected that one evening at tea, such a teapot had been broken, when my mother remarked that she had purchased it that day. Of course, such a trifling incident made no impression on my memory; but it appears to have done so on that of my mother, and as I asked for trifling incidents she gave this. Being unable to complete the communication, she endeavored to produce an apparition of the teapot; but from some cause, although her recollection was perfect, she happened at the moment to have the more familiar one in her mind.

Some time after my sister became able, with the aid of Mrs. S., to converse orally with me, owing to the fact that she was frequently personated by Mrs. S., I became suspicious that she had not conversed with me at all, but had given the incidents which satisfied me of her presence to Miss M., who, at that time, I supposed was the one assisting. I, therefore, one evening requested my sister, if she had actually conversed with me direct, to satisfy me of the fact ; and it occurred to me that a satisfactory mode would be to produce her appearance in dresses which I had forgotten, but which might be recalled to my recollection. She then appeared in a dress—a figured one—which I thought I perfectly recognized ; but I was told there was a stripe in it which I did not see; then I saw and recollected the stripe, a very narrow one. This shows how clearly she could perceive what my perceptions were, and also that minute images are not as distinctly reproduced as larger ones. While the dress was presented to my view, I saw no bonnet, the latter not being in her mind ; but immediately afterward several bonnets appeared in succession on her head, the appearance being as though one changed into another. Three thus made their appearance ; the two first I recognized, the third I did not; it appeared to me to be made of dark silk or satin, but I was told it was velvet; even then, however, I could not distinctly recollect it.

Such, when not merely the product of a disordered nervous system, are the visions of "seers ; " though some of the seers pretend to have visions when they have not even hallucinations. As the matter of the other world, whether animate or inanimate, does not reflect the light by which objects become visible to us, no one of our world can see the other or its inhabitants.

There are many persons who do not believe in Spiritualism, and do believe in clairvoyance. But the latter is also a delusion; there is no such faculty in man. Many occurrences attributed to clairvoyance should be attributed to the agency of beings of the other world. I have stated in the introductory narrative that one of the invisible beings with me at Trenton went to another hotel and found a gentleman seated at a small desk. She might have ascertained what he was doing, and, except as to color, have described with tolerable accuracy his dress and appearance. Once at Long Branch, to test their accuracy, I requested one of them to go and ascertain the number of individuals seated where from my position I could not see all of them. On receiving the report, I went and counted them, and found the number given me to be correct. Information of this nature can be given by those of the other world; they see the *forms* of our world; and where the *rapport* is such that the information is conveyed to one of our world by *impression* solely, the latter may honestly believe, and may induce others to believe, that he possesses an abnormal faculty of perception. But as those of the other world cannot distinguish colors of our world, it is easy to test this faculty of clairvoyance. Place a slip of paper containing either written or printed matter—the matter being unknown to any one of our world—in an envelope, or where it cannot be read by any one of good natural eyesight, and it will be found that no clairvoyant or seer can read the paper.

This connection between one of the other world and one of ours, does not differ, except in degree, from what is known as mesmerism. And it differs in degree partly because the connection is longer and more constant.

One of the other world may be, and often is, with one of this constantly for months and even years; the mesmerizer is with his subject occasionally for two or three hours, at most, at a time.

One common phenomenon is, answering letters by mediums without opening them. During my earlier investigations, I sent to a celebrated medium in Boston, who devoted his whole time to this business, a letter containing two classes of questions. The first class could be answered by any one who read the letter; the second class could only be answered by the person to whom the letter was addressed. The letter was enclosed in two envelopes, the outer one carefully sealed with wax stamped with a peculiar seal. No name was written on this envelope, the package was simply enclosed in a letter addressed to the medium. The package was returned, as I *know*, without having been opened, with a letter over the signature of the individual to whom mine was addressed, answering the first series of questions only; those questions which the individual whose name was signed to the letter could have answered, were not noticed at all.

The simple explanation of the matter is, that one of the other world was with me when I wrote the letter, and obtained from my mind—not by reading the letter—a knowledge of the contents; she, or another one, then went to Boston and communicated to the one in control of the medium the contents; the envelope, which was duplicated in matter of the other world, having been marked so as to be identified when it came before the medium. These mediums do not pretend to be able to answer all letters sent them; and if any person, having accidentally heard of such a medium, should at once sit down and write a letter, the probability is that it would not be answered. But most, if not all, of these letters are written by individuals who have visited mediums, or sat in "circles," and thus become interested in the subject; and a large proportion of such individuals are accompanied by those of the other world.

The idea entertained by most who are not Spiritualists, that the medium opens the letters—which is tantamount to saying that it is impossible so carefully to enclose and seal a letter as to prevent it being opened without detection—is really about as absurd as anything in Spiritualism. The truth is, it is not necessary that the medium should be given an opportunity to open the letter. The writer may carry it to the medium, and not suffer it to pass out of his sight until answered. The answers, as might be expected, are unsatisfactory except to credulous persons; they show little more, as a rule, than the fact that the writer, or dictator, has a knowledge of the contents of the letter.

But it is the second class of phenomena, the physical, which has excited the greatest interest; and, in fact, modern Spiritualism owes its rise and rapid spread mainly to these startling occurrences. Writing-mediums would, probably, never have been developed but for the fact that a belief in the presence of invisible beings was created by the physical phenomena. This belief formed, individuals were induced—sometimes being so directed by the "raps"—to sit and hold their hands passively for the "spirits" to write. The development of a writing-medium requires considerable time;

the *rapport* necessary for the use of the medium's electricity in the production of physical phenomena can be speedily acquired. Seers have existed in all ages ; but belief in their visions was nearly extinct when the " Rochester knockings," to some extent, revived the faith.

The first thing to be here explained, if such explanation were possible, would be *matter ;* but I find that my invisible informants know no more about matter, solely as such, than we do. But this much, at least, I have learned to be a certainty ; namely, that what to us is a granite rock, offers no resistance to the passage of another individual ; and what to another individual is solid substance, may be imperceptible in any way by us. One thing further relative to matter I have learned, provided, of course, that my informants are not deliberately deceiving me as to facts within their knowledge ; that is, that our only knowledge of it is through the agency of electricity. Of course, we have no knowledge of electricity other than the effects it produces.

As the matter of our world, whether living or inanimate, offers no resistance to that of the other in its normal condition, living or inanimate, the question arises, How can the inhabitants of the other world move a body—say a table—of our world ? The matter of the two worlds does not differ so greatly as would naturally be supposed ; and that of either world is capable of undergoing changes which assimilate it to the matter of the other. The agent which effects this change is electricity.

For the purpose of moving bodies of our world, writing without using the hand of a medium, playing on

musical instruments, and performing other like phenomena by one of the other world, a pair of gloves to
be worn by the latter are subjected to a certain chemical
process. Now, strange as it may seem, whether one
body offers resistance to another, or not, depends upon
the electrical condition of the bodies. In their normal
electrical condition, a table of our world would offer no
resistance to the gloves. But the individual who wears
these gloves is *en rapport* with one of our world; the
electricity of the two has become assimilated, and is
therefore not precisely the natural electricity of either
world, but of an intermediate quality. This electricity,
in passing from the hands of the wearer, penetrates the
gloves, and, in consequence of the chemical· process to
which they have been subjected, effects a change in
them of such a nature that, while the gloves are permeated by· the electricity, they resist matter of both
worlds : that is, they offer resistance to the hands of the
wearer and to a table of our world. The table is then
moved by the wearer of the gloves precisely as we would
move it with our hands. When a body of any considerable weight is to be lifted, similar covering is prepared
for the feet, so that the floor will also offer resistance.

These gloves sometimes become so far changed as to
reflect the particles of light by which objects are rendered visible to us ; they are then called "spirit-hands"
by the Spiritualists. Sometimes a portion of the arm
is covered with the prepared material; and thus the
singular spectacle is presented of, apparently, a hand
with a portion of the arm suspended in the air supported by nothing. Sometimes—but this is a *very* rare
phenomenon—a dress with a mask, are thus changed,

and made visible to those of our world; and Spiritualists believe that in such cases a spirit is actually seen;
though they appear to have no definite idea as to how
a spirit could make itself visible at one time, when it is
invisible at another. As the masks would not bear
critical examination, these figures are always exhibited
in a very feeble light; a fact, however, which excites
no suspicion in the minds of Spiritualists. An exhibition of this kind is, as I have said, very rare; it requires
a very good medium, and considerable care and time in
the preparation of the dress. I have never witnessed one
myself, and have read but few accounts of such which
I considered authentic.

Of course, for tipping tables, and various other phenomena, it is not essential that the prepared material
should be in the form of gloves; sometimes it is merely
a covering for the hand like a mitten without a thumb;
sometimes the whole hand is not covered; all that is
necessary is that the material should be interposed between the hand and the body to be moved. There is a
celebrated medium now in New York who, to satisfy
visitors that writing is performed by the "spirits," puts
a mere morsel of pencil on a slate and holds the slate
close against the under side of a table, the slate being
kept from actual contact with the table by the frame;
and in this position communications are written on the
slate. In this case, merely a bit of material, to be
placed on the tip of one finger, is chemically prepared.
The one of the other world then reaching through the
table which offers no resistance to his hand, and placing
himself *en rapport* with the medium, writes as one of

our world might, if the slate was on the top of the table, by placing his finger on the morsel of pencil.

The "raps" are literally such; being made with the changed material, just as we would make them with our fist, or some hard body; though the material does not become visible to us. There is no particular difficulty in understanding the latter fact, since, theoretically at least, glass might be so perfectly transparent as to be invisible. But all "tipping-mediums" will not serve for "rapping-mediums;" for the latter purpose the material must undergo greater change than is necessary for the former.

I think the reader will be able to understand, from what I have said, how most phenomena of this class are produced. There is, however, one somewhat common phenomenon, the method of producing which would not, probably, occur to him, and I will therefore explain it. I refer to the production of letters and words on the person—generally, for convenience of exhibition, on the arm—of the medium.

It will readily be understood, from what I have said, how *indentations* of any form, might be made by those of the other world. But to cause *names* to appear by indentations would be difficult without preparing a plate for the purpose; and this is impracticable for the reason that it is not known what name, or names, will be wanted until the visitor calls. For this purpose, a plate of soft material is chemically prepared, in which, when the visitor calls, the name ascertained to be wanted is written with a pointed instrument, the letters formed being concave. The plate being then placed on the arm of the medium, undergoes through his electricity

the change described, and being formed of material of
an attractive or drawing nature—somewhat like a draw-
ing-plaster—the flesh of the arm is forcibly drawn into
the indentations of the plate, forming on the arm raised
or convex letters, which are of a purplish tint in consequence of the blood being unnaturally drawn into the
convexities.

For the production of these phenomena, the electricity of some individuals is much more serviceable
than that of others. In all cases, the operation is injurious to the medium, because it produces an unnatural
discharge and consequent exhaustion of electricity.
No person can endure the discharge of electricity required for the production of these phenomena for any
great length of time; not even when the medium sits
in a "circle," which, to a certain extent, supplies him
with electricity. The amount of electricity required
varies with the quality, which also varies in different
individuals. With a large proportion of men, the
amount required would be so great that the exhaustion
would soon cause the death of the individual.

I have stated that Mrs. S. attempted to choke me by
creating the so-called "spirit-hands." According to my
recollection, this was attempted on three successive
nights, for a short period each night. These comparatively brief operations produced violent palpitation of
the heart, and partial paralysis of the limbs; and a continuance of the operations would soon have caused my
death. Of course, therefore, I would be a very poor
medium for the production of the physical phenomena.
As I have already said, if there is an appearance of ego-
tism in these explanations, it is unavoidable. The truth

is, that the best mediums for the production of the physical phenomena are very unintellectual individuals.
This is what I am told, and the statement accords with
my own observations. So far as I have any knowledge
of these mediums, they are either women, or men low in
the scale of intellectuality.

That the one of the other world is able to cause an
unnatural discharge of electricity from the medium, is
a fact which may require explanation. This power
differs only in degree from that possessed by individuals of our world. The simple explanation is, that the
vital electricity is controlled by the will. It is the will
which sends the electricity into the muscles which move
the limbs; and long-continued efforts of the will produce an exhaustion of electricity. Now, those of the
other world possess this power of directing the electricity by the will to a greater degree than we do. They
can, for example, when they have the gloves on, cause
an enormous flow of electricity into their hands, and
thus produce a corresponding discharge from their hands
through the gloves. This produces rapid exhaustion
of electricity; and as the one of the other world is *en
rapport* with the medium, the exhaustion in the former
produces exhaustion in the latter. For some reason,
those of the other world do not suffer so much from
this exhaustion of electricity as those of our world.

When my mother and sister were endeavoring to
overcome the power of Miss McCauley, I was repeatedly cautioned not to think of past occurrences, and,
especially, to avoid thinking of myself. The occurrences which I was cautioned to avoid thinking of,
were such as took place when Miss McCauley was with

me, and my mother and sister were not. It seems that the *rapport* is increased by harmony, or coincidence of thought; and these occurrences would be more distinct in the mind of Miss McCauley than in that of my mother or sister, who had only heard of them, or learned of them for the first time by my thinking of them. This is all the explanation I am able to give of the first caution.

The second was for a different reason. Self-consciousness did not increase the *rapport* of Miss McCauley, but it diminished that of my mother and sister. The *rapport* is due to an interchange of electricity. Now, when an individual is thinking of anything outside of himself, there is a constant flow of electricity from the brain. When one person is engaged in *earnest* conversation with another, or when one merely fixes his mind intently on another without speaking, there is a flow of electricity from the former to the latter. But when a person's thoughts are concentrated upon himself, or turned inwards, the outward flow of electricity is in a measure stopped. Self-consciousness on my part therefore broke the connection, or stopped the interchange of electricity, between my mother, sister, and myself. And this explains the fact that thinking of either of the individuals with me, brought him, or her, more intimately *en rapport;* there was a more free interchange of electricity.

When Mrs. S., at Trenton, undertook to overcome entirely the power of Miss McCauley, as she was unwilling to give her own name, she told me my father was present, and directed me to think of him. Miss McCauley could perceive the image in my mind; but as Mrs. S.

had been acquainted with my father, and Miss McCauley had not, the thoughts of the former would more nearly coincide with my own than those of the latter. A great change could not, however, be effected in so short a time ; and therefore the night's operations had no very important result. I have since wondered, as Mrs. S. and Miss M. are not very wise, that they did not remove Miss McCauley by force. The explanation given me is, that such connections are now so common it is understood by almost every one in their world that a forcible removal is dangerous to the individual of our world.

By substantially the same process as that through which matter of the other world is rendered visible and perceptible to the touch of an inhabitant of this, matter of our world may be rendered invisible to us, and imperceptible to our touch ; and when a body has been thus changed, other matter of our world in its normal condition offers no resistance to the body. In this case, it is the electricity of the other world which effects the change ; the only use of the medium being to enable those of the other world to handle the body and give it the chemical preparation. Some of the phenomena occurring in the presence of mediums are explained by this fact ; but such phenomena are not so common as others, for the obvious reason that it is more difficult for those of the other world to prepare a body of our world than one of their own.

If the explanations given are correct, it is, of course, impossible thus to change *living* matter, either of our own or the other world. So far as I can recollect, I have never heard or read of an occurrence in the United States where it was pretended that a living body was carried through solid matter.   But some time since I read, in the London *Spiritual Magazine*, an account of a woman (a medium) being carried by the " spirits " from her own house in London to another, and into a room where a " circle " was seated, the openings of the room being closed.   This was the statement of the woman and the belief of the writer of the article; the facts *known* by the writer were simply, that when the room was darkened the woman was not in it, when it was again lighted she was standing on a table in the room.

It is unnecessary to explain such performances as the above, or all the phenomena reported by Spiritualists as occurring in darkened rooms.   It would be very strange, considering what kind of persons many of the mediums are, if there was never any trickery when ample opportunity for it is given.   But it should be evident, even to Spiritualists, that the phenomena must be governed by some law, and therefore must be of an uniform character. Now, those generally recognized as being the best mediums, such as the Fox sisters in this country and Mr. Home in England, do not pretend that they are ever carried through solid walls.

- Another performance in darkened rooms never occurs, so far as I am informed, when either of these individuals is the medium ; namely, speaking by the " spirits," as pretended, in audible voices ; that is, voices audible to all in the room.   Sometimes the " spirits " and mediums combine for deception.   There are, or have been, public mediums who practice speaking through trumpets, pretending that the speaking is done by the spirits. As the medium's limbs are fastened, and the trumpet is placed beyond his reach before the room is darkened, and is in the same position when it is again lighted, the inference that the speaking was by the spirits is a natural one. But the "spirits" merely placed the trumpet to the mouth of the medium, and the speaking was by the latter.

Most persons, however, naturally conclude that all performances in darkened rooms, and in dark cabinets, are merely attempts at deception. The conclusion is a natural one, since no sensible reason is given why the phenomena only occur in darkness. It is, nevertheless, an erroneous conclusion; but no sensible reason can be given why darkness is preferred, except upon the hypothesis that the performers are not sensible persons. Of course, darkness is preferred because the performers wish to conceal the mode of operation; but there is nothing gained in *always* concealing entirely the mode of operation.

For example, many of the most startling phenomena are produced, as I have stated, by creating what Spiritualists call "spirit-hands." The so-called spirits voluntarily exhibit these hands, asserting that they are their own hands, which they have power to make visible and perceptible to the touch of those of our world. This is deception, and for that reason practiced; but that bodies of our world are lifted with these hands, whatever they are, is fact, and therefore concealed. The gloves are not always so far changed that they would be visible to us in the light; but those of the other world cannot always determine how far they will be changed, and therefore certain phenomena are generally performed in the dark, or under a table. Now, there is nothing gained by this, it is simply stupidity; for if the gloves were made visible, and the phenomena occurred in the light, the number of believers in Spiritualism would certainly be increased.

But the stupidity is not confined to those of the other world; Spiritualists, as a class, so far as relates to this subject, are about as stupid. They, or a large proportion of them, have seen and felt these so-called hands; and those who have not, believe that they can be produced. It would seem that any person of ordinary intelligence who believes that these hands can be produced, ought to believe that bodies of our world can be moved by them; but it is a remarkable fact that, so far as my knowledge extends, not a single Spiritualist believes that bodies are thus moved. The cause of this is that the "spirits" give other explanations, if explanations they can be called. In the chapter on Spiritualism, I have given the explanations of Andrew Jackson Davis and Prof. Hare; all that I have heard or read are of the same character, equally silly and incoherent.

Before closing this chapter, I will notice a remarkable phenomenon occurring with Mr. Home, the only well-authenticated instance of the kind of which I have ever heard or read. Mr. Home, as is stated, is frequently lifted and carried about his room. There is no difficulty in understanding this; he can be lifted in the same way that a table is. But there is this difference in the two cases: So many of the other world are, or can become, *en rapport* with Mr. Home, that he can be very nearly deprived, for a short time, of gravity. It is the electricity with which a body is permeated that determines its gravity; and those of the other world can so permeate the body of Mr. Home with their electricity that he becomes nearly as devoid of gravity as themselves.

The occurrence to which I refer is this: I have seen an apparently well-authenticated account of Mr. Home having been, in one instance, carried out of the house through one window, and brought in again through an adjoining one. Both windows were open; but as they were at a considerable height from the ground, the reader may not understand how this could be done if the surface of the other world is coincident with that of ours.

In considering these phenomena, it is necessary to bear constantly in mind what pains—or what to us would be such—these creatures are willing to take in the execution of their senseless performances. My informants aver that, in this instance, they constructed a platform on the outside of the building, on a level with, and supported by, the floor of Mr. Home's room, and extending from one window to the other, upon which, he having been nearly deprived of gravity, Mr. Home was carried.

That extraordinary preparations must have been made, is evident from the fact that such a phenomenon is very rare. This is the only well-authenticated account I have ever seen of even the lightest body being raised more than a few feet from a surface of our world. But if the views of Spiritualists as to the "spirit-world" are correct, then certainly, if the "spirits" can lift a man at all, they can lift a lighter body to any height.

CHAPTER XIII.

IN the fifth chapter I have endeavored to give the reader some understanding of the theories held by Spiritualists relative to the phenomena which I have undertaken to explain. I propose in this chapter to examine a variety of narratives of so-called spiritual manifestations and communications, that the reader may judge for himself whether the theories of Spiritualists, or those which I have propounded, best explain the phenomena. And I shall devote considerable space to this purpose, for it is only by a test of this kind that the soundness or unsoundness of a theory can be ascertained.

I have stated that there is no such faculty as clairvoyance. The following, taken from Wm. Howitt's "History of the Supernatural," is a very fair example of the experiments made to test this faculty; and is given by Mr. Howitt as indisputable proof of its existence:

" A doctor of Antwerp was allowed at a *séance* to impose his own tests; the object of the *séance* being to demonstrate vision by abnormal means. He said beforehand, 'If the somnambulist tells me what is in my pocket, I will believe.' The patient having entered into somnambulism, was asked by him the question, 'What is in my pocket?' She immediately replied, 'A case of lancets.' 'It is true,' said the doctor, somewhat startled; 'but the young lady may know that I am one of the medical profession, and that I am likely to carry lancets, and this may be a guess ; but if she will tell me the number of the lancets in the case I will believe.' The number of lancets was told. The skeptic still said, 'I cannot yet believe ; but if the form of the case is accurately described, I must yield to conviction.' The form of the case was accurately described. ' This certainly is very singular,' said the doctor, ' very indeed ; but still I cannot believe; but if the young lady can tell me the color of the velvet that lines the case that contains the lancets, I really must believe.' The question being put, the young lady directly said, ' The color is dark blue.' The doctor allowed that she was right; yet he went away repeating, ' Very curious, yet still I cannot believe.'"

Now, mark the character of the questions and answers. The doctor must have had several pockets in his clothes, and there was probably something in each pocket; at all events, it is not probable that the case of lancets was all that they contained. Yet instead of designating a particular pocket, he simply asked, " What is in *my pocket?*" And when the young lady replied, " A case of lancets," the readiness with which he accepted the reply as an answer to his question, shows that his mind was fixed upon that particular article. Again, if the young lady had not read his mind, when such a question was put, she would naturally have inquired which pocket was meant. And as to the succeeding questions, it is evident the doctor had the correct answers in his mind, from the fact that he did not examine the case to ascertain their correctness. The anecdote shows that one mind can read another; and, in my judgment, that is all that it does show.

Aside from this one anecdote, there is nothing in the work of Mr. Howitt suitable for my purpose. The best collection of narratives that I have seen, is contained in a work by Hon. Robert Dale Owen, enti led, "Footfalls on the Boundary of Another World." * I will, therefore, so far as possible, confine myself to a selection of narratives from this work. Aside from the convenience of selecting from one volume, I have another object in doing so, namely, to enable the reader who may be sufficiently interested in the subject to take the trouble, to ascertain whether I do, or do not, select mainly such narratives as most favor my own views. As the work of Mr. Owen has had an extensive circulation, it is well adapted for this purpose. I will here state that I shall confine my examination mainly to such narratives as are considered by Mr. Owen to confirm theories which I have stated to be false; and I design noticing *every narrative* of this kind in the work; while of such as do not seem to conflict with the doctrines I have propounded I shall notice a few only, by way of illustration.

It will be readily understood, that owing to the extraordinary nature of the phenomena under consideration, the statements given by individuals witnessing them are

* "Footfalls on the Boundary of Another World." By Robert Dale Owen. Philadelphia: J. B. Lippincott & Co., 1865.

liable to great exaggeration. It appears to be absolutely impossible for a large class of individuals to state occurrences of this startling character precisely as they took place; and, unfortunately, a large proportion of the narratives bearing upon this subject are given by persons of this class. And in so large a collection of narratives as this of Mr. Owen—numbering about sixty—it is to be expected, remembering the fondness of many persons for inventing tales of the supernatural, that some will be entirely fictitious. If, therefore, the theories which I have given will explain a large majority of the narratives, it is all that can reasonably be expected. And if it shall be found that they explain *all* the well-known phenomena which during the past twenty years have been witnessed by thousands of individuals on both sides of the Atlantic, while the narratives which conflict with these theories are of occurrences of an exceptional nature, and of doubtful authority, then the correctness of the theories is established as far as is possible by a test of this kind. Again, as the phenomena must be governed by certain laws, if I have stated correctly the laws governing a large majority of the cases cited, and the exceptional occurrences, stated to have taken place, would conflict with these laws, it is a logical deduction that the narrative must be wholly false, or partially incorrect.

The narratives in Mr. Owen's work are classified under the following heads :—*Dreams ; Disturbances popularly termed Hauntings; Apparitions of the Living ; Apparitions of the Dead; Retribution;* and *Guardianship.*

First, then, as to dreams : In certain stages of sleep the mind is in a more receptive, or impressible condition than when the individual is fully awake, and his mind,

or thinking faculties, in active exercise. Hence, inhabitants of the other world, who are unable at any other
time to do so, are sometimes able to communicate *impressions* to those of our world when the latter are
asleep, or partially so. Sometimes, when unable to
convey ideas, or the impression of words being spoken,
it is possible to produce an impressional apparition; and
this is occasionally done to convey intelligence of the
death of a relative or friend of the person receiving the
impression; it being, of course, as well known in the
other world as in ours, that most persons, on seeing an
apparition, conclude that the individual whose "spirit"
is supposed to be seen, is an inhabitant of the other
world. These impressional apparitions, conveying intelligence of deaths, have occasionally been produced
where the individual never before or afterward experienced anything of the kind; and so frequently have
they occurred immediately after the death of the person
whose likeness is seen, that it is believed by some that
individuals, or "spirits," can appear to us immediately
after their death, but not at any considerable length of
time afterward. I have myself heard this opinion expressed; and Mr. Owen states that a society was formed
in the year 1851 by members of Cambridge University,
England, "for the purpose of instituting, as their printed
circular* expresses it, 'a serious and earnest inquiry
into the nature of the phenomena, which are vaguely
called supernatural.'" And in a note, Mr. Owen states
that the son of a British peer, who was one of the leading
members of the society, informed him "that the re-

---

* Published in an appendix to Mr. Owen's work.

searches of the society had resulted in a conviction, shared, he believed, by all its members, that there *is* sufficient testimony for the appearance, about the time of death or after it, of the apparitions of deceased persons; while in regard to other classes of apparitions, the evidence, so far as obtained, was deemed too slight to prove their reality."

Yet nothing is really seen in such a case; nor is the apparition, or hallucination, produced by the individual deceased, but by some friend or relative in the invisible world. And, compared with the number of deaths, these apparitions are very rare for several reasons: first, it is only occasionally that a friend of the deceased person is able to produce the apparition; second, the death of the individual is not always known, at the time, by his friends in the other world; and third, there is usually no reason for attempting to make the death known in this way.

The principal difference between the views of Mr. Owen and myself in reference to dreams produced by those of the other world is, that he thinks some dreams indicate the faculty of prevision, others that of clairvoyance, and still others a faculty which I hardly know how to designate otherwise than as omniscience; while I contend that no such faculty as either of these is possessed by an inhabitant of either world.

I consider it unnecessary to notice dreams of a very common class, evidently produced by natural apprehension; such, for example, as that a ship in which a friend has sailed, or is about to sail, is lost. As dreams of this kind, caused by natural apprehension, are frequent, it is not strange that occasionally one is fulfilled.

If I understand Mr. Owen, he does not claim that such occasional coincidences prove the existence of the faculty of prevision. In dreams of this class those of the other world have usually no agency.

I also consider it unnecessary to notice dreams indicating the approaching death of a relative or friend, and which are fulfilled, where the death occurs from natural causes. I agree with Mr. Owen, that such dreams are frequently produced by those of the other world; but deny that the dream indicates the faculty of prevision. A man may be in apparent health, and yet those of the other world may perceive a change taking place in his system which indicates that he will soon die; this is not what is meant by prevision. And those of the other world are not infallible in this respect; but when the death does not occur in accordance with the dream, the latter is not often narrated, and is supposed to have originated from natural causes.

" The Visit Foretold."

This narrative is taken by Mr. Owen from a work on Sleep by Macario. I will give the substance:

Madame Macario and daughter went to the Bourbon baths. A cousin of Madame Macario, residing at Moulins—which, it appears, was the point at which they left the railway and took the diligence for the baths— dreamed, on the night before they started, that he saw them take the railway cars for the baths, and in the morning told his wife to prepare to receive them, as they would pay them a visit.

As it was raining when Madame Macario and daughter arrived at Moulins, and the cousin lived in a distant quarter of the town, they did not visit him—as I infer they intended—but stopped at the house of a friend near the railway station.

The dream, then, was accurate as to what was *intended*, but not as to what actually occurred. The power of those of the other world to produce dreams does not differ, except in degree, from that of individuals of our world. And, like common electricity, vital electricity. which causes the dream, will travel to any distance provided the conditions for transmission are sufficiently favorable.

I presume that this dream was produced either by Madame Macario or her daughter, probably by the former. In the night she thought, or dreamed of the intended journey, and of a visit to the cousin. This produced a corresponding impression on the mind of the latter, who, it is stated, " habitually dreams of anything extraordinary that is to happen to him." Stripped of exaggeration, this simply implies that when asleep he was very impressible. If he had possessed the "faculty of foresight, or prophetic instinct," as Mr. Owen terms it, he would have dreamed what actually occurred.

" The Indian Mutiny."

Mr. Owen says that in this dream, "a highly improbable event was foreshadowed with distinctness a year before it occurred."

"Mrs. Torrens, the widow of General Torrens, now residing at South Sea, near Portsmouth, about a year previous to the Indian mutiny dreamed that she saw her daughter, Mrs. Hayes, and that daughter's husband,

Captain Hayes, attacked by sepoys; and a frightful, murderous struggle ensued, in which Captain Hayes was killed."

Captain Hayes and his wife were at Lucknow during the siege of that place, where the former was captured by the sepoys and killed. It does not appear that his wife was attacked or molested in any way, except that she shared in the privations of the siege.

This dream is called a distinct foreshadowing of the great Indian mutiny. I venture to say that if the narrative was not headed "The Indian Mutiny," most readers would see no intimation of that event in the dream. Mrs. Torrens dreamed simply that her daughter and son-in-law were attacked by a party of sepoys; this has no resemblance to the siege of a city by an army. The dream was caused by natural apprehension, and is of the same class as where one dreams that a vessel in which a friend has sailed is lost. I have no doubt that similar dreams occur frequently to persons in England having relatives in India. But if one or a dozen individuals in England had, before the event occurred, dreamed of a general mutiny in India, the fact would be no proof of prophetic instinct, or prevision; because more or less apprehension of such an occurrence has always existed.

" The Negro-Servant."

" A lady dreamed that an aged female relative had been murdered by a black servant; and the dream occurred more than once. She was then so much impressed by it that she went to the house of the lady to whom it related, and prevailed upon a gentleman to watch in an adjoining room during the following night. About three o'clock in the morning, the gentleman hearing footsteps on the stairs, left his place of concealment, and met the servant carrying up a quantity of coals. Being questioned as to where he was going, he replied, in a confused and hurried manner, that he.was going to mend his mistress's fire, which at three o'clock in the morning, in the middle of summer, was evidently impossible; and on further investigation, a strong knife was found concealed beneath the coals."

This narrative is taken from Abercrombie's "Intellectual Powers," and its accuracy is vouched for by him. Mr. Owen, when in Edinburgh, where the occurrences took place, in 1858, obtained an additional voucher, with the names of the parties—which he gives—and the following additional facts, namely, that the dreamer did not know, until she went to her relative's house after the dream, that the latter had a black servant, he having been engaged but a short time previous; and that the servant was afterward hung for murder, and confessed before his execution that he had intended to assassinate the lady.

The vouchers for this remarkable dream appear to be as perfect as it is possible to produce; and it would be unphilosophical to consider the dream a natural one, when the dreamer did not know that her relative had a black servant. I assume, then, that this dream was produced by some relative or friend of the lady, in the other world, who occasionally visited her, or possibly, as she was aged, remained most of the time with her; and who perceived, being able to read his mind, that the servant designed murdering her; for it is a reasonable supposition that the servant had contemplated the murder for some time previous to the night of the discovery. This would not indicate that the one of the other world had the faculty of prevision, or the power of seeing into futurity; but merely the power of ascertaining a determination already formed.

It will be noticed that "the dream occurred more than once." This is not usual in the case of a natural dream; but I can testify from my own experience, that it is a common occurrence when the dream is produced by one of the other world. One of the annoyances which I experienced was unpleasant, and sometimes distressing dreams produced by Miss McCauley; and when I awoke from such a dream, it was necessary thoroughly to rouse myself, and fix my mind upon something else, or it would be repeated when I again fell asleep.

Mr. Owen says: "It is true that, with that inexplicable dimness of vision which seems so often to characterize similar phenomena, the coming event is indicated only, not distinctly foretold. The daughter's dream was that her mother *had been* murdered; and this had not taken place."

I see nothing inexplicable in the matter. The one of the other world was able merely to produce a dream, not to communicate a message; and having in his (or her) mind the images of the negro servant and the aged lady, with the fact that the former designed murdering the latter, the dream produced would naturally be such as occurred. If a person should, in any way, get the impression when awake that a certain individual intended to kill a certain other individual, and this impression caused him to dream of the subject, the dream would probably be that the event had occurred, or that he witnessed it. We rarely dream that an event is to occur in the future.

"*Bell and Stephenson.*"

" In the year 1768 my father, Matthew Talbot, of Castle Talbot, county Wexford, was much surprised at the recurrence of a dream three several times during the same night, which caused him to repeat the whole circumstance to his lady the next morning. He dreamed that he had arisen as usual, and descended to his library, the morning being hazy. He then seated himself at his *secretaire* to write; when, happening to look up a long avenue of trees opposite the window, he perceived a man in a blue jacket, mounted on a white horse, coming toward the house. My father arose and opened the window: the man, advancing, presented him with a roll of papers, and told him they were invoices of a vessel that had been wrecked and had drifted in during the night on his son-in-law's (Lord Mount Morris') estate, hard by, and signed ' *Bell and Stephenson.*'

" My father's attention was called to the dream only from its frequent recurrence; but when he found himself seated at his desk on the misty morning, and beheld the identical person whom he had seen in his dream, in the blue coat, riding on a gray horse, he felt surprised, and, opening the window, waited the man's approach. He immediately rode up, and drawing from his pocket a packet of papers, gave them to my father, stating that they were invoices belonging to an American vessel which had been wrecked and drifted upon his lordship's estate ; that there was no person on board to lay claim to the wreck; but that the invoices were signed '*Stephenson and Bell.*'

"I assure you, my dear sir, that the above actually occurred, and is most faithfully given; but it is not more extraordinary than other examples of the prophetic powers of the mind or soul during sleep, which I have frequently heard related.

"Yours, most faithfully,

"WILLIAM TALBOT.

"Alton Towers, October 23, 1842."

This narrative is taken from a work by Edward Binns, M.D., entitled "The Anatomy of Sleep." It is the only narrative in the chapter on dreams which clearly indicates the prophetic faculty; and I admit that this, assuming it to be true, can only be explained upon such an hypothesis. The only point for examination, then, is the authority for the narrative; and as what is alleged to have occurred is of an exceptional and extraordinary character, the authority should be proportionally strong to warrant belief. On this point the last paragraph of the communication has an important bearing, as it evinces excessive credulity in the narrator. Probably most persons "have frequently heard related" stories as extraordinary as the foregoing; but no person of sound judgment believes that he has *frequently* heard such that were *true.* Another thing; the narrative is given *seventy-four years* after the period at which the events are stated to have occurred, and yet we are not informed how or when Mr. Talbot heard the story. When a man is called upon to testify in a court of justice, he is required to state not only *what* he knows, but, also, *how* he knows; and the latter is especially important when seventy-four years have elapsed between the occurrence and the testimony. We have then solely, as authority for this narrative, the belief of a man who thinks such occurrences not uncommon, that the events described did occur seventy-four years previous to the time when he gave the statement. Hardly sufficient, I think, to establish the existence of prophetic powers. ·

In reference to one point Mr. Owen says :—" In the above we find the same strange element of slight inaccuracy mixed with marvelous coincidence of detail already several times noticed. The man with his blue coat ; the white or gray horse ; the vessel wrecked on Lord Mount Merris' estate ; the roll of invoices presented—all exhibit complete correspondence between the foreshadowing dream and the actual occurrences. The names on the invoices, too, correspond ; but the order in which they stand is reversed : in the dream, ' Bell and Stephenson ; ' on the invoices themselves, ' Stephenson and Bell.' "

I have no doubt that the narrator intended to make the coincidences appear complete, and that the above discrepancy is his ; and it is not the only one. In the dream it appears that the vessel had drifted upon the estate of Matthew Talbot's son-in-law ; but in the second paragraph, the man who brought the invoices is represented as stating, as I understand the sentence, that it had drifted upon the estate of Matthew Talbot. Trifling matters of this kind deserve notice when we are examining a narrative of alleged supernatural occurrences ; for the slightest inaccuracy may make wholly inexplicable occurrences which, if the account was correctly given, could be easily understood.

I have stated that this narrative of Mr. Talbot is the only one in the chapter on dreams which, if true, would indicate prevision. This is true; but I find that, in a subsequent chapter, Mr. Owen, in noticing the disturbances in the Fox family—called "knockings"—at Hydesville, N. Y., states, that several of the ancestors and connections of this family possessed the power of, what he here calls, "second-sight;" and he gives one story of a dream, which, if correct, would support the assertion. But, as he gives no authority for the anecdote, and has not, as I infer, thought the vouchers sufficient to authorize it being placed in the proper chapter, it is unnecessary to notice it; and I will pass to the examination of narratives which Mr. Owen thinks indicate "farsight or natural clairvoyance."

The following is taken from Abercrombie's work:—
"A lady in Edinburgh had sent her watch to be repaired. A long time elapsed without her being able to recover it; and, after many excuses, she began to suspect that something was wrong. She now dreamed that the watchmaker's boy, by whom the watch was sent, had dropped it in the street, and had injured it in such a manner that it could not be repaired. She went to the master, and, without any allusion to her dream, put the question to him directly, when he confessed that it was true."

Upon which Mr. Owen comments as follows:—"In this case nothing can be more ridiculous than to imagine that there was miraculous intervention for the purpose of informing a lady why her watch was detained at the maker's; yet how extreme the improbability, also, that, among the ten thousand possible causes of that detention, chance should indicate to her, in a dream, the very one, though apparently among the most far-fetched and unlikely, that was found exactly to coincide with the fact as it occurred!

"The attempt is futile to explain away even such a simple narrative as the foregoing, unless we impeach the good faith of the narrator; imagining, let us suppose, that he has willfully concealed some essential attendant circumstance, as, for instance, that the lady whose watch was injured had reason, from information obtained, to surmise that the boy might have dropped it. But, when Abercrombie vouches for the narrative as authentic, his voucher excludes, of course, suppositions which would deprive the anecdote of all value whatever in the connection in which he publishes it."

Mr. Owen seems to admit, that if the lady had reason to surmise that the boy might have dropped the watch, the dream was a natural one, and does not substantiate the faculty of farsight, or natural clairvoyance. But, as will, I presume, be admitted, if the lady surmised the same without any particular reason, the dream would be equally natural. The question then is, as to the probability of the lady having felt apprehension that the boy had dropped the watch.

Now, under the circumstances stated, is this accident, "apparently among the most far-fetched and unlikely," of "ten thousand possible causes" of the detention? Omitting the *thousands*, can the reader think of *ten* probable causes? But, the inquiry in this case, as to what causes would probably occur to the lady, is much

narrowed from the fact stated, that "she began to suspect that something was wrong." What would she be
likely to suspect this "something" to be? It appears
to me that her suspicion would naturally be one of these
two: namely, that the watchmaker had sold or pawned
the watch; or, that it had been so injured, either by
himself or some one in his employ, that it could not
readily be repaired. . I can, at this moment, think of no
other suspicion that appears at all likely to have occurred; and, in fact, I think we may assume the first
to be rather improbable. That the watchmaker was so
crowded with business that he neglected this watch,
would not be what is meant by "something wrong."

Now, that the boy *would* drop the watch, was, when
he took it, an improbable event; that he *had* dropped
it, was, at the time the lady's suspicions were excited,
much less improbable. The question, however, is not
as to the chances for or against the watch having been
dropped, but as to the probability of the lady being ap-
prehensive that the boy had dropped it. I venture to
say, that nine out of ten ladies, sending their watches
by a boy, would feel a little (in some cases almost unconscious) apprehension that he might drop it. I am
frequently conscious of this feeling in myself, even when
handing a watch, or any delicate instrument, to a gentleman for examination. It appears to me, therefore, that
there is nothing unreasonable in the supposition that
this dream occurred from natural apprehension.

If the reader thinks this explanation unsatisfactory,
let him consider the possibility of the lady seeing, by
clairvoyance, the boy drop the watch, not at the time
of the occurrence, but a long time afterward. I can

imagine that there might be such a faculty as clairvoyance (clear-seeing); and if the lady, in her dream, had seen the watch, in the watchmaker's shop, broken, that would be an instance of what is meant by the word; but I cannot even imagine a faculty by which she could see occur an event not taking place at the time.

I shall not review any more of this class of narratives, which I think can be explained without resorting to the hypothesis of clairvoyance, but will next notice those which I think cannot. There are two such in the chapter, both given by sailors—very doubtful authority in such matters. The first is taken from a work of which I never before heard, entitled, " Early Years and Late Reflections," by C. Carlyon, M.D.

" *The Murder near Wadebridge.*"

"On the evening of the 8th of February, 1840, Mr. Nevell Norway, a Cornish gentleman, was cruelly murdered by two brothers of the name of Lightfoot, on his way from Bodium to Wadebridge, the place of his residence. At that time, his brother, Mr. Edmund Norway, was in the command of a merchant vessel, the 'Orient,' on her voyage from Manilla to Cadiz; and the following is his own account of a dream which he had on the night when his brother was murdered:—

" ' About 7.30 P.M. the island of St. Helena N.N.W. distant about seven miles : shortened sail and rounded to with the ship's head to to the eastward ; at night, set the watch and went below ; wrote a letter to my brother, Nevell Norway. About twenty minutes or a quarter before ten o'clock, went to bed ; fell asleep, and dreamt I saw two men attack my brother and murder. him.

One caught the horse by the bridle, and snapped a pistol twice, but I heard no report; he then struck him a blow, and he fell off the horse. They struck him several blows, and dragged him by the shoulders across the road and left him. In my dream, there was a house on the left-hand side of the road. At four o'clock I was called, and went on deck to take charge of the ship. I told the second officer, Mr. Henry Wren, that I had had a dreadful dream—namely, that my brother Nevell was murdered by two men on the road from St. Columb to Wadebridge, but that I felt sure it could not be there, as the house there would have been on the right-hand side of the road; so that it must have been somewhere else. He replied, "Don't think anything about it; you west-country people are so superstitious! You will make yourself miserable the remainder of the voyage." He then left the general orders and went below. It was one continued dream from the time I fell asleep until I was called at four o'clock in the morning.' "

The difficulty with this dream is, that it is too *minutely* accurate. It agrees with the facts, as stated, in every particular, even the snapping twice of a pistol occurred just as represented in the dream. I confess my inability to explain such perfect coincidence in minute particulars. As the Captain had been writing to his brother before going to bed, it would be no remarkable coincidence if he happened to dream of him the same night; and under such circumstances—the Captain thinking of his brother—if the latter, at the time he was being murdered, happened to think of the former, some impression of the murder might be produced on the mind of the Captain. The dream, however, could not be as minutely accurate as represented. In fact, two wit-nesses, who were on the spot and saw the murder, would not be likely to coincide so minutely in their statements. It is quite probable that the Captain on that night dreamed of his brother, but the accuracy of the narra-tive I must doubt.

Mr. Owen says: " The precise correspondence between the dream and the actual occurrences is not left to be proved by recollections called up weeks or months af-ter the dream; for the evidence is an extract taken *ver-batim* from the ship's log—the record of the 'moment, when everything was fresh on the memory."

If this was true, the evidence would be unquestionable; if the Captain asserted that the narrative was an extract from the ship's log, without producing the log, the as-sertion would be sufficient to prove the story a fiction; for it is not customary to enter dreams in the ship's log. But neither Dr. Carlyon or the Captain pretend that the narrative is taken from the ship's log. Mr. Owen ap-pears to have so inferred from the fact that it is dated " Ship Orient, from Manilla to Cadiz, February 8, 1840." We have, solely, so far as appears from Mr. Owen's ex-tracts, the narrative of a sailor, given after he had learned the facts of the murder.

" *The Two Field-Mice.*"

" On the night of the 17th of February, 1836, Cap-tain Clarke, then on board of the schooner referred to,* had a dream of so vivid a character that it produced a

* A schooner frozen up in the Bay of Fundy. It is stated that Captain Clarke had not heard of the illness of his grandmother, who resided at Lyme-Regis, England.

great impression upon him. He dreamed that, being at Lyme-Regis, he saw pass before him the funeral of his grandmother. He took note of the chief persons who composed the procession, observed who were the pall-bearers, who were the mourners, and in what order they walked, and distinguished who was the officiating pastor. He joined the procession as it approached the churchyard gate, and proceeded with it to the grave. He thought (in his dream) that the weather was stormy, and the ground wet, as after a heavy rain ; and he noticed that the wind, being high, blew the pall partly off the coffin. The graveyard which they entered, the old Protestant one, in the centre of the town, was the same in which, as Captain Clarke knew, their family burying place was. He perfectly remembered its situation ; but, to his surprise, the funeral procession did not proceed thither, but to another part of the churchyard, at some distance. There (still in his dream) he saw the open grave, partially filled with water, as from the rain ; and, looking into it, he particularly noticed floating in the water two drowned field-mice. Afterward, as he thought, he conversed with his mother ; and she told him that the morning had been so tempestuous that the funeral, originally appointed for ten o'clock, had been deferred till four. He remarked, in reply, that it was a fortunate circumstance ; for, as he had just arrived in time to join the procession, had the funeral taken place in the forenoon he could not have attended it at all.

"This dream made so deep an impression on Captain Clarke that in the morning he noted the date of it. Some time afterward there came the news of his grandmother's death, with the additional particular that she was buried on the same day on which he, being in North America, had dreamed of her funeral.

"When, four years afterward, Captain Clarke visited Lyme-Regis, he found that every particular of his dream minutely corresponded with the reality. The pastor, the pall-bearers, the mourners, were the same persons he had seen. Yet this, we may suppose, he might naturally have anticipated. But the funeral *had* been appointed for ten o'clock in the morning, and, in consequence of the temptestuous weather and the heavy rain that was falling, it *had* been delayed until four in the afternoon. His mother, who attended the funeral, distinctly recollected that the high wind blew the pall partially off the coffin. In consequence of a wish expressed by the old lady shortly before her death, she was buried, not in the burying-place of the family, but at another spot, selected by herself: and to this spot Captain Clarke, without any indication from the family or otherwise, proceeded at once, as directly as if he had been present at the burial. Finally, on comparing notes with the old sexton, it appeared that the heavy rain of the morning had partially filled the grave, and that there were actually found in it two field-mice, drowned. This last incident, even if there were no other, might suffice to preclude all idea of accidental coincidence."

This narrative was given Mr. Owen by Captain Clarke, on board his schooner, lying at the New York docks, in July, 1859.

The objection to this narrative is the same as that applied to Captain Norway's, namely, that it is too minutely accurate. No one person present at the funeral

would have noticed, and recollected, all the particulars
named.   Again, there is precisely the same difficulty in
considering it a case of " far-sight," as in the dream of
the lady about her broken watch.   The dream is said
to have occurred in the night, while the funeral took
place, in England, at four o'clock in the afternoon—corresponding to an earlier hour at the spot where Captain
Clarke was; and, if the story is true, he saw, by " far-
sight," what was not taking place at the time.   I can
only say that I do not believe the narrative.   I shall
have occasion hereafter to notice a far more wonderful
and inexplicable story, told by this Captain Clarke ; and
if the reader is satisfied that it is wholly or mainly an
invention of the Captain, he should conclude that the
foregoing narrative is not entitled to belief.

Mr. Owen believes, in common with Spiritualists generally, that there is a spiritual body, and that it can
leave, temporarily, the natural body during the life of
the latter.   In the chapter on dreams he gives several
narratives in support of this theory.   In my opinion,
they are properly placed in this chapter, being simply
dreams, or what may be called such ; but why, holding
the views Mr. Owen does, he has placed them here, I do
not understand, and the reason is unimportant.

The following is taken from Abercrombie's work.
The dream occurred to Joseph Wilkins, at the time
usher of a school in Devonshire, England, afterward
dissenting clergyman at Weymouth ; and the narrative
was written by himself.   It may be proper to state that
the titles of these narratives are added, or prefixed, by
Mr. Owen.

" The Mother and Son."

" One night, soon after I was in bed, I fell asleep, and dreamed I was going to London. I thought it would not be much out of my way to go through Gloucester-shire and call upon my friends there. Accordingly, I set out, but remembered nothing that happened by the way till I came to my father's house; when I went to the front door and tried to open it, but found it fast. Then I went to the back door, which I opened, and went in; but, finding all the family were in bed, I crossed the rooms only, went up-stairs, and entered the chamber where my father and mother were in bed. As I went by the side of the bed on which my father lay, I found him asleep, or thought he was so; then I went to the other side, and, having just turned the foot of the bed, I found my mother awake, to whom I said these words:—' Mother, I am going a long journey, and am come to bid you good-by.' Upon which she answered in a fright, ' Oh, dear son, thou art dead!' With this I awoke, and took no notice of it more than a common dream, except that it appeared to me very perfect. In a few days after, as soon as a letter could reach me, I received one by post from my father: upon the receipt of which I was a little surprised, and concluded something extraordinary must have happened, as it was but a short time before I had a letter from my friends, and all were well. Upon opening it I was more surprised still; for my father addressed me as though I was dead, desiring me, if alive, or whoever's hands the letter might fall into, to write immediately; but if the letter should find me living, they concluded I should not live long, and gave this as a reason of their fears : That on a certain night, naming it, after they were in bed, my father asleep and my mother awake, she heard somebody try to open the front door ; but, finding it fast, he went to the back door, which he opened, came in, and came directly through the rooms up-stairs, and she perfectly knew it to be my step ; but I came to her bedside, and spoke to her these words :—' Mother, I am going a long journey, and have come to bid you good-by.' Upon which she answered me, in a fright, ' Oh, dear son, thou art dead ! '—which were the circumstances and words of my dream. But she heard nothing more and saw nothing more ; neither did I in my dream. Upon this she awoke and told my father what had passed ; but he endeavored to appease her, persuading her it was only a dream. She insisted it was no dream, for that she was as perfectly awake as ever she was, and had not the least inclination to sleep since she was in bed. From these circumstances I am apt to think it was at the very same instant when my dream happened, though the distance between us was about one hundred miles ; but of this I cannot speak positively. This occurred while I was at the academy at Ottery, Devon, in the year 1754 ; and at this moment every circumstance is fresh upon my mind. I have, since, had frequent opportunities of talking over the affair with my mother, and the whole was as fresh upon her mind as it was upon mine. I have often thought that her sensations as to this matter were stronger than mine. What may appear strange is, that I cannot remember anything remarkable happening hereupon. This is only a plain, simple narrative of a matter of fact."

Whether the mother was really asleep, or not, is immaterial; she was lying in bed, her mind in a receptive condition; and I assume that this is an instance of one mind acting upon another at a distance. As I have given in a preceding chapter what I consider a correct explanation of such phenomena, I will here merely notice the absurdity of the spiritual-body hypothesis, as applied to such a case.

Upon the latter hypothesis, it is necessary to suppose that the spiritual body of the son could leave the natural body, and the house in which it lay, without difficulty; and could travel one hundred miles in, let us say, an instant; but, when it came to the residence of the parents, it could not enter without opening the door, and, finding the front door fastened, was obliged to go to the back door. Again, on entering the house, it walked precisely as the natural body would have done, and the tread was so firm that the mother, up-stairs, heard and recognized it. This being the case, how could it travel one hundred miles in, at farthest, a few minutes? Once more, as the spirit was heard to open the door and walk across the rooms on entering, why was it not heard to do the same on leaving? And why should he leave so suddenly when spoken to by the mother, without assuring her that he was not dead? Possibly the reply to the latter question would be, that the awakening of the natural body recalled the spiritual body. Then it must be assumed that there was some kind of a connection existing between the natural and spiritual bodies, extending over the distance of one hundred miles. It strikes me that it is as difficult to understand how this could be as to understand how the mind of the son could influence that of the mother at that distance. But what kind of a phenomenon would the awaking of the natural body be in such a case, the mind being with the spiritual body, one hundred miles distant? The spiritual hypothesis, as applied to such a phenomenon as that described in this narrative, appears to me, in every respect, an utter absurdity.

I will notice one more narrative of this class, which, if true, proves clearly, I think, that one mind can produce an impression upon another at a distance of several hundred miles. The following, Mr. Owen says, "was communicated to me in March, 1859, by Miss A. M. H——, the talented daughter of a gentleman well known in the literary circles of Great Britain. I give it in her words."

" One Dream the Counterpart of Another."

"We had a friend, S——, who some years ago was in a delicate state of health, believed to be consumptive. He lived several hundred miles from us, and, although our family were intimately acquainted with himself, we knew neither his home nor any of his family; our intercourse being chiefly by letters, received at intervals. One night, when there was no special cause for my mind reverting to our friend or to his state of health, I dreamed that I had to go to the town where he resided. In my dream I seemed to arrive at a particular house, into which I entered, and went straight up-stairs into a darkened chamber. There, on his bed, I saw S—— lying as if about to die. I walked up to him; and, not mournfully, but as if filled with hopeful assurance, I took his hand and said, 'No, you are not going

to die. Be comforted: you will live.' Even as I spoke
I seemed to hear an exquisite strain of music sounding
through the room. On awaking, so vivid were the impressions remaining that, unable to shake them off even
the next day, I communicated them to my mother, and
then wrote to S——, inquiring after his health, but giving him no clew to the cause of my anxiety. His reply
informed us that he had been very ill—indeed, supposed to be at the point of death—and that my letter,
which for several days he had been too ill to read, had
been a great happiness to him.

"It was three years after this that my mother and I
met S—— in London ; and, the conversation turning
on dreams, I said, ' By the way, I had a singular dream
about you three years ago, when you were so ill ; ' and
I related it. As I proceeded, I observed a remarkable
expression spread over his face ; and when I concluded
he said, with much emotion, ' This is singular indeed ;
for I too had, a night or two before your letter arrived,
a dream the very counterpart of yours. I seemed to
myself on the point of death, and was taking final leave
of my brother. "Is there anything," he said, "I can
do for you before you die ?" " Yes," I replied, in my
dream ; " two things. Send for my friend A. M. H——.
I must see her before I depart." " Impossible ! " said
my brother ; " it would be an unheard-of thing : she
would never come." " She would," I insisted, in my
dream, and added, " I would also hear my favorite sonata by Beethoven, ere I die." " But these are trifles,"
exclaimed my brother, almost sternly. " Have you no
desires more earnest at so solemn an hour ? " " No : to
see my friend A. M. and to hear that sonata, that is all I

wish." And, even as I spoke, in my dream I saw you enter. You walked up to the bed with a cheerful air; and, while the music I had longed for filled the room, you spoke to me encouragingly, saying 'I should not die.'"

This narrative will be best understood by reading the second part first; when it will be evident, that if the spiritual body of Miss H—— visited Mr. S——, the visit was in consequence of the desire of the latter, impressed upon her mind. But if this impression could be made at the distance named, a dream might be produced at the same distance by the mind of Mr. S—— acting upon hers.

Mr. Owen calls this a phenomenon of "two concurring and synchronous dreams;" and he uses the word *dream* in speaking of the Wilkins narrative; but he appears to use it as merely implying that the natural body was asleep. He will not admit that one mind can influence another at such a distance; and claims— quite logically, I think—that such precise coincidences cannot be accidental. He says: "In another chapter will be adduced such evidence as I have obtained that the appearance of a living person at a greater or less distance from where that person actually is, and perhaps usually where the thoughts or affections of that person may be supposed, at the moment, to be concentrated, is a phenomenon of not infrequent occurrence. If it be admitted, it may furnish the true explanation of the Wilkins dream, the Goffe dream,* and others similar in character."

* This narrative is very similar to that of Mr. Wilkins.

The chapter here alluded to is that on "Apparitions of the Living," which will be noticed in its proper order. The narrative of Miss H—— is not referred to in this extract, but I think it will not be disputed that if this was an example of synchronous dreams, as the word *dreams* is generally understood, then the cases named may be considered as being of the same character.

Now, is it possible to suppose that the narrative of Miss H—— describes real occurrences, and not dreams? Was the music real? If this was an illusion, then, of course, the whole was an illusion. Mr. S—— wished Miss H—— to come and perform his favorite sonata; but seems to have had no idea in his mind as to the kind of instrument it was to be performed upon. It does not appear, and is not probable, that he had any musical instrument in his room. When Miss H—— came, he heard the music, but—an incoherence common in dreams—it did not appear to be performed by her, and he had no idea by whom, or on what, it was performed. The dream of Miss H. was equally vague and indefinite on this point. In short, the two dreams precisely corresponded, terminating at the same point: both dreamt of the entrance of Miss S—— into the room, and neither of her leaving it. The same was the case in the Wilkins dream; and in every well-authenticated instance of the kind, the dreams coincide too minutely to be real occurrences. If a visit was really made by a "spirit," and a conversation took place, the recollection of the occurrence by the two parties would not be so precisely alike, and so entirely confined to the same particulars.

I presume that these synochronous dreams occur

much more frequently than is generally supposed. People rarely tell their dreams; in fact, unless the impression is very vivid, they do not recollect them; and it may be considered an accidental circumstance that a coincidence of the kind becomes known. Three years elapsed, it appears, before Miss H—— and Mr. S—— learned of each other's dream.

I will now pass to the chapter of Mr. Owen's work, on "Disturbances popularly termed Hauntings."

If a large portion of the inhabitants of the invisible world arc such as I have described; if they can find nothing to interest them in the world to which they now belong; then, we can readily imagine that they will haunt the scenes of former pleasure, and be drawn to certain spots by recollections of events of special interest which there occurred.

I contend it is not true, however, that there are now, or ever were, houses in which disturbances of the kind alluded to in the chapter under notice could be made without the presence of what are now called *mediums ;* that is, without the presence of one of our world whose electricity could be used to create the disturbances. The point for examination, then, is, whether there is any evidence that the invisible beings have power to create these disturbances otherwise than in the manner I have pointed out. The following narrative conveys more nearly than any other in the chapter the popular idea of a haunted house, as the building appears to have been uninhabited previous to the visit of the parties named:

" *The Castle of Slawensik.*"

This narrative is too lengthy to copy entire, but I will give the substance.

In the month of November, 1806, Councilor Hahn, attached to the court of the reigning Prince of Hohenlohe, Neuenstein-Ingelfingen, received orders from the prince to proceed to the above castle, situated in Upper Silesia, and there await his orders. Hahn was accompanied by Cornet Charles Kern. They both occupied the same room in the castle, which was a corner room on the first floor, having no opening without except the windows. The only residents of the castle at the time were Hahn, Kern, Hahn's servant, and two of the prince's coachmen.

" On the third evening after their arrival in the castle, the two friends were sitting reading at a table in the middle of the room. About nine o'clock their occupation was interrupted by the frequent falling of‹ small bits of lime over the room. They examined the ceiling, but could perceive no signs of their having fallen thence. As they were conversing of this, still larger pieces of lime fell around them. This lime was cold to the touch, as if detached from an outside wall.

· " They finally set it down to the account of the old walls of the castle, and went to bed and to sleep. The next morning they were astonished at the quantity of lime that covered the floor, the more so as they could not perceive on walls or ceiling the slightest appearance of injury. By evening, however, the incident was forgotten, until not only the same phenomenon recurred, but bits of lime were thrown about the room, several of which struck Hahn. At the same time loud knockings, like the reports of distant artillery, were heard, sometimes as if on the floor, sometimes as if on the ceiling. Again the friends went to bed ; but the loudness of the knocks prevented their sleeping. Kern accused Hahn of causing the knockings by striking on the boards that formed the under portion of his bedstead, and was not convinced of the contrary till he had taken the light and examined for himself. Then Hahn conceived a similar suspicion of Kern. The dispute was settled by both rising and standing close together, during which time the knockings continued as before. Next evening, besides the throwing of lime and the knockings, they heard another sound, resembling the distant beating of a drum.

" Thereupon they requested of a lady who had charge of the castle, Madame Knittel, the keys of the rooms above and below them ; which she immediately sent them by her son. Hahn remained in the chamber below, while Kern and young Knittel went to examine the apartment in question. Above they found an empty room, below a kitchen. They knocked ; but the sounds were entirely different from those that they had heard, and which Hahn at that very time continued to hear, in the room below. When they returned from their search, Hahn said, jestingly, 'The place is haunted.' They again went to bed, leaving the candles burning ; but things became still more serious, for they distinctly heard a sound as if some one with loose slippers on were walking across the room ; and this was accompanied also with a noise as of a walking-stick on which some one was leaning, striking the floor step by step ; the person seeming, as far as one could judge by the sound, to be walking up and down the room. Hahn jested at this, Kern laughed, and both went to sleep, still not seriously disposed to ascribe these strange phenomena to any supernatural source.

"Next evening, however, it seemed impossible to ascribe the occurrences to any natural cause. The agency, whatever it was, began to throw various articles about the room—knives, forks, brushes, caps, slippers, padlocks, a funnel, snuffers, soap, in short, whatever was loose about the apartment. Even candlesticks flew about, first from one corner, then from another. If the things had been left lying as they fell, the whole room would have b.en strewed in utter confusion. At the same time there fell, at intervals, more lime; but the knockings were discontinued. Then the friends called up the two coachmen and Hahn's servant, besides young Knittel, the watchman of the castle, and others; all of whom were witnesses of these disturbances."

After the disturbances had continued about three weeks, Hahn and Kern removed into the room immediately over the one they had been occupying; but the same phenomena followed them to their new apartment. The story of the disturbances spread over the neighborhood, and others visited the castle and witnessed them. Finally, the two friends moved into another room—the third occupied—when, as it appears, the disturbances ceased.

The narrative is taken by Mr. Owen, from Dr. Kerner's life of the "Seeress of Prevorst," it having been communicated to Dr. Kerner by Hahn, and it is attested by the latter, as follows: "I saw and heard everything, exactly as here set down: observing the whole carefully

and quietly. I experienced no fear whatever; yet I
am wholly unable to account for the occurrences nar
rated.

"Written this 19th of November, 1808.

"COUNCILOR HAHN."

Two subsequent letters from Hahn to Dr. Kerner,
upon the subject, are given by Mr. Owen, the last letter
being written in the year 1831, and both affirming the
correctness of the narrative. It is also stated that a
gentleman of the utmost respectability, residing in
Stuttgart, visited Slawensik in the year 1830, for the
purpose of verifying the narrative; and that, while
some ridiculed it, the only two men he met with that
had witnessed the events, confirmed its accuracy in
every particular.

"This gentleman further ascertained that the castle
of Slawensik had been since destroyed; and that, in
clearing away the ruins, there was found a male skeleton walled in, and without coffin, with the skull split
open. By the side of this skeleton lay a sword."

This last story is not very well authenticated. Some
tragedy may have been enacted in the castle which was
the cause of its being haunted by former occupants;
but it is equally probable that the cause was the latter
having lived there a life of pleasure.

No phenomena of the kind—so far as appears from
the narrative of Hahn, and the report of the gentleman
who subsequently visited the place—were ever wit
nessed in the castle before or after the visit of Hahn
and Kern. In that portion of the narrative which I
have copied, it is stated that when Kern and young
Knittel went into the room above, Hahn continued to

hear the knockings, but Kern and Knittel heard nothing. And in a subsequent portion it is stated that Hahn witnessed the disturbances when entirely alone in the castle.

" Hahn resolved that he would investigate them seriously. He accordingly, one evening, sat down at his writing-table, with two lighted candles before him— being so placed that he could observe the whole room, and especially all the windows and doors. He was left, for a time, entirely alone in the castle—the coachmen being in the stables, and Kern having gone out. Yet the very same occurrences took place as before ; nay, the snuffers, under his very eyes, were raised and whirled about."

It does not appear that the disturbances ever occurred without the presence of Hahn in the vicinity ; and as they occurred in his presence when alone, it is evident that he was the instrument employed.

The disturbances in the residence of the Fox family, at Hydesville, N. Y., commenced, like those at Slawensik, soon after the family had moved into the house. Certain members of the family were probably the first occupants through whom beings of the other world, visiting the house, could cause the disturbances ; as Hahn was the first at the castle. The great difference in the results of the two cases is owing to the fact that a member of the Fox family discovered a mode of communicating with the invisible beings, in consequence of which she and her two sisters became known as " mediums," being followed from place to place by these beings. Had Hahn made the same discovery, he too would, undoubtedly, have been followed in the same

way. So far as I have been able to learn, no disturbances occurred in the house at Hydesville after the Fox
family left it; and, as I have stated, none occurred in
the castle after Hahn left it. The two cases are very
similar, except as to the results following the discovery
in the one of a mode of communication.

There is in this narrative an account of an apparition,
which, I think, tends to confirm my statement that
they are mostly impressional, or hallucinations. One
evening, when the disturbances were taking place,
" Kern, half undressed, paced the room in deep thought.
Suddenly he stopped before a mirror, into which he
chanced to look. After gazing upon it for some ten
minutes, he began to tremble, turned deadly pale, and
moved away. Hahn, thinking that he had been suddenly taken ill from the cold, hastened to him and
threw a cloak over his shoulders. Then Kern, naturally a fearless man, took courage, and related to his
friend, though still with quivering lips, that he had
seen in the mirror the appearance of a female figure, in
white, looking at him, and apparently before him, for
he could see the reflection of himself behind it. It was
some time before he could persuade himself that he
really saw this figure ; and for that reason he remained
so long before the glass. Willingly would he have believed that it was a mere trick of his imagination ; but
as the figure looked at him full in the face, and he
could perceive its eyes move, a shudder passed over
him, and he turned away. Hahn instantly went to the
mirror and called upon the image to show itself to him ;
but, though he remained a quarter of an hour before it,
and often repeated his invocation, he saw nothing.

Kern told him that the figure exhibited old but not disagreeable features, very pale but tranquil looking; and that its head was covered with white drapery, so that the face only appeared."

As Kern saw the reflection of himself *behind* what appeared to him the reflection of a female figure, and the latter appeared to be looking at him, it is evident that it was a case of hallucination; for, in the first place, if there had been any one between him and the mirror, he could not have seen the reflection of that person, looking at *him* "full in the face;" and, in the second place, as the image of an object reflected from a plane mirror is rather less distinct than the object viewed directly, if there had been any person between him and the mirror, he would have seen that person more distinctly than the reflected image; while the fact is, that as soon as he ceased looking into the mirror he lost sight of the image.

But, assuming this and similar narratives to be mainly correct, it can be easily understood how the popular belief as to haunted houses has originated. Disturbances of the kind here described are witnessed in a certain house, when an individual whose electricity can be used for the purpose happens to be in it; the report of the strange phenomena spreads in the neighborhood, and others visiting the house, who have heard the story, hear noises which they do not understand, and therefore imagine to be produced by the same invisible cause; some, perhaps, excited by what they have heard, and thinking there must be a "ghost" in the house, fancy, as Kern did, that they see one; and thus the house acquires its bad reputation. The popular belief is correct on the main point; the error consisting in supposing that the invisible beings have power, of themselves, to create such disturbances; when, in fact, the presence of a "medium" of our world is always necessary.

In some of the remaining narratives given by Mr. Owen in the chapter under notice, the *medium* is plainly indicated; in others, this indication is not so clear, from the fact that several members of the family in which the disturbances occurred were always present at the time they were taking place. As narratives of the latter kind do not conflict with the theory I have advanced, it is unnecessary to notice them. But in some there is, as might be expected, considerable exaggeration, allowance for which must be made. The following, taken from a work by Mackay, on "Popular Delusions," will show the necessity for making such allowance when examining narratives of such phenomena ·

" The Farm-House of Baldarroch."

" On the 5th of December, 1838, the inmates of the farm-house of Baldarroch, in the district of Banchory, Aberdeenshire (Scotland), were alarmed by observing a great number of sticks, pebble stones, and clods of earth flying about their yard and premises. They endeavored, but in vain, to discover who was the delinquent, and, the shower of stones continuing for five days in succession, they came at last to the conclusion that the devil and his imps were alone the cause of it. The rumor soon spread all over that part of the country, and hundreds of persons came from far and near to witness the antics of the devils of Baldarroch. After the fifth day, the showers of clods and stones ceased on the outside of the premises, and the scene shifted to the interior. Spoons, knives, plates, mustard-pots, rolling-pins, and flat-irons, appeared suddenly endued with the power of self-motion, and were whirled from room to room, and rattled down the chimneys, in a manner nobody could account for. The lid of a mustard-pot was put into a cupboard by a servant-girl, in the presence of scores of people, and in a few minutes afterward came bouncing down the chimney, to the consternation of everybody. There was also a tremendous knocking at the doors and on the roof, and pieces of stick and pebble stones rattled against the windows and broke them. The whole neighborhood was a scene of alarm; and not only the vulgar, but persons of education, respectable farmers within a circle of twenty miles, expressed their belief in the supernatural character of these events."

If the narrative terminated here, it would be one of the most difficult of explanation, consistently with the theory given in this work, that I have seen, appearing to be as well authenticated. But Mackay's account closes as follows:

"After a fortnight's continuance of the noises, the whole trick was discovered. The two servant-lasses were strictly examined, and then committed to prison. It appeared that they were alone at the bottom of the whole affair, and that the extraordinary alarm and credulity of their master and mistress in the first instance, and of the neighbors and country people afterward, made their task comparatively easy. A little common dexterity was all they had used; and, being themselves unsuspected, they swelled the alarm by the wonderful stories they invented. It was they who loosened the bricks in the chimneys and placed the dishes in such a manner on the shelves that they fell on the slightest motion."

Mr. Owen remarks: "The proof that the girls were the authors of all the mischief appears to have rested on the fact that 'no sooner were they secured in the county gaol than the noises ceased;' and thus, says Mackay, 'most people were convinced that human agency alone had worked all the wonder.' Others, however, he admits, still held out in their first belief, and were entirely dissatisfied with the explanation, as indeed they very well might be, if we are to trust to the details given by Mackay himself of these disturbances."

If either of the servant-girls was the medium through whom the disturbances were produced by invisible beings, of course the disturbances would cease when both girls were removed. But what I wish to show by this narrative is, the tendency in most persons toward exaggeration, when giving an account of such occurrences; whether really caused by invisible beings, or only supposed to be, makes no difference. As these disturbances ceased when the girls were removed, it is evident that they could only have occurred in their vicinity; and consequently the account must be highly exaggerated. Assuming that invisible beings had no agency in the matter, the girls could not have performed what is described without immediate detection, if, indeed, they could have performed it at all. They might loosen bricks in the chimney, and place dishes so that they would fall easily ; but that is not even an approach to an explanation of the phenomena described in the first part of the narrative. Now, supposing that in this case the girls had not been removed from the house, then there would have been, founded upon these disturbances, an apparently well-authenticated account of occurrences totally inexplicable upon any other hypothesis than that they were caused by invisible beings, and that, too, without the intervention of a "medium" of our world ; while, as it is, the narrative confirms, instead of conflicting with, the theory I have given.

There is one (and only one) narrative in Mr. Owen's work in which, if true, it appears that disturbances in our world were caused by invisible beings without the presence of a medium. The narrative is quite lengthy, but I will give a pretty full synopsis, with the authority, and the reader can judge as to its credibility.

"The Cemetery of Ahrensburg."

"In the immediate vicinity of Ahrensburg, the only town in the island of Oesel,* is the public cemetery. Tastefully laid out and carefully kept, planted with trees and partly surrounded by a grove dotted with evergreens, it is a favorite promenade of the inhabitants. Besides its tombs,—in every variety, from the humblest to the most elaborate—it contains several private chapels, each the burying-place of some family of distinction. Underneath each of these is a vault, paved with wood, to which the descent is by a stairway from inside the chapel and closed by a door. The coffins of

* In the Baltic.

the members of the family more recently deceased usually remain for a time in the chapel. They are afterward transferred to the vaults, and there placed side by side, elevated on iron bars. These coffins it is the custom to make of massive oak, very heavy and strongly put together.

" The public highway passes in front of the cemetery, and at a short distance therefrom. Conspicuous, and to be seen by the traveler as he rides by, are three chapels, facing the highway. Of these the most spacious, adorned with pillars in front, is that belonging to the family of Buxhoewden, of patrician descent, and originally from the city of Bremen. It has been their place of interment for several generations."

It was in this chapel, which previously had the reputation of being haunted, that the disturbances are stated to have taken place. Country people visiting the cemetery were in the habit of fastening their horses immediately in front of, and close to this chapel.

On the 22d of June, in the year 1844, a woman visited the cemetery, and fastened her horse, as usual, in front of the chapel. While kneeling in prayer by the grave of her mother, situated behind the chapel, she had an indistinct perception, as she afterward remembered, of hearing noises in the direction of the chapel. On returning to her horse, after completing her prayers, she found it covered with sweat and foam, its limbs trembling, and apparently in mortal terror. It was scarcely able to walk, and she was obliged to call a veterinary surgeon. He said the horse must have been excessively terrified from some cause ; bled it, administered a remedy, and it recovered.

The following Sunday several persons, who had fastened their horses in front of the chapel, reported that they found them in a somewhat similar condition; and some of them stated that they heard, seeming to proceed from the vaults of the chapel, rumbling sounds which occasionally assumed the character of groans.

" And this was but the prelude to further disturbances, gradually increasing in frequency. One day in the course of the next month (July) it happened that eleven horses were fastened close to the columns of the chapel. Some persons, passing near by, and hearing, as they alleged, loud noises, as if issuing from beneath the building, raised the alarm ; and when the owners' reached the spot they found the poor animals in a pitiable condition. Several of them, in their frantic efforts to escape, had thrown themselves on the ground, and lay struggling there ; others were scarcely able to walk or stand ; and all were violently affected, so that it became necessary immediately to resort to bleeding and other means of relief. In the case of three or four of them these means proved unavailing. They died within a day or two.

" This was serious. And it was the cause of a formal complaint being made by some of the sufferers to the Consistory—a court holding its sittings at Ahrensburg and having charge of ecclesiastical affairs.

" About the same time, a member of the Buxhoewden family died. At his funeral, during the reading in the chapel of the service for the dead, what seemed groans and other strange noises were heard from beneath, to the great terror of some of the assistants, the servants especially. The horses attached to the hearse and to

the mourning-coaches were sensibly affected, but not so
violently as some of the others had been. After the interment, three or four of those who had been present,
bolder than their neighbors, descended to the vault.
While there they heard nothing; but they found, to
their infinite surprise, that of the numerous coffins which
had been deposited there in due order side by side, almost all had been displaced and lay in a confused pile.
They sought in vain for any cause that might account
for this. The doors were always kept carefully fastened, and the locks showed no signs of having been
tampered with. The coffins were replaced in due order."

The excitement increasing, and renewed complaints
reaching the Consistory, an inquiry was proposed, which
the family at first objected to. But the Baron de Guldenstubbé, president of the Consistory, having visited
the vault in company with two members of the family,
and found the coffins again in the same disorder—which
were again replaced—an official investigation was assented to.

"The persons charged with this investigation were
the Baron de Guldenstubbé, as president, and the bishop
of the province, as vice-president, of the Consistory;
two other members of the same body; a physician,
named Luce; and, on the part of the magistracy of the
town, the burgomaster, named Schmidt, one of the syn-
dics, and a secretary.

"They proceeded, in a body, to institute a careful
examination of the vault. All the coffins there deposited, with the exception of three, were found this time
as before, displaced. Of the three coffins forming the

exception, one contained the remains of a grandmother of the then representative of the family, who had died about five years previous; and the two others were of young children. The grandmother had been, in life, revered almost as a saint, for her great piety and constant deeds of charity and benevolence."

The commission found, on examination, that nothing had been carried off: the ornaments of the coffins were found untouched, and the articles of jewelry, which had been buried with the corpses, remained in the coffins. They had the pavement of the vault taken up, and the foundations of the chapel examined, to ascertain if there was any subterranean entrance, but found none. The coffins were replaced, and ashes strewed over the pavement of the vault, the stairs leading down to it from the chapel, and the floor of the chapel. Both doors, the inner and the outer, after being carefully locked, were doubly sealed; first with the official seal of the Consistory, then with that bearing the arms of the city. Finally, guards, selected from the garrison of the town, were set for three days and nights to watch the building and prevent any one from approaching it.

" At the end of that time the commission of inquiry returned to ascertain the result. Both doors were found securely locked and the seals inviolate. They entered. The coating of ashes still presented a smooth, unbroken surface. Neither in the chapel nor on the stairway leading to the vault was there the trace of a footstep of man or animal. The vault was sufficiently lighted from the chapel to make every object distinctly visible. They descended. With beating hearts, they gazed on the spectacle before them. Not only was every coffin,

with the same three exceptions as before, displaced, and
the whole scattered in confusion over the place, but many
of them, weighty as they were, had been set on end, so
that the head of the corpse was downward. Nor was
even this all. The lid of one coffin had been partially
forced open, and there projected the shrivelled right arm
of the corpse it contained, showing beyond the elbow:
the lower arm being turned up toward the ceiling of
the vault!"

No trace of footstep was discovered in the vault, and
this time, as before, the commission found that nothing
had been carried off.

"They approached, with some trepidation, the coffin
from one side of which the arm projected; and, with a
shudder, they recognized it as that in which had been
placed the remains of a member of the Buxhoewden
family who had committed suicide. The matter had ·
been hushed up at the time, through the influence of
the family, and the self-destroyer had been buried with
the usual ceremonies; but the fact transpired, and was
known all over the island, that he was found with his
throat cut and the bloody razor still grasped in his right
hand—the same hand that was now thrust forth to human view from under the coffin lid; a ghastly memo-
rial, it seemed, of the rash deed which had ushered the
unhappy man, uncalled, into another world!"

The commission, it is stated, made an official report,
which is to be found in the archives of the Consistory.

"It remains to be stated that, as the disturbances
continued for several months after this investigation,
the family, in order to get rid of the annoyance, resolved
to try the effect of burying the coffins. This they did,

covering them up, to a considerable depth, with earth. The expedient succeeded. From that time forth no noises were heard to proceed from the chapel; horses could be fastened with impunity before it; and the inhabitants, recovering from their alarm, frequented with their children, as usual, their favorite resort."

This narrative was given Mr. Owen, in the year 1859, by Mademoiselle de Guldenstubbé, daughter of the baron referred to. According to the narrative, these remarkable disturbances do not appear to have depended upon the presence in the vicinity of any particular person or persons. And it must be admitted that the authority for the story seems, on first view, very strong; as the narrator was the daughter of a baron, and, as is stated, "was residing in her father's house at the time, and was cognizant of each minute particular." Here again, then, but for an accidental circumstance, would have been an apparently well-authenticated account, going to disprove the theory I have given.

In the copy of Mr. Owen's work which I have, I find, on page 345, the following:

"*Note to tenth thousand.*—In the first editions of this work, another narrative, bearing upon the habitual appearance of a living person, was here given. It is now replaced by that of the 'Two Sisters,' for the following reasons: A friend of one of the parties concerned, having made inquiries regarding the story, kindly furnished me with the result; and the evidence thus adduced tended to invalidate essential portions of it. A recent visit to Europe enabled me to make further inquiries in the matter; and though, in some respects, these were confirmatory, yet I learned that a considerable portion of the narrative in question, which had been represented to me as directly attested, was in reality sustained only by second-hand evidence. This circumstance, taken in connection with the conflicting statements above referred to, places the story outside the rule of authentication to which in these pages I have endeavored scrupulously to conform; and I therefore omit it altogether."

On examining a copy of the first edition of the work, I find the narrative above referred to is one entitled, " Why a Livonian School-teacher lost her Situation; " which was given Mr. Owen by this Mlle. de Guldenstubbé. It is as wonderful, and, had it remained in the work, would have been as inexplicable a story as this of the chapel. The narrator stated that she was an inmate of the school in which the events took place at the time of their occurrence; and professed to describe what she had herself witnessed. That narrative, therefore, was more likely to be correct than this of the cemetery. It appears that some friend of the school-teacher, having seen Mr. Owen's work, took the trouble to advise him of the incorrectness of the story relative to that lady. Whether he became satisfied that the story was incorrect, or only that the narrator had not seen what she professed to have witnessed, does not matter; as he thought proper to omit the story for one or both of these reasons, he should, at the same time, have withdrawn this story of the chapel also, given him by the same individual.

It appears from Mr. Owen's remarks, that the narrative relative to the school-teacher had some foundation; and it is altogether probable that this of the chapel had also. In reference to one point, Mr. Owen says: "Finally, if these disturbances are to be ascribed to trickery, why should the tricksters have discontinued their persecution as soon as the coffins were put under ground? This last difficulty, however, exists equally in case we adopt the spiritual hypothesis. If to interference from another world these phenomena were due, why should that interference have ceased from the moment the coffins were buried?"

The last sentence shows what unlimited power Mr. Owen supposes the "spirits" to possess. Whether the invisible beings operate, in similar cases, in the way I have described, or not, it does not follow as a necessary consequence, that if they have power to move coffins placed in a vault, they must have power to do the same when the coffins are buried in the earth.

Let us suppose that these coffins were disturbed by invisible beings, in the manner I have explained, when some one whose electricity could be used for the purpose happened to be in the chapel, and that the only noises heard were caused by the moving of the coffins; then, evidently, these disturbances must cease when the coffins were buried to the depth of several feet in the earth. I do not, however, wish this to be considered as an attempt to explain the narrative; for, after reading the story of the school-teacher, I should consider an attempt to explain a story told by this narrator a hopeless task.

In a fictitious narrative there is generally something by which its character may be detected. In this case we have the unaccountable terror of men and horses, and the death from fright of three or four of the latter.

Now, animals cannot distinguish between noises made by "spirits," and those originating from any other cause. Some horses are easily frightened by unusual noises; and it is possible there may have been instances of horses dying from such a cause; but I am quite certain that no one ever knew of three or four horses dying at the same time from fright. Such an instance, I venture to say, was never known. And the story appears still more incredible from the fact that there appears to have been no cause for excessive fright. The woman, kneeling behind the chapel, scarcely heard the noises; while her horse, fastened outside of the cemetery, was, as represented, frightened almost to death. Notice, also, the description of the terror of men and horses at the funeral. And, after the services, it was only a few, "bolder than their neighbors," that dared descend to the vault. Now, this is the only narrative in the chapter in which it is represented that the spectators of the occurrences experienced such terror; and in several cases children were present. When the well-known occurrences in the Fox family at Hydesville took place, two members of the family, in the house, were girls of nine and twelve years of age; yet it does not appear that these girls, or any of the family, felt any alarm. Almost, if not quite as well known is the account of disturbances in the family of which the celebrated John Wesley was a member; from which it appears that the family regarded the occurrences simply as an annoyance, not as a terror. And the same may be said of the account given by Mr. Owen of disturbances in the family of a Mr. Mompesson, in which there were also children.

The story under consideration has not the appearance of a statement of actual occurrences. The terror of men and animals; the exemption of the coffins of the saintly grandmother and the two children from molestation; the suicidal hand that had held the bloody razor raised toward the ceiling—such things occur only in fictions.

Finally, as to this branch of the subject, the fact that these physical manifestations, as they are called, have, within the past few years, been witnessed by thousands, —who never elsewhere witnessed anything of the kind— in the presence of certain individuals known as *mediums*, is very strong, if not convincing proof that they occur only in the vicinity of such individuals.

The next two chapters of Mr. Owen's work are on "Apparitions of the Living," and "Apparitions of the Dead."

My views upon this branch of the subject will, I have no doubt, be altogether unsatisfactory to Spiritualists, while most of my readers will, probably, require no argument to be convinced that the apparitions described were mostly hallucinations. The only difficulty with the latter class will be, to convince them that the apparitions are ever anything but hallucinations or impositions. The phenomena of apparitions are the most difficult of satisfactory treatment of any that I shall have occasion to notice. On the one hand, instances of apparitions, other than hallucinations, are, for the reasons given in a preceding chapter, extremely rare. But, on the other hand, when individuals of integrity state positively that they have seen "spirits" as distinctly as they ever saw anything, how can such

statements be disproved? The great difficulty in the
case is, as I assume, that the statements are exaggerated. I do not assume, or admit, that it is impossible
for an individual, in a sound state of health, to discriminate between hallucinations and actual vision.
A man of discrimination, when he experiences a hallucination, perceives that it is such, and, if he thinks
the fact worth mentioning, will state the occurrence as
an instance of the kind ; while a female, experiencing
the same, will state in the most positive terms that she
actually saw the object. I shall only attempt to show
that the supposition of a " spirit" being seen in the
cases here cited is an absurdity ; that the apparitions
occurred at a time or place favorable for hallucinations ;
and—which ought to be to Spiritualists a convincing
fact—that, in the case cited from another work, where
an apparition was unquestionably seen and *felt*, it required months to produce it.

The following extract from the chapter on appari·
tions of the dead will show that Mr. Owen considers
apparitions of the living, and of the dead, to be of the
same character; and that the evidence for the one is as
strong as that for the other; hence, it may be assumed
that if the former doctrine is an absurdity, there is no
satisfactory evidence for the latter :

" If, as St. Paul teaches and Swedenborgians believe,
there go to make up the personality of man a natural
body and a spiritual body; if these co-exist while
earthly life endures, in each one of us; if, as the apos-
tle further intimates and the preceding chapter seems
to prove, the spiritual body—a counterpart, it would
seem, to human sight, of the natural body—may, dur·

ing life, occasionally detach itself, to some extent or other and for a time, from the material flesh and blood which for a few years it pervades in intimate association ; and if death be but the issuing forth of the spiritual body from its temporary associate : then, at the moment of its exit, it is that spiritual body which through life may have been occasionally and partially detached from the natural body, and which at last is thus entirely and forever divorced from it, that passes into another state of existence.

" But if that spiritual body, while still connected with its earthly associate, could, under certain circumstances, appear distinct and distant from the natural body, and perceptible to human vision, if not to human touch, what strong presumption is there against the supposition that after its final emancipation the same spiritual body may still at times show itself to man ?"

I should say, that, granting the premises, there could be no presumption of the kind. It appears to me very strange, however, that Spiritualists quote St. Paul in support of their theories. If there is anything clearly taught by the writings of Paul, it must be conceded that he taught the doctrine of the resurrection of the body, as generally understood by Christians; and if, as Spiritualists believe, he was mistaken on that point, he was liable to be mistaken as to the existence of a spiritual body.

In reference to illusions and hallucinations, Mr. Owen makes the following remarks :

" An illusion, unlike a hallucination, has a foundation in reality. We actually see or hear something, which we mistake for something else. The mirage of the Desert, the Fata Morgana of the Mediterranean, are well-known examples. . . . There are collective illusions; for it is evident that the same false appearance which deceives the senses of one man is not unlikely to deceive those of others also. . . . But I know of no well-authenticated instance of collective hallucinations. No two patients that I ever heard of imagined the presence of the same cat or dog at the same moment.

"This is a distinction of much practical importance. If two persons perceive at the same time the same phenomenon, we may conclude that that phenomenon is an objective reality—has, in some phase or other, actual existence."

The distinction between illusions and hallucinations is neither so broad, or, as bearing upon this subject, so important, as Mr. Owen appears to think. As he cites Mrs. Catherine Crowe's "Night Side of Nature," I will copy from that work two narratives, in illustration of this point:

"During the Seven Years' War in Germany, a drover lost his life in a drunken squabble on the high road. For some time there was a sort of rude tombstone, with a cross on it, to mark the spot where his body was interred; but this has long fallen, and a mile-stone now fills its place. Nevertheless, it continues to be commonly asserted by the country people, and also by various travelers, that they have been deluded in that spot by seeing, as they imagine, herds of beasts, which on investigation prove to be merely visionary. Of course, many people look upon this as a superstition; but a very singular confirmation of the story occurred in the year 1826, when two gentlemen and two ladies were passing the spot in a post carriage. One of these was a clergyman, and none of them had ever heard of the phenomenon said to be attached to the place. They had been discussing the prospects of the minister, who was on his way to a vicarage to which he had just been appointed, when they saw a large flock of sheep, which stretched quite across the road, and was accompanied by a shepherd and a long-haired black dog. As to meet cattle on that road was nothing uncommon, and indeed they had met several droves in the course of the day, no remark was made at the moment, till suddenly each looked at the other and said, ' What is become of the sheep?' Quite perplexed at their sudden disappearance, they called to the postilion to stop, and all got out, in order to mount a little elevation and look around, but still unable to discover them, they now bethought themselves of asking the postilion where they were; when, to their infinite surprise, they learnt that he had not seen them. Upon this, they bade him quicken his pace, that they might overtake a carriage that had passed them shortly before, and inquire if that party had seen the sheep; but they had not."

" About the year 1750, a visionary army was seen in the neighborhood of Inverness by a respectable farmer of Glenary and his son. The number of troops was very great, and they had not the slightest doubt that they were otherwise than substantial forms of flesh and blood. They counted at least sixteen pairs of columns, and had abundance of time to observe every particular. The front ranks marched seven abreast, and were accompanied by a good many women and children, who were carrying tin cans and other implements of cookery.

The men were clothed in red, and their arms shone brightly in the sun. In the midst of them was an animal, a deer, or a horse, they could not distinguish which, that they were driving furiously forward with their bayonets. The younger of the two men observed to the other, that every now and then the rear ranks were obliged to run to overtake the van; and the elder one, who had been a soldier, remarked that that was always the case, and recommended him, if he ever served, to try and march in the front. There was only one mounted officer; he rode a gray dragoon horse, and wore a gold-laced hat, and blue Hussar cloak, with wide open sleeves lined with red. The two spectators observed him so particularly, that they said afterward they should recognize him anywhere. They were, however, afraid of being ill-treated, or forced to go along with the troops, whom they concluded had come from Ireland, and landed at Kyntyre; and while they were climbing over a dyke to get out of their way, the whole thing vanished."

It is a peculiarity of Mrs. Crowe that she seldom gives her authority for the narrative; but these have the appearance of being genuine. Whether they are correct or not, there are well-authenticated instances of similar occurrences. Let us assume, then, that these are *substantially* correct: that the accounts are exaggerated is altogether probable.

In the first case, four persons think they see, at the same time, a flock of sheep, a shepherd, and a black dog, neither of which have existence. I presume the ground taken by Mr. Owen would be, that there was some "objective reality" which caused the illusion.

Let this be admitted, for such was probably the fact. The most probable hypothesis that occurs to me is, that clouds, *seen through the small window of the carriage*, in a hilly country, in connection with impressions left on the minds of the party of flocks they had actually passed, were the exciting cause. Still, their illusions would not have so completely coincided unless the minds of the party had, to some extent, operated upon each other. Let it be admitted that they did not all think, at the time, that they saw the shepherd and dog, and that it was only after subsequent conversation they imagined their perceptions corresponded so minutely ; even then, the occurrence cannot be explained except upon the hypothesis of one mind influencing another. The party had been for some time in the same carriage, engaged in conversation, and had, probably, become more or less *en rapport.*

In the second case, it may be presumed that the father and son were, to some extent, *en rapport ;* and an image of what the former had, probably, actually witnessed, having been a soldier, being from some cause produced in his mind, was, by his influence, aided by the original cause, reproduced in the mind of the son. Whether the visions were or were not as vivid as represented, is not material.

But it does not matter how these delusions were caused ; nor whether they are called illusions or hallu-cinations. All I wish to show is, that several persons, at the same time, think they see the same object, when there is nothing at all resembling the object within their range of vision.

In reference to the position taken, that there can be

no collective hallucinations, Mr. Owen says: "The results of what have been usually called electro-biological experiments cannot with any propriety be adduced in confutation of this position. The biologized patient knowingly and voluntarily subjects himself to an artificial influence, of which the temporary effect is to produce false sensations; just as the eater of hasheesh, or the chewer of opium, conjures up the phantasmagoria of a partial insanity, or the confirmed drunkard exposes himself to the terrible delusions of delirium tremens. But all these sufferers know, when the fit has passed, that there was nothing of reality in the imaginations that overcame them."

There is no parallel in the cases cited. The delusions of several persons, under the effects, at the same time, of either of the drugs named, would not coincide. And the biologized patient is not given anything, either to eat or drink, in order that the hallucinations may be produced; he simply assumes a passive state of mind; and the effect is produced, solely, by the will of the operator acting upon his own will. The results of such experiments prove that, under favorable conditions, the will of one person can produce, at the same time, in the minds of half a dozen others, coinciding hallucinations. The phenomena of electro-biology, mesmerism, and the *involuntary* action of one mind upon another, are all of the same character.

The biologized patients know, when the experiments are over, that there was nothing of reality in what they thought they saw, because they are told, in the first place, the nature of the experiments. But let us suppose that—having never learned the nature of the experiments—they are told that the operator can open their "interior perception," or "spiritual vision," so that they will be able to perceive spirits, and things invisible to them in their normal condition: can any one doubt that some of them, at least, would continue in the belief, after the conclusion of the experiments, that they had really perceived the objects?

Mr. Owen maintains that, while the fact that two or more persons perceive at the same time the same object is evidence that it is not a case of hallucination, it does not follow that if only one person among many present perceives—or thinks he does—an object, it is a hallucination.

"There is nothing, then, absurd or illogical in the supposition that some persons may have true perceptions of which we are unconscious. We may not be able to comprehend *how* they receive these; but our ignorance of the mode of action does not disprove the reality of the effect. I know an English gentleman who, if a cat had been secreted in a room where he was, invariably and infallibly detected her presence. *How* he perceived this, except by a general feeling of uneasiness, he could never explain; yet the fact was certain."

Admitting the fact to be certain, it does not support Mr. Owen's position. The gentleman did not see the cat, nor even think he saw it. He could not describe its appearance: could not even tell whether it was white or black. The cat produced in him a "feeling of uneasiness;" that was all. A dog can detect the presence of an animal without seeing it. But how do such examples prove that there are individuals who can *see* spir-

its ? for that is the point in dispute.   If it was only con-
tended that there were individuals who were sensible
of the presence of what are called spirits, when others
are not, the point would not be disputed by me, for that
is my belief.   What I assert is, that no one of our world
can see (or perceive, if the latter word is preferred) the
form and color of beings of the invisible world.

I will now copy, from the two chapters upon this
branch of the subject, a few narratives which Mr. Owen
thinks confirm his views.

"*Apparition in Ireland.*"

In the summer of 1802, a clergyman of the Established Church, living in Ireland, was invited by the
bishop to dinner.   He accepted the invitation, leaving
his wife, quite unwell, at home.   Returning from the
bishop's about ten o'clock, the clergyman approached
his own residence through the garden attached to it.

" It was bright moonlight.   On issuing from a small
belt of shrubbery into a garden walk, he perceived, as
he thought, in another walk, parallel to that in which
he was, and not more than ten or twelve feet from him,
the figure of his wife, in her usual dress.   Exceedingly
astonished, he crossed over and confronted her.   It *was*
his wife.   At least, he distinguished her features, in the
clear moonlight, as plainly as he· had ever done in his
life.   ' What *are* you doing here ? ' he asked.   She did
not reply, but receded from him, turning to the right,
toward a kitchen-garden that lay on one side of the
house.   In it there were several rows of peas, staked
and well grown, so as to shelter any person passing behind them.   The figure passed round one end of these.

Mr. —— followed quickly, in increased astonishment, mingled with alarm; but when he reached the open space beyond the peas the figure was nowhere to be seen. As there was no spot where, in so short a time, it could have sought concealment, the husband concluded that it was an apparition, and not his wife, that he had seen. He returned to the front door and, instead of availing himself of his pass-key as usual, he rung the bell. While on the steps, before the bell was answered, looking round, he saw the same figure at the corner of the house. When the servant opened the door, he asked him how his mistress was. 'I am sorry to say, sir,' answered the man, 'she is not so well. Dr. Osborne has been sent for.' Mr. —— hurried up-stairs, found his wife in bed and much worse, attended by the nurse, who had not left her all the evening. From that time she gradually sank, and within twelve hours thereafter expired."

This was communicated to Mr. Owen by a son of the clergyman, in the year 1859.

Now, which is the most probable—admitting the existence of a spiritual body—that the whole was a hallucination, or, that the spirit of the wife, *in her usual dress*, was dodging around the peas, and the corner of the house, while the wife in bed *was not aware that her spirit was absent?* I think that an unusual quantity of wine drank at the bishop's dinner will account for this apparition, and also for the fact that the clergyman did not avail himself of his pass-key, as usual.

" *Sight and Sound.*"

"During the winter of 1839–'40, Dr. J—— E——

was residing with his aunt, Mrs. L——, in a house on Fourteenth street, near New York avenue, in the city of Washington. Ascending one day from the basement of the house to the parlor, he saw his aunt descending the stairs. He stepped back to let her pass, which she did, close to him, but without speaking. He instantly ascended the stairs and entered the parlor, where he found his aunt sitting quietly by the side of the fire. The distance from where he first saw the figure to the spot where his aunt was actually sitting was between thirty and forty feet. The figure seemed dressed exactly as his aunt was; and he distinctly heard the rustle of her dress as she passed."

"The above was related to me by Dr. E—— himself, in Washington, on the 5th of July, 1859; and the MS. was submitted to him for revision."

In this case, Mr. Owen says, "if it be one of hallucination, two senses were deceived."

There is nothing more natural, or common, than that a hallucination of sight should produce a hallucination of hearing. If Dr. E—— thought he saw his aunt descending the stairs, he would be quite likely to think that he heard the rustle of her dress.

Look at the absurdity of the spiritual hypothesis: The spiritual body of Mrs. L—— is supposed to leave her natural body, and to procure a dress exactly like that worn by the natural body, and so substantial that its rustle can be heard; and yet, the Mrs. L—— sitting by the fire knows nothing of the transaction. For the time being, then, there must have been two Mrs. L——s.

In defining hallucinations, Mr. Owen says: "I knew

well a lady who, more than once, distinctly saw feet ascending stairs before her. Yet neither her physician nor she herself ever regarded this apparent marvel in other light than as an optical vagary dependent on her state of health."

This he considers an instance of hallucination, because the lady so considered it. But where is the difference between this case, and those of Dr. E—— and the clergyman? The only difference, as I have before remarked, in all such cases is, that one person has the sense to perceive that it is a hallucination, and another has not. I consider it unnecessary to notice any more narratives precisely resembling these two.

"Apparition of the Living, seen by Mother and Daughter."

"In the month of May and in the year 1840, Dr. D——, a noted physician of Washington, was residing with his wife and his daughter Sarah (now Mrs. B——) at their country-seat, near Piney Point, in Virginia, a fashionable pleasure-resort during the summer months. One afternoon, about five o'clock, the two ladies were walking out in a copse-wood not far from their residence; when, at a distance on the road, coming toward them, they saw a gentleman. 'Sally,' said Mrs. D——, 'there comes your father to meet us.' 'I think not,' the daughter replied; 'that cannot be papa: it is not so tall as he.' As he neared them, the daughter's opinion was confirmed. They perceived that it was not Dr. D——, but a Mr. Thompson, a gentleman with whom they were well acquainted, and who was at that time, though they then knew it not, a patient of Dr. D——'s. They observed also, as he came nearer, that he was dressed in a blue frock-coat, black satin waistcoat, and black pantaloons and hat. Also, on comparing notes afterward, both ladies, it appeared, had noticed that his linen was particularly fine, and that his whole apparel seemed to have been very carefully adjusted. He came up so close that they were on the very point of addressing him; but at that moment he stepped aside, as if to let them pass; and then, *even while the eyes of both the ladies were upon him*, he suddenly and entirely disappeared."

The ladies afterward learned from Dr. D—— that Mr. Thompson had been confined to his room during the entire day. The narrative was communicated to Mr. Owen by Mrs. D—— in the year 1859.

"How strong in this case," Mr. Owen remarks, "is the presumptive evidence against hallucination! Even setting aside the received doctrine of the books, that there is no collective hallucination, how can we imagine that there should be produced, at the very same moment, without suggestion or expectation, or unusual excitement of any kind, on the brain of two different persons, a perception of the self-same image, minutely detailed, without any external object to produce it? Was that image imprinted on the retina in the case both of mother and daughter? How could this be if there was nothing existing in the outside world to imprint it? Or was there no image on the retina? Was it a purely subjective impression; that is, a false perception, due to disease? But among the millions of impressions which *may* be produced, if imagination only is the creative agent, how infinite the probabilities *against* the contingency that, out of these millions, this one especial ob-

ject should present itself in two independent cases!—
not only a particular person, dressed in a particular
manner, but that person advancing along a road, approaching within a few steps of the observers, and then
disappearing! Yet even this is not the limit of the ad-
verse chanc s. There is not only identity of object, but
exact coincidence of time. The two perceive the very
same thing at the very same moment; and this coincidence continues throughout several minutes.

"What is the natural and necessary conclusion?
That there *was* an image produced on the retina, and
that there *was* an objective reality there to produce it.

"It may seem marvelous, it may appear hard to believe, that the appearance of a human being, in his usual
dress, should present itself where that human being is
not. It would be a thing a thousand times more marvelous, ten thousand times harder to believe, that the
fortuitous action of disease, freely ranging throughout
the infinite variety of contingent possibilities, should
produce, by mere chance, a mass of coincidences such
as make up, in this case, the concurrent and cotempora-
neous sensations of mother and daughter."

I am not aware that it is a "received doctrine of the
books" that there are no collective hallucinations. Mr.
Owen himself quotes several writers who appear to have
different opinions. I copy the following mainly for the
purpose of showing, if the reader can understand it, Mr.
Owen's ideas upon the point:

"De Boismont reminds us that considerable assem-
blages of men have been the dupes of the same illusions.
'A cry,' he says, 'suffices to affright a multitude. An
individual who thinks he sees something supernatural,

soon causes others, as little enlightened as he, to share his conviction.' As to *illusions*, both optical and oral, this is undoubtedly true; more especially when these present themselves in times of excitement—as during a battle or a plague—or when they are generated in twilight gloom or midnight darkness. But that the contagion of example, or the belief of one individual under the actual influence of hallucination, suffices to produce, in others around, disease of the retina or of the optic or auditory nerve, or, in short, any abnormal condition of the senses, is a supposition which, so far as my reading extends, is unsupported by any reliable proof whatever."

That is, in short, in times of excitement, in twilight gloom or midnight darkness, an individual may cause others to share his *illusions;* but an individual under the influence of hallucination cannot produce in others *disease of the retina or optic nerve.* I presume that neither of these assertions will be disputed by any one. How the facts support Mr. Owen's theory, however, I do not perceive; unless it is assumed that a hallucination is always produced by disease of the eye or optic nerve, while an illusion is not. Such a supposition would be extremely absurd. It would make necessary the assumption that in biological experiments the operator always produces such disease in the subject—the disease changing as often as the operator, by his will, produces a change of hallucination; while in illusions, although, in the cases supposed by Mr. Owen, the operator produces precisely the same effect, there is no disease of the kind. I am here supposing the distinction between illusions and hallucinations to be, that in the former case *something* is actually seen, while in the latter there is no "objective reality." As a matter of fact, however, this distinction must in some cases be a very fine one; for example, where the object actually seen has not the slightest resemblance to what is supposed to be seen.

I deny that what are properly called hallucinations are always produced by disease of the organs of sight. So far as regards the narrative under notice, however, it makes no difference whether the occurrence is called a hallucination or an illusion, for it is probable that *something* was seen. As Mr. Owen admits that, under favorable circumstances, one individual may cause others to share his illusions, let us call the occurrence by the latter name.

Assuming the narrative to be substantially correct, the following, I think, is the true explanation: The ladies were walking in a copse-wood—a place favorable for illusions. Persons unaccustomed to walking in woods are very liable to be the victims of illusions. A shadow, a stump, or the body of a tree, is mistaken for a human being—the motion of the observer giving the object the appearance of motion. The ladies were mother and daughter, and, consequently, there was an affinity existing between them. Some object was seen which was mistaken for a man approaching them. Whether the daughter thought it was a man before the mother called her attention to it, cannot be determined from the narrative; at all events, she then shared the illusion of the mother; but, while the mother thought it was her husband, the daughter thought it was a taller man. The probability is that the latter at once thought of the acquaintance Thompson. However this may

have been, one or the other suggested that it was Mr
Thompson, and then their illusions coincided and became very strong.   The coincidence of their illusions as
to dress followed as a matter of course ; the appearance
being, undoubtedly, such as they had seen him wear.
When the illusion vanished—probably in consequence
of their approach to the object—the ladies commenced
" comparing notes ; " and they continued afterward
comparing notes, and talking of the subject, until the
story assumed a character somewhat marvelous.   On
the latter point I would remark, and I speak advisedly,
not one woman in t n thousand could give an unexag-
gerated account of such an occurrence.   But the account
does not show that the coincidence lasted " several minutes," as Mr. Owen states ; nor even that it lasted one
minute.

It is not easy to understand Mr. Owen's views regarding illusions and hallucinations.   He seems to believe
that a " spirit " can produce the latter in an individual
of our world.   The dream narrated under the heading
of " The Negro Servant " was caused, as he evidently
believes, by a being of the invisible world ; and it is
stated that the dreamer " was astonished, on entering her
mother's house, to meet the very black servant whom
she had seen in her dream, as he had been engaged during her absence."   Now, if the lady was made to perceive the servant by a " spirit," as supposed, there is but
one mode by which this could be effected, namely, by
the " spirit " first forming the image in his, or her, own
mind, and reproducing the same in the mind of the
lady.   And there is no ground for the assumption, that
the power of an individual of our world, in this respect,

is not of the same *kind* (though it may be less in degree) as that of an inhabitant of the invisible world. It is true, that in the one case the lady was asleep, while in the other both ladies were awake. But here, again, there is no ground for assuming that the power of one mind over another in the two cases differs in *kind*, although it undoubtedly does in degree.

The fact that such occurrences (two or more, thinking they see the same object at the same time) are unusual, instead of supporting the spiritual hypothesis, is very strong evidence that they are hallucinations or illusions. If, as Mr. Owen insists, "there *was* an image produced on the retina, and there *was* an objective reality there to produce it"—the objective reality being assumed to be the spirit of Thompson—why should it be an unusual event for two or more persons to see a spirit at the same time? Why are they not seen in the streets of New York and London by hundreds of individuals on the same day?

Let us look again at the absurdity of the spiritual hypothesis as applied to such a case. The fact will not be disputed, that the same individual cannot be in two places at the same time. Then, admitting that there was, at the time, *a* Mr. Thompson walking in the copse-wood, it certainly was not the Thompson that was in his room at the time. The Thompson walking in the copse-wood may have resembled the other Thompson; he may have been "dressed in a blue frock-coat, black satin waistcoat, and black pantaloons and hat;" his linen may have been "particularly fine;" and, in short, his whole apparel may have been "very carefully adjusted," so as to resemble that of the other Thompson;

but, after all, it could not have been the other Thompson ; nor could one Thompson be responsible, either legally or morally, for the actions of the other. The subject of dress is one which Spiritualists always evade ; but I can conceive of no reason why the spiritual Thompson should dress precisely as the other Thompson dressed ; nor, in fact, why spirits should at all consult the fashion of our world as to dress.

" *The Two Sisters.*"

"In the month of October, 1833, Mr. C——, a gentleman, several members of whose family have since become well and favorably known in the literary world, was residing in a country-house, in Hamilton County, Ohio. He had just completed a new residence, about seventy or eighty yards from that in which he was then living, intending to move into 'it in a few days. The new house was in plain sight of the old, no tree or shrub intervening ; but they were separated, about half-way, by a small, somewhat abrupt ravine. A garden stretched from the old house to the hither edge of this ravine, and the farther extremity of this garden was about forty yards from the newly erected building. Both buildings fronted west, toward a public road, the south side of the old dwelling being directly opposite to the north side of the new. Attached to the rear of the new dwelling was a spacious kitchen, of which a door opened to the north.

"The family, at that time, consisted of father, mother, uncle, and nine children. One of the elder daughters, then between fifteen and sixteen years old, was named

Rhoda; and another, the youngest but one, Lucy, was between three and four years of age.

"One afternoon in that month of October, after a heavy rain, the weather had cleared up; and between four and five o'clock the sun shone out. About five o'clock Mrs. C—— stepped out into a yard on the south side of the dwelling they were occupying, whence, in the evening sun, the new house, including the kitchen already referred to, was distinctly visible. Suddenly she called a daughter, A——, saying to her, 'What can Rhoda possibly be doing there, with the child in her arms? She ought to know better, this damp weather.' A——, looking in the direction in which her mother pointed, saw, plainly and unmistakably, seated in a rocking-chair just within the kitchen door of the new residence, Rhoda, with Lucy in her arms. 'What a strange thing!' she exclaimed: 'it is but a few minutes since I left them up-stairs.' And, with that, going in search of them, she found both in one of the upper rooms, and brought them down. Mr. C—— and other members of the family soon joined them. Their amazement—that of Rhoda especially—may be imagined. The figures seated at the hall-door, and the two children now actually in their midst, were absolutely identical in appearance, even to each minute particular of dress.

"Five minutes more elapsed, in breathless expectation, and there still sat the figures; that of Rhoda appearing to rock with the motion of the chair on which it seemed seated. All the family congregated, and every member of it—therefore twelve persons in all— saw the figures, noticed the rocking motion, and became convinced, past all possible doubt, that it *was* the appearance of Rhoda and Lucy.

"Then the father, Mr. C——, resolved to cross over and endeavor to obtain some solution of the mystery; but, having lost sight of the figures in descending the ravine, when he ascended the opposite bank they were gone.

"Meanwhile the daughter A——.had walked down to the lower end of the garden, so as to get a closer view : and the rest remained gazing from the spot whence they had first witnessed this unaccountable phenomenon. Soon after Mr. C—— had left the house, they all saw the appearance of Rhoda rise from the chair with the child in its arms, then lie down across the threshold of the kitchen door ; and, after it had remained in that recumbent position for a minute or two, still embracing the child, the figures were seen gradually to sink down out of sight. When Mr. C—— reached the entrance there was not a trace nor appearance of a human being."

This narrative was communicated to Mr. Owen by two of the daughters in the year 1860.

Twenty-seven years had elapsed, then, between the occurrence and the time when the account was given ; and, as it is stated that one of the eldest daughters was, at the time, between fifteen and sixteen years old, the two from whom Mr. Owen received the account must have been quite young when the events took place. Assuming the narrative to be substantially correct, I can only explain it upon the supposition that the setting sun, shining out after the rain, produced in some way the illusion. It will be observed that all the members of the family, with the exception of the mother, were told

what the appearance was before they perceived the like-
nesses. Instances of illusions like this are too common
to need explanation. Mr. Owen himself admits that
such illusions do occur.

If it is possible that Rhoda and Lucy were actually
looking at their own "spirits," and not aware that their
spirits were absent from their "natural" bodies, nor
sensible of their return, then, the spirits were separate
and distinct beings. It is admitted by the most intelligent class of Spiritualists that the only benefit Spiritualism has, as yet, conferred upon mankind is, that it
has confirmed our belief in immortality. But what is
this immortality, if these appearances were the spirits
of the two daughters? There is, existing within me,
according to this doctrine, a being that will continue to
live after my death. But it is not *me*, it is not the individual who is writing these lines, that will continue to
exist. The immortal being may be, at this moment,
off on an excursion, taking a walk, perhaps, in some
copse-wood, while I am trying to prove that he has no
existence. But whether he has, or has not, an existence, is a matter of no particular moment to *me*.

"*The Dying Mother and her Babe.*"

A lady residing in Cambridgeshire, England, being
ill, went to London for medical advice, leaving a child
at home. The mother became worse, and was unable
to return. In the mean time the child sickened and
died. A young lady, staying in the house, who, it is
stated, had from infancy been accustomed to the occasional sight of apparitions, went alone into the room

where the body of the infant lay in its coffin, and there saw, reclining on a sofa near the coffin, the appearance of the mother.

On account of her critical condition, the mother had not been advised of the death of the child; but, reviving as from a swoon about the time of the appearance to the young lady, as was afterward ascertained, she asked her husband why she had not been informed of the death, and said: "It is useless to deny it, Samuel, for I have just been home, and have seen her in her little coffin."

This occurred in the year 1843, and was related to Mr. Owen, by the lady who saw the apparition of the mother, in 1859.

I infer from the narrative that the mother was asleep, or, at least, partially so; and she was probably dreaming or thinking of her child, and of the young lady in whose charge it was left. This young lady was accustomed to the sight of apparitions; that is, according to my views, she was impressible, and subject to hallucinations. On going into the room where the corpse lay, she would naturally think of the mother; and as the latter was at the same time thinking of her, the two were brought, intimately *en rapport*. The room was probably, as is usual, partially darkened. Now, if one mind can produce an effect upon another, that a young lady subject to hallucinations should, under such circumstances, experience one, is not at all strange. When the two ladies became, for a moment, perfectly *en rapport*, their perceptions coincided. The mother really saw nothing, for she was asleep; the young lady saw the apparition of the mother and the dead child in its coffin; or at least had the latter in her mind, which would have the same effect as if she was looking at it. Whether the mother retained the impression of having reclined on the sofa, or not, does not appear from the narrative, and is not material. Sometimes only the strongest impressions are retained; and the vision of the dead child in its coffin may have been all that was recollected.

Mr. Owen does not trouble himself with seeking for any coherence in his theory as applied to the different narratives. In this, and the two narratives entitled "The Mother and Son," and "One Dream the Counterpart of Another," the parties experienced the sensation of being where their apparitions were seen; and in such cases the "spirit" is represented as being *the* individual, or, as Spiritualists express it, as containing the *soul*. But it is evident from the narratives entitled, "Sight and Sound," "Apparition of the Living seen by Mother and Daughter," and "The Two Sisters," that in these cases the parties had no knowledge or sensation of being where their spirits were supposed to be seen; in fact, in the latter cases there appears to have existed, at least for the time being, no more connection between the "spiritual body" and the "natural body" than between the latter and any other individual; and therefore each body—the natural and spiritual—must have possessed its own distinct "soul," whatever the latter may be.

"*The Visionary Excursion.*"

"In June of the year 1857, a lady whom I shall designate as Mrs. A—— (now Lady ——), was residing with her husband, a colonel in the British army, and their infant child, on Woolwich Common, near London.

" One night in the early part of that month, suddenly awaking to consciousness, she felt herself as if standing by the bedside and looking upon her own body, which lay there by the side of her sleeping husband. Her first impression was that she had died suddenly; and the idea was confirmed by the pale and lifeless look of the body, the face void of expression, and the whole appearance showing no sign of vitality. She gazed at it with curiosity for some time, comparing its dead look with that of the fresh countenances of her husband and of her slumbering infant in a cradle hard by. For a moment she experienced a feeling of relief that she had escaped the pangs of death; but the next, she reflected what a grief her death would be to the survivors, and then came a wish that she could have broken the news to them gradually. While engaged in these thoughts, she felt herself carried to the wall of the room, with a feeling that it must arrest her further progress. But no: she seemed to pass through it into the open air."

The lady was, as she thought, thus carried along, without action or volition on her part, past familiar objects, until she found herself in the bed-chamber of an intimate friend, Miss L—— M——, at Greenwich; with whom she entered into conversation, the purport of which she did not recollect.

This occurred during a Wednesday night. On the succeeding Friday Miss L—— M—— visited Mrs. A——, when the two ladies began conversing about bonnets; and Mrs. A—— said, " My last was trimmed with violet; and I like the color so much, I think I shall select it again." "Yes," her friend replied, "I know that is your color." "How so?" Mrs. A—— asked. "Because when you came to me the other night—let me see; when was it?—ah, I remember, the night before last—it was robed in violet that you appeared to me." "I appeared to you the other night?" "Yes, about three o'clock; and we had quite a conversation together. Have you no recollection of it?"

This narrative was given Mr. Owen in 1859 by one of the ladies, and confirmed by the other. To assume that it was precisely accurate as to the actual conversation, would be equivalent to assuming that Miss L—— M—— was an idiot; but this is a matter of little consequence; and we will suppose the narrative to be substantially correct. It is so similar to others which I have copied that it requires no additional explanation; and my only reason for noticing it is, that Mr. Owen here advances more definitely than in the preceding cases his theory upon the subject. He says:

"Resembling in its general character the Wilkins dream, the above differs from it chiefly in this, that the narrator appears to have observed more minutely the succession of her sensations, thus suggesting to us the idea that the apparently lifeless body which seemed to her to have remained behind might, for the time, have parted with what we may call a spiritual portion of itself; which portion moving off without the usual means of locomotion, might make itself perceptible, at a certain distance, to another person. Let him who may pronounce this a fantastical hypothesis, absurd on its face, suggest some other sufficient to explain the phenomenon we are here examining."

This hypothesis does not explain *this* phenomenon at all; for the principal portion of the figure which Miss L—— M—— thought she saw, was a violet dress; not a spiritual portion, or any other portion of the body of Mrs. A——. She probably thought that she saw her face, and nothing more. Now, the supposition that a spiritual portion of the body of Mrs. A—— could assume the form and appearance of a violet dress, would certainly be a "fantastical hypothesis." And it would be equally absurd to suppose that the spirit procured, in some way, the dress, and that Mrs. A—— had no recollection of this, while she recollected so many other less important occurrences. But, in fact, as all the movements of the spirit were involuntary, how *could* it have procured the dress? Spiritualists entirely ignore the question as to the dress of the spirits. Mr. Owen's work contains about five hundred pages; and yet he makes no attempt to explain this point.

But what could have carried the spirit, without its own volition, into the bed-chamber of Miss L—— M——? Not the volition of the "natural body;" for, according to the narrative, the "soul" was with the "spiritual body." And look once more at the utter incoherence of Mr. Owen's views. In this case, the natural body is supposed to be left in a lifeless condition in consequence of the spirit's exit; in other cases, the spirit is not missed by the natural body at all.

It is stated in the narrative that Mrs. A—— was expecting the visit of Miss L—— M——. In the night she dreamed of visiting her; and as violet was her favorite color, dreamed that she was dressed in violet; this produced a coinciding dream in her friend. The narrative does not state that Mrs. A—— thought she was dressed in violet; but, even according to Mr. Owen's theory, she must have thought, or, as he would probably say, have *known* that she was.

In the Wilkins narrative, and in that entitled "One Dream the Counterpart of Another," the original dreamer —the one who produced the corresponding dream in another—dreamed that certain words were spoken; and each party recollected precisely the same words. In this case, Mrs. A—— merely dreamed that she had a conversation with her friend; she did not dream of any particular words being spoken. Such, at least, appears to have been her recollection. And the recollection of her friend appears to have been precisely the same; she only remembered they had a conversation; not, apparently, recollecting a single word that was spoken. Such precise coincidences in the recollections of the parties would be very strange if the visits were real, and not imaginary ones.

The chapter on "Apparitions of the Living" contains one narrative which, if true, cannot be explained otherwise than upon the spiritual hypothesis. It was given Mr. Owen by the Captain Clarke, who also gave him the inexplicable narrative entitled "The Two Field-mice." The narrative is quite lengthy, covering about eight pages of Mr. Owen's work: and I can give only a synopsis.

"*The Rescue.*"

In the year 1828 Robert Bruce was first mate of a bark bound from* Liverpool to St. John's, New Brunswick. One day, having taken an observation at noon, the captain and mate descended to make their calculations; the captain to the cabin, and the mate to his stateroom, from which he could see into the cabin. The captain, having finished his calculations, went on deck. When Bruce had finished his, supposing the captain to be still in the cabin, he inquired as to how their calculations agreed. Receiving no answer, he looked into the cabin, and saw the captain, as he supposed, writing on his slate. As Bruce rose, and was about entering the cabin, the person that he thought the captain raised his head, when Bruce perceived that the individual was an entire stranger.

The narrative asserts that "Bruce was no coward;" but immediately contradicts this by the statement that when he perceived it was a stranger he became frightened, rushed on deck, and refused to descend again and ascertain who the individual was, as the captain requested, until the latter led the way. No one was found in the cabin when the captain and Bruce entered it; but upon examining the slate, they found written on it, " *Steer to the nor'west.*"

In obedience to this mysterious mandate, the captain decided to change the course of the bark from south of west to northwest; and after sailing in the latter direction for several hours, a vessel was discovered wrecked in a field of ice. This vessel had several passengers; and when these were transferred to the bark, Bruce recognized one of them as the person he had seen writing on the slate. This individual was then asked to write the words, " Steer to the nor'west," which he did, when the hand-writing was found to precisely resemble that of the original sentence.

It seems to me unnecessary to discuss the credibility of this story, for the reason that if such an extraordinary occurrence had taken place, *with as many witnesses as is represented*, the facts would have been made known wherever a newspaper was published. The only point worth examining, and this only as bearing upon the credibility of the preceding narrative of this Captain Clarke, is, who was the liar in this case, Clarke or Bruce?

Mr. Owen says: "I asked Captain Clarke if he knew Bruce well, and what sort of man he was. 'As truthful and straightforward a man,' he replied, 'as ever I met in all my life. We were as intimate as brothers; and two men can't be together, shut up for seventeen months in the same ship, without getting to know whether they can trust one another's word or not.'"

But Mr. Owen should first have ascertained what sort of man Clarke was. So far as appears, he knew nothing about Clarke, except that he had learned, in some way, that the latter had these marvelous stories to relate; when he went down to the New York docks and received the narratives. What sort of a man Bruce was, was certainly a very *naive* inquiry. Bruce was probably a myth; at any rate, it is very obvious that Clarke never received the story from Bruce; for if he had, he would have given the names of the bark and wrecked vessel, with other items, by means of which the truth of the story could be ascertained. It will be perceived, and Mr. Owen should have noticed, that Clarke did not give a single item of the kind. Now, he could not have heard such a wonderful story, and have been seventeen months in the same ship with the narrator, the two " as intimate as brothers," without having learned all the items in the case.   It is evident that Clarke, not Bruce, was the liar in this case; and we have, therefore, a right to conclude that the preceding narrative given by the former, entitled " The Two Field-mice," is also a fiction.

In this case, again, if there is any truth in the narrative, the spirit was dressed in a suit precisely like that worn by the natural body.   But why *do* the spirits always imitate the natural body in dress?   Why copy the fashions of our world at all; and especially for a short excursion like this, where a more simple dress would serve as well?   The truth appears to be, that Mr. Owen has written this book without having once thought about the matter of dress.

And, once more, look at the incoherence of his theories, in common with those of all Spiritualists.   Sometimes it appears from the narratives he gives, that the spirits can only communicate with our world by means of a medium; at other times, as in this case, there is no necessity for a medium, the spirit can make itself visible, and write on a slate without any such aid.

From the chapter on " Apparitions of the Dead," I will take two narratives of such occurrences where the apparitions were, as I think, produced by beings of the other world; selecting such as are of most recent date, and which appear to be best authenticated.

The following, Mr. Owen says, was communicated to him, under date of April 25, 1859, in a letter from the Rev. Dr., a clergyman of the Church of England, and Chaplain to the British Legation at ——; who informed him that "the relation is in the very words, so far as his memory serves, in which the narrator, his brother, repeated it to him. Though not at liberty to print the reverend gentleman's name, he has permitted me to furnish it privately in any case in which it might serve the cause to advance which these pages have been written."

" *The Stains of Blood.*"

"In the year 185– I was staying, with my wife and children, at the favorite watering-place ——. In order to attend to some affairs of my own, I determined to leave my family there for three or four days. Accordingly, on the —th of August, I took the railway, and arrived that evening, an unexpected guest, at —— Hall, the residence of a gentleman whose acquaintance I had recently made, and with whom my sister was then staying.

"I arrived late, soon afterward went to bed, and before long fell asleep. Awaking after three or four hours, I was not surprised to find I could sleep no more; for I never rest well in a strange bed. After trying, therefore, in vain again to induce sleep, I began to arrange my plans for the day.

"I had been engaged some little time in this way, when I became suddenly sensible that there was a light in the room. Turning round, I distinctly perceived a female figure; and what attracted my special attention was, *that the light by which I saw it emanated from itself.* I watched the figure attentively. The features were not perceptible. After moving a little distance, it disappeared as suddenly as it had appeared.

"My first thoughts were that there was some trick. I immediately got out of bed, struck a light, and found my bedroom-door still locked. I then carefully examined the walls, to ascertain if there were any other concealed means of entrance or exit; but none could I find. I drew the curtains and opened the shutters; but all outside was silent and dark, there being no moonlight.

"In doubt and uncertainty I passed the rest of the night; and in the morning, descending early, I immediately told my sister what had occurred, describing to her accurately everything connected with the appearance I had witnessed. She seemed much struck with what I told her, and replied: 'It is *very* odd; for you have heard, I dare say, that a lady was, some years ago, murdered in this house; but it was not in the room you slept in.' I answered, that I had never heard anything of the kind, and was beginning to make further inquiries about the murder, when I was interrupted by the entrance of our host and hostess, and afterward by breakfast. After breakfast I left, without having had any opportunity of renewing the conversation.

"On the Wednesday following I received a letter from my sister, in which she informed me that, since I left, she had ascertained that the murder *was* committed in the very room in which I had slept. She added that she purposed visiting us next day, and that she would like me to write out an account of what I had seen, together with a plan of the room, and that on that plan she wished me to mark the place of the appearance, and of the disappearance of the figure.

"This I immediately did; and the next day, when my sister arrived, she asked me if I had complied with her request. I replied, pointing to the drawing-room table, 'Yes: there is the account and the plan.' As she rose to examine it, I prevented her, saying, 'Do not look at it until you have told me all you have to say, because you might unintentionally color your story by what you may read there.'

"Thereupon she informed me that she had had the carpet taken up in the room I had occupied, and that the marks of blood from the murdered person were there, plainly visible, on a particular part of the floor. At my request she also then drew a plan of the room, and marked upon it the spots which still bore traces of blood. The two plans—my sister's and mine—were then compared, and we verified the most remarkable fact, *that the places she had marked as the beginning and ending of the traces of blood coincided exactly with the spots marked on my plan as those on which the female figure had appeared and disappeared.*"

Of course the sister could not have ascertained which was the beginning and which the ending of the traces of blood; that was a subsequent inference. I call attention to this, merely for the purpose of showing with what caution these marvelous narratives must be received. This narrator evidently intended to state the facts, and nothing more; and yet, he has stated as a fact what was merely an inference. It is a matter of no great importance here; but in some cases it is a point of vast importance whether what is stated as a remarkable coincidence is a known fact, or an inference.

And this inaccuracy has in this case a bearing upon the question as to the nature of the phenomenon. I presume the apparition was produced by one of the other world, probably by the murdered lady; but I think it was merely a hallucination which was produced, and that the gentleman really saw nothing.

I have had a somewhat similar experience myself. One night in the month of November, or December, 1863, while lying awake, I perceived what appeared to be a draped female statue in marble, standing with the left side toward me, about four feet from the foot of the bed. It was not the likeness of any one I knew; and I had not recently seen any statues, nor, so far as I can recollect, read or thought of any. At first it was very indistinct; that is, the room appeared to be dark; but while looking at it, and endeavoring to make out the features more clearly, the face and upper portion of the bust appeared to be suddenly illuminated, and then the whole figure as suddenly disappeared. I could have marked on a plan of the room the spot where the statue appeared to stand; and yet I could have seen nothing, for my eyes were closed.

Of course it is possible for any one to ascertain whether the light in such a case is real or not, by observing whether it renders other objects visible; but the difficulty is that the attention is entirely concentrated upon the figure supposed to be seen, and other facts are not observed. It would be useless to speculate as to the object of the murdered lady in producing the apparition; probably she had no definite object whatever.

It will be understood that I have here given my views as to this particular phenomenon; not that I believe it would be an impossibility for one of the other world to produce a dress (which appears to be all that the gentleman thought he saw) which might be actually seen by one of our world; and it is possible the dress might be made luminous in the dark. But, as I shall hereafter show, considerable time is required in the pre paration of such dresses.

" *The Fourteenth of November.*"

"In the month of September, 1857, Captain G——
W——, of the 6th (Inniskillin) Dragoons, went out to India to join his regiment.

"His wife remained in England, residing at Cambridge. On the night between the 14th and 15th of November, 1857, toward morning, she dreamed that she saw her husband, looking anxious and ill; upon which she immediately awoke, much agitated. It was bright moonlight; and, looking up, she perceived the same figure standing by her bedside. He appeared in his uniform, the hands pressed across the breast, the hair disheveled, the face very pale. His large dark eyes were fixed full upon her; their expression was that of great excitement, and there was a peculiar contraction of the mouth, habitual to him when agitated. She saw him, even to each minute particular of his dress, as distinctly as she had ever done in her life; and she remembers to have noticed between his hands the white of the shirt bosom, unstained, however, with blood. The figure seemed to bend forward, as if in pain, and to make an effort to speak; but there was no sound. It remained visible, the wife thinks, as long as a minute, and then disappeared.

"Next morning she related all this to her mother, expressing her conviction, though she had noticed no marks of blood on his dress, that Captain W—— was either killed or grievously wounded. So fully impressed was she with the reality of that apparition that she thenceforth refused all invitations. A young friend urged her, soon afterward, to go with her to a fashionable concert, reminding her that she had received from Malta, sent by her husband, a handsome dress-cloak, which she had never yet worn. But she positively declined, declaring that, uncertain as she was whether she was not already a widow, she would never enter a plac˙ of amusement until she had letters from her husband (if, indeed, he still lived) of later date than the 14th of November."

Some time in the succeeding month (December) a telegram was published in London, stating that Captain W—— was killed before Lucknow on the *fifteenth* of November; and official intelligence was afterward received at the War Office to the same effect.

When Mr. Wilkinson, a London solicitor who had in charge Captain W——'s affairs, met Mrs. W——, after the publication of the telegram, she informed him of the apparition, saying she felt sure that her husband could not have been killed on the 15th of November, inasmuch as it was during the night between the 14th and 15th that he appeared to her. The certificate from the War Office, however, which it became Mr. Wilkinson's duty to obtain, confirmed the date given in the telegram.

After the interview with Mrs. W——, Mr. Wilkinson visited a friend, called Mr. N——, "whose lady has all her life had perception of apparitions, while her husband is what is usually called an impressible medium."

"Mr. Wilkinson related to them, as a wonderful circumstance, the vision of the captain's widow in connection with his death, and described the figure as it had appeared to her. Mrs. N——, turning to her husband, instantly said, 'That must be the very person I saw, the evening we were talking of India, and you drew an elephant, with a howdah on his back. Mr. Wilkinson has described his exact position and appearance; the uniform of a British officer, his hands pressed across his breast, his form bent forward as if in pain. The figure,' she added to Mr. Wilkinson, 'appeared just behind my husband, and seemed looking over his left shoulder.'

" ' Did you attempt to obtain any communication from him ? ' Mr. Wilkinson asked.

" ' Yes : we procured one through the medium of my husband.'

" ' Do you remember its purport ? '

" ' It was to the effect that he had been killled in India that afternoon, by a wound in the breast ; and adding, as I distinctly remember, " That thing I used to go about in is not buried yet." I particularly marked the expression.' "

This occurred, as was found by looking at the date of a bill which had been paid on the same evening, on the 14th of November.

In the month of March, 1858, the family of Captain W—— received a letter from India, informing them that the captain had been killed in the afternoon of the 14th of November ; having been struck in the breast by a fragment of shell. And the War Office, more than a year after the event occurred, made the correction as to the date of the death, altering it from the 15th to the 14th of November.

"This extraordinary narrative," Mr. Owen says, "was obtained by me directly from the parties themselves. The widow of Captain W—— kindly consented to examine and correct the manuscript, and allowed me to inspect a copy of Captain C——'s letter, giving the particulars of her husband's death. To Mr. Wilkinson, also, the manuscript was submitted, and he assented to its accuracy so far as he is concerned. That portion which relates to Mrs. N—— I had from that lady herself. I have neglected no precaution, therefore, to obtain for it the warrant of authenticity.

"It is, perhaps, the only example on record where the appearance of what is usually termed a ghost proved the means of correcting an erroneous date in the dispatches of a commander-in-chief, and of detecting an inaccuracy in the certificate of a War Office.

"It is especially valuable, too, as furnishing an example of a double apparition. Nor can it be alleged (even if the allegation had weight) that the recital of one lady caused the apparition of the same figure to the other. Mrs. W—— was at the time in Cambridge, and Mrs. N—— in London; and it was not till weeks after the occurrence that either knew what the other had seen.

"Those who would explain the whole on the principle of chance coincidence have a treble event to take into account: the apparition to Mrs. N——, that to Mrs. W——, and the actual time of Captain W——'s death; each tallying exactly with the other."

It does not appear from the narrative that the apparition had any connection, either directly or indirectly, with the correction of the date at the War Office; and such a supposition is rather absurd. The statement on this point is, that Mr. Wilkinson, having occasion to apply for a second certificate, found that the date had been changed. There is no evidence that the apparition had even been heard of at the War Office. This, however is a matter of no particular consequence. The main facts in the case are as well authenticated as anything of the kind can be. I recollect reading in an English newspaper—or copied from such, I am not certain which —shortly after the date of the occurrences, an article upon the subject, from which it appeared that there was no dispute as to the facts; but the position was taken that the coincidence might have been accidental, and that the facts were not sufficient to prove that the spirit of Captain W—— was actually seen. I do not recollect whether the appearance and communication to Mr. and Mrs. N—— were alluded to, and, in my judgment, that part of the narrative is not of the slightest importance.

I might, perhaps, have selected a narrative which would be better evidence of an apparition produced by an inhabitant of the invisible world. All that this narrative shows to that effect is, that Mrs. W——, during the night succeeding the afternoon on which her husband was killed, saw the apparition described. As she knew that her husband was fighting in India, that he should appear to her, as described, that night in a dream, and that the vision of the dream should continue for a few seconds after she awoke, might be considered an accidental coincidence. But, as the facts have become so well known, and have been, more than once, triumphantly quoted by Spiritualists in confirmation of their doctrines, I have thought it best to give the substance of the narrative, with my views regarding the occurrences.

As apparitions, occurring soon after the death of the person whose appearance is seen, are, as formerly stated, frequent, it is very probable that this one was produced by a relative or friend of the captain in the invisible world, who, knowing the danger to which he was to be exposed, had accompanied him. The invisible being producing the apparition, would naturally have in his (or her) mind the image of the captain as he appeared on being struck by the fragment of shell. It is stated that he almost instantly expired.

Now, let us examine that part of the narrative relating to Mr. and Mrs. N——. They were talking of India, probably of the war there. Mrs. N——, a lady who "has all her life had perception of apparitions," thought she saw a British officer, who appeared to have been wounded in the breast—a part of the person which, somehow, we are apt to think most likely to be struck by a ball, or pierced by a bayonet. Mr. N——, an *impressible* medium, on being told by his wife that she saw an officer standing just behind him, looking as described, *thought* that he received a communication (by *impression*, it will be recollected) from the officer, corroborative of the vision of his wife, and to the effect that the death had occurred that afternoon. The vision of the seeress, and the communication to the impressible medium, may all have been merely effects of the imagination.

But let us assume, which is quite probable, that the communication was from an inhabitant of the invisible world. It could not have been from Captain W——, for he would, of course, if he communicated at all with Mr. N——, have given his name, and a message for his widow. A narrative like this shows how entirely Spiritualist discard common sense as a foundation for their belief. That Captain W—— should journey from India to England to make his death known to Mrs. W——, and that when, on reaching London, he found a medium through whom he might have sent her a message, he merely stated to the medium that he was killed in India that afternoon, and that the thing he used to go about in was not buried yet—without even giving his name—does not to Spiritualists appear at all improbable.

I presume that Mr. and Mrs. N—— were impressible mediums; and that, like all other mediums, they were surrounded by degraded beings of the invisible world, ready at all times to communicate. These beings may, possibly, have learned that a battle had been fought that day in India; but it is equally probable that the communication was owing to the fact that Mr. and Mrs. N—— were talking of the war. At any rate, it is quite certain that the one giving the communication had not learned the name of any officer who had been killed; for if any such name had been learned it would have been given. The silly and vulgar language of the sentence, "That thing I used to go about in is not buried yet," must be familiar to all who have often visited mediums.

I assume that the apparition, seen by Mrs. W——,

could not have been produced by her husband so soon after his death. But my principal object in copying this narrative was, to show that what may be called the respectable class of the other world will not communicate through the mediums; and that therefore it is useless for people to visit mediums for the purpose of receiving communications from departed friends. Even upon the assumption that this was the spirit of Captain W——, which had procured a dress resembling a captain's uniform—it is evident that the spirit was unwilling to send a message to Mrs. W—— through any medium; for if this were not so, a message would have been sent.

"*The Brother's Appearance to the Sister.*"

This narrative was communicated to Mr. Owen, in the year 1859, by William Howitt, who, in reference to it, says:

"The circumstance you desire to obtain from me is one which I have many times heard related by my mother. It was an event familiar to our family and the neighborhood, and is connected with my earliest memories; having occurred, about the time of my birth, at my father's house at Heanor, in Derbyshire, where I myself was born."

"One fine calm afternoon my mother, shortly after a confinement, but perfectly convalescent, was lying in bed, enjoying, from her window, the scene of summer beauty and repose; a bright sky above, and the quiet village before her. In this state she was gladdened by hearing footsteps which she took to be those of her brother Frank, as he was familiarly called, approaching the chamber-door. The visitor knocked and entered. The foot of the bed was toward the door, and the curtains at the foot, notwithstanding the season, were drawn, to prevent any draught. Her brother parted them and looked in upon her. His gaze was earnest, and destitute of its usual cheerfulness, and he spoke not a word. 'My dear Frank,' said my mother, 'how glad I am to see you! Come round to the bedside: I wish to have some talk with you.'

" He closed the curtains as complying; but, instead of doing so, my mother, to her astonishment, heard him leave the room, close the door behind him, and begin to descend the stairs. Greatly amazed, she hastily rang, and when her maid appeared she bade her call her brother back. The girl replied that she had not seen him enter the house. But my mother insisted, saying, 'He was here but this instant. Run! quick! call him back! I must see him.' "

About the time of this occurrence the brother had been stabbed in the street of the village, and killed on the spot.

" On comparing the circumstances and the exact time at which each occurred, the fact was substantiated that the apparition presented itself to my mother almost instantly after her brother had received the fatal stroke."

I at once admit that this narrative, *as given*, cannot be explained consistently with the theories I have propounded; and it would be equally difficult to explain it upon any theory advanced by Mr. Owen. If this narrative is a correct account of the visit of a spirit, then most of those in his work have no bearing what-

ever upon the subject. In the two preceding narratives
the spirits are represented as appearing and disappearing without opening any door. And in the narrative
entitled " The Visionary Excursion," where Mr. Owen
states more definitely than elsewhere his views, the
" spiritual portion "—that is, the spiritual body—is supposed to pass, without the least difficulty, through a
solid wall. But in this narrative, the spirit is represented as being like an individual of our world in every
respect except that it could not, or would not, talk. It
even observed the etiquette of knocking at the door before opening it.

Then again, this spirit, apparently, could not speak a
word; others converse without difficulty. And if Mr.
Owen's narratives are accounts of the actual visits of
spirits, then it would seem that all spirits are idiots, as
I have represented those to be who communicate through
mediums. This spirit took the trouble to visit his sister; but instead of going to the side of the bed, as a
sensible person would have done, he opened the curtains at the foot; and when the sister requested him to
go around to the side, so that she might converse with
him, he left the room. What object could he have had
in visiting the sister at all?

I presume that this was simply another instance of
one mind operating upon another. The sister was lying
in a receptive or impressible condition, and the dying
brother probably thought of her, which produced a hallucination of some kind. We have no means of determining the accuracy of the narrative; for the voucher
is of the same defective character as that for the narrative entitled " Bell and Stephenson; " and the question

again arises, *How* do you know? or, in this case, when did you last hear the story? the incident having occurred when the narrator was a child. After reading Mr. Howitt's "History of the Supernatural," I conclude the story would lose nothing of the marvelous in being told by him.

"*The Nobleman and his Servant.*"

"The late Lord M——, having gone to the Highlands about the end of the last century, left his wife perfectly well in London. The night of his arrival at his Highland home he was awakened by seeing a bright light in his room. The curtains of his bed opened, and he saw the appearance of Lady M—— standing there. He rang for his servant, and inquired of him what he saw; upon which the man exclaimed, in terror, 'It's my lady!' Lady M—— had died suddenly in London that night. The story made a great noise at the time; and George the Third, sending for Lord M—— and ascertaining from him the truth of it, desired him to write out the circumstances as they happened; and the servant countersigned the statement.

"About a year afterward, a child five years old, the youngest daughter of Lord M——, rushed breathlessly into the nursery, exclaiming, 'I have seen mamma standing at the top of the stair and beckoning to me.' That night the child, little Annabella M——, was taken ill, and died. "

Mr. Owen says: "I can vouch, in an unqualified manner, for the authenticity of both the above circumstances; having received the account, in writing, from a member of Lord M——'s family."

That portion of the narrative relating to the child requires no further comment than that it indicates a family liability to hallucination. It is quite possible the mother perceived the approaching death, or at least illness, of the child, and that her presence produced in the latter a hallucination.

But the preceding portion of the narrative cannot, as it reads, be assumed to be merely an account of a hallucination; for it is stated that the bed-curtains were opened, and not by Lord M.——. The account of this apparition would, to most persons, appear no more incredible than the accounts I shall hereafter give of what I believe to have been real and tangible apparitions. But the difficulty in the case is, that these apparitions can be produced through the mediumship of but very few individuals; and only after a considerable length of time spent in preparing the materials.

In this case, again, the narrative was given a long time—at least sixty years—after the occurrences took place, and by one who must at the time have been quite young. If we had the account written at the time by Lord M——, the occurrence might, perhaps, be explained; but there is a lack of detail in this given, which makes such explanation impossible.

It is stated that, "the curtains of his bed opened;" but who, or what, opened them? If the apparition of Lady M—— opened them, Lord M—— would, naturally, have so stated. Lord M—— "was awakened by seeing a bright light in his room;" which must mean, I suppose, that the light awoke him. But there is no explanation as to what caused this light, or what it appeared to emanate from; which is a very strange omission. The servant, apparently, perceived nothing unusual until asked by his master what he saw; and even then, so far as the narrative shows, he perceived no unnatural light. It seems to me quite certain that there was no unnatural light in the room; for if there had been, it would have been noticed, and stated what the light appeared to emanate from. I presume that this was another case of hallucination, produced by the action of one mind upon another; the account of which is incorrectly given.

"Apparition of a Stranger."

This narrative was given Mr. Owen, in May, 1859, by Baron de Guldenstubbé, brother of Mlle. de Guldenstubbé, who gave him the two inexplicable narratives entitled, " Why a Livonian School-teacher lost her Situation," and "The Cemetery of Ahrensburg ; " the former of which, it will be recollected, Mr. Owen has thought proper to omit from the later editions of his work.

" In March of the year 1854 the Baron de Guldenstubbé was residing alone in apartments, at Number 23 Rue St. Lazare, Paris. On the 16th of that month, returning thither from an evening party, after midnight, he retired to rest; but finding himself unable to sleep, he lit a candle and began to read. Very soon his attention was drawn from the book by experiencing first one electric shock, then another, until the sensation was eight or ten times repeated. This greatly surprised him, and effectually precluded all disposition to sleep : he rose, donned a warm dressing-gown, and lit a fire in the adjoining saloon."

Returning a few minutes afterward to the bedroom
for a pocket-handkerchief, without a candle, the baron
observed, just before the fireplace, what seemed like a
dim column of grayish vapor, slightly luminous; of
which, however, he took no particular notice at the time.
But, returning again, after a while, for a stick of wood,
the appearance in front of the fireplace arrested his attention.   It reached nearly to the ceiling of the apartment, which was fully twelve feet high; and its color
had changed from gray to that shade of blue exhibited
when spirits of wine are burned.   As the baron gazed
at it, the outlines of a human figure became visible.

"Gradually the outlines of the figure became marked,
the features began to assume exact form, and the whole
to take the colors of the human flesh and dress.   Finally,
there stood within the column, and reaching about half
way to the top, the figure of a tall, portly old man, with
a fresh color, blue eyes, snow-white hair, thin white
whiskers, but without beard or mustache; and dressed
with some care.   He seemed to wear a white cravat and
long white waistcoat, high stiff shirt collar, and a long
black frockcoat, thrown back from his chest, as is the
wont of corpulent people like him in hot weather.   He
appeared to lean on a heavy white cane.   After a few
minutes, the figure detached itself from the column and
advanced, seeming to float slowly through the room,
till within about three feet of its wondering occupant.
There it stopped, put up its hand, as if in form of salu-
tation, and slightly bowed."

"After a time the figure moved toward the bed, which
was to the right of the entrance-door and immediately
opposite the fireplace, then turning to the left, returned

to the spot before the fireplace, where it had first appeared, then advanced a second time toward the baron. And this round it continued to make (stopping, however, at intervals) as often as eight or ten times. The baron heard no sound, either of voice or footstep.

" The last time it returned to the fireplace, after facing the baron, it remained stationary there. By slow degrees the outlines lost their distinctness ; and, as the figure faded, the blue column gradually reformed itself, inclosing it as before. This time, however, it was much more luminous—the light being sufficient to enable the baron to distinguish small print, as he ascertained by picking up a Bible that lay on his dressing-table and reading from it a verse or two. He showed me the copy : it was in minion type. Very gradually the light faded, seeming to flicker up at intervals, like a lamp dying out."

The baron now concluded to go to bed again. In a dream, the same figure again appeared to him. It seemed to sit down on the side of the bed, and, to say to him, " Hitherto you have not believed in the reality of apparitions, considering them only the recallings of memory : now, since you have seen a stranger, you cannot consider it the reproduction of former ideas."

The next morning, on inquiring of the wife of the concierge, the baron learned that the last occupant of the apartments had died, about two years before, in the bed he now occupied ; and the woman's description of this individual corresponded in every respect, as to person, dress, and cane, with the apparition. The woman also stated that she had seen the same figure several times, in different places, and that a maid-servant had once seen it on the stairs. Finally, the daughter of the individual, whose appearance was seen, caused masses to be said for the soul of her father, since which, as alleged, the apparition has not been seen.

As the baron confirmed the narrative of the cemetery of Ahrensburg—occurrences which had taken place ten years previous—I cannot understand why this old gentleman considered him skeptical upon the subject of " spirits."

This spirit differed from all others described in Mr. Owen's work in its mode of making itself visible to persons of our world ; and, while in some narratives it is stated that the spirit's footsteps could be heard as distinctly as those of an individual of our world, in this case the baron heard not the slightest sound.

As the baron stated that he had previously seen apparitions, and, also, that before the appearance of this one he experienced several electric shocks, I might assume that this narrative did not conflict with my explanations of such phenomena. But, as my object is to make the phenomena understood, I feel bound to state that apparitions—such as are actually seen—are not produced as here represented. The baron's description meets the views of Spiritualists, who believe the bodies of spirits to consist of attenuated matter, or *ether*, and that they have the power, either of changing this body so that it will be visible to us, or of clothing it with another body formed from matter of our world. And the intimation that the spirit was quieted by the performance of masses, agrees with the popular superstition of Catholic countries. Masses would have no more

effect toward quieting the "spirits" than "Yankee
Doodle" played on a hand-organ.

I can only account for these marvelous stories of the
de Guldenstubbés upon the supposition that, having
a passion for telling "ghost-stories," they constructed
these upon some slight foundation. They cannot be
accounted for upon the supposition that these two persons were wonderful mediums; for, in all three of the
stories it is stated that the phenomena were witnessed
by others when they were not present.

In reference to this last narrative, Mr. Owen says
"The story derives much of its value from the calm
and dispassionate manner in which the witness appears
to have observed the succession of phenomena, and the
exact details which, in consequence, he has been enabled
to furnish." This refers, I suppose, to the statement of
the baron, that "He experienced little or no alarm,
being chiefly occupied during the period of its stay in
seeking to ascertain whether it was a mere hallucination
or an objective reality." He was so calm that he picked
up a Bible and read a verse or two, to ascertain how
strong the light was; but, although the figure came
close to him eight or ten times, he did not *touch* it, or
attempt to; which would have shown him whether it
was, or was not, an objective reality, the point he was
calmly endeavoring to ascertain. This is rather absurd.

It is not necessary that I should review the chapter
on "Retribution," the purport of which is, that individuals of the other world sometimes punish, or persecute
those who have done them an injury before their death.
As they frequently annoy those who have done them

no injury, there is no reason to doubt that they sometimes persecute such as have. The only reason that
such persecutions are not more often experienced is, the
lack of ability in those of the other world to inflict
them.

In opening the final chapter of narratives, which is
on "Guardianship," Mr. Owen says : " A pleasanter
task remains ; to speak, namely, of the indications that
reach us of ultramundane aid and spiritual protection."

Of course, with the knowledge of the subject which
Mr. Owen has, and the views which he holds, he cannot
discriminate, on this point, between those of the other
world who produce the physical phenomena and communicate through the mediums, and those who can do
neither. This is the principal difference between his
views and my own upon this point ; I believe that any
connection with the former class is far from desirable.
That the latter class has sometimes, though not very
often, rendered valuable services to friends in our world,
I readily admit. The narrative entitled "The Negro
Servant" gives a remarkable instance of the kind; and
why Mr. Owen has not placed it in this chapter, in pref-
erence to some which are here, I cannot understand.

There are in this chapter but two narratives relating
to that class producing the physical phenomena ; and
the reader shall be enabled to judge for himself how
far these indicate "ultramundane aid and spiritual protection."

"*Gaspar.*"

About the year 1820 an English family were residing

in France. One evening the father saw, enveloped in a large cloak and seated on a fragment of rock a few yards from the door, what he called a ghost; and that night noises and disturbances similar to those described in the narratives on "hauntings," occurred in the house. After these annoyances had continued for several weeks, the family, as stated, became able to hear the "spirit" speak. He gave his name as *Gaspar*, but refused to give any account of himself, or to state why he had annoyed them, or, in short, what he wanted. He continued with the family while they remained in France—a period of more than three years—followed them when they returned to England, and remained with them there several weeks, when he left them; assigning as a reason for leaving them, that harm would come to them if he communicated with them in England.

While in France one of the children—a boy aged about twelve years—said, one evening, "'Gaspar, I should like to see you;' to which the voice replied, 'You shall see me. I will meet you if you go to the farthest side of the square.' He went, and returned presently, saying, 'I have seen Gaspar. He was in a large cloak, with a broad-brimmed hat. I looked under the hat, and he smiled upon me.' 'Yes,' said the voice, joining in, 'that was I.'"

On one occasion, while in France, the father was extremely desirous to recover some valuable papers which he feared might have been lost. "Gaspar told him exactly where they were, in our old house in Suffolk; and there, sure enough, in the very place he designated, they were found."

"He never spoke on subjects of a religious nature or

tendency, but constantly inculcated Christian morality, seeming desirous to impress upon us the wisdom of virtue and the beauty of harmony at home.   Once, when my sister and myself had some slight dispute, we heard the voice saying, 'M—— is wrong; S—— is right.' From the time he first declared himself he was continually giving us advice, *and always for good.*"

This narrative was given Mr. Owen, in writing, by Mr. S. C. Hall, of England, in June, 1859.   Mr. Hall received the account the same year, orally, from one of the daughters of the family, whom he accidentally met; and he states that he gives the narrative as nearly as he can in the lady's words.   It is proper to state that Mr. Hall is known as a Spiritualist; for some persons always wish to be advised upon this point when a narrative of the kind is given.

Nearly forty years, then, had elapsed between the date of these occurrences and their recital to Mr. Hall; and the latter repeated the narrative to Mr. Owen from recollection.   "Spirits" are not now, in America, seen sitting on rocks; they do not, when performing in a room, agree to show themselves if one of the party will go into the street; nor can they talk so that several persons can hear them at the same time.   I do not believe that their powers were any greater forty or fifty years ago, in France, than at the present time in America.   This is, I believe, the only narrative in Mr. Owen's work in which it is stated that a number of individuals could, at the same time, hear the same spirit talk.   In a narrative entitled "The Old Kent Manor-House" it is stated, that "every inmate of the house had been more or less disturbed at night—*not* usually during the day—by knockings and sounds as of footsteps, but more especially by voices which could not be accounted for. These last were usually heard in some unoccupied adjoining room; sometimes as if talking in a loud tone, sometimes as if reading aloud, occasionally as if screaming." But, on reading the narrative through, it appears that only one individual in the house—a Miss S——, a visitor who "had been in the habit of seeing apparitions"—ever understood a word that was spoken. It may reasonably be assumed, then, that the others heard only noises which they imagined to be voices.

But, as indicating "spiritual protection," let it be assumed that this narrative of " Gaspar " is literally correct. We have, then, an account of a "spirit" entering a house and alarming the family—disturbing their rest at night for several weeks—and, when able to communicate, refusing to give any account of himself, or to explain why he had annoyed them; giving, however, good advice, and inculcating Christian morality. What would be thought of an individual of our world who should take the same course? for there is scarcely a drunken wretch in the world that will not give plenty of good advice, and preach Christian morality. I think no one but a Spiritualist would desire such companionship as that of *Gaspar.*

" *The Rejected Suitor.*"

Mr. and Mrs. W—— resided in England, not far from London. A short time previous to the date of the following occurrences, an aged gentleman, who had resided with them about four years, died.

Mrs. W. had been to some extent interested in the
subject of Spiritualism, and had, on one or two occasions, held her hand, as writing mediums do, to see if
the "spirits" would write with it; and "a few unintel-
ligible figures, or unimportant words" written, were the
result. She went one morning into the garden, feeling
much depressed on account of the death of her aged
friend; and had been there but a few minutes, when
she felt a strong impulse to return to the house and
write.*

"The impulse to write gradually increasing, and attended with a nervous and uneasy sensation in the right
arm, became so strong that she yielded to it; and, returning to the house and picking up a sheet of note-
paper and a small portfolio, she sat down on the steps
of the front door, put the portfolio on her knee, with
the sheet of note-paper across it, and placed her hand,
with a pencil, at the upper left-hand corner, as one usually begins to write. After a time the hand was gradually drawn to the lower right-hand corner, and began
to write *backward;* completing the first line near the
left-hand edge of the sheet, then commencing a second
line, and finally a third, both on the right, and completing the writing near to where she had first put down
her pencil. Not only was the last letter in the sentence
written first, and so on until the commencing letter was
written last, but each separate letter was written backward, or inversely; the pencil going over the lines
which composed each letter from right to left.

---

* I give the words of Mr. Owen, but it is evident from what follows that the impulse was to let the "spirits" write.

" Mrs. W. stated to me that (as may well be conceived) she had not the slightest perception of what her hand was writing ; no idea passing through her mind at the time. When her hand stopped, she read the sentence as she would have read what any other person had written for her. The handwriting was cramped and awkward, but, as the fac-simile* will show, legible enough. The sentence read thus :—' *Ye are sorrowing as one without hope. Cast thy burden upon God, and he will help thee.*' "

Mrs. W. placed her pencil at the foot of the paper, that the " spirit " might subscribe its name—expecting the name of her aged friend to be given.

" The event, however, wholly belied her expectation. The pencil, again drawn nearly to the right-hand edge of the paper, wrote, backward as before, not the expected name, but the initials R. G. D."

These were the initials of a gentleman who, eighteen years before, had sought her in marriage, but whom she had rejected ; and the gentleman had died about six years previous, a bachelor.

" This occurred on the afternoon of Tuesday, March 1, 1859. A little more than a month afterward, to wit, on Monday, April 4, about four o'clock in the afternoon, while Mrs. W. was sitting in her parlor, reading, she suddenly heard, apparently coming from a small side-table near her, three distinct raps. She listened ; and again there came the same sounds. Still uncertain whether it might not be some accidental knocking, she said, ' If

---

* Fac-similes of this, and a sentence written afterward, are given in Mr. Owen's work.

it be a spirit who announces himself, will he repeat the sound?' Whereupon the sounds were instantly and still more distinctly repeated : and Mrs. W. became assured that they proceeded from the side-table.

"She then said, 'If I take pencil and paper, can I be informed who it is?' Immediately there were three raps, as of assent; and when she sat down to write, her hand, writing backward, formed the same initials as before—R. G. D. Then she questioned, 'For what purpose were these sounds?' To which the reply, again written backward, was, ' *To show you that we are thinking and working for you.*' "

Ten days after the last incident, Mrs. W., happening to recollect that R. G. D. had once given her a Newfoundland dog, thought she would then like to have such an animal, and said to a servant who happened to be near, " I wish I had a fine large Newfoundland for a walking companion." The next morning a gentleman from a neighboring town, whom Mrs. W. did not remember to have ever before seen, brought and presented to her a noble black Newfoundland dog; stating as his reason for doing so, that he did not intend for the future to keep dogs, and that he felt assured that in Mrs. W. the dog would find a kind mistress. Mrs. W. stated that she had ascertained, to an absolute certainty, that the girl to whom she had spoken on the matter had not mentioned to any one her wish to have a dog.

The foregoing is all there is of the narrative. It was communicated to Mr. Owen by Mrs. W. a few days after the occurrence of the last incident.

The result, then, of the "thinking and working" of the spirits for a period of about six weeks, was the gift of a Newfoundland dog; that is, assuming that this presentation was brought about by them. People of our world can employ their time to better advantage.

In reference to the ungrammatical construction of the sentence, "Ye are sorrowing as one without hope," Mr. Owen says: "If I am asked whence this error in the grammatical construction of the sentence, I reply that I can no more account for it than I can for the writing itself. No one could write more correctly or grammatically than does Mrs. W. It was not through her, therefore, as in the case of an illiterate scribe we might have imagined it, that the error occurred. Its occurrence is additional proof that her mind had no agency in the matter; though it would probably be stretching conjecture too far to imagine that it was so intended."

Yes, I should say that would be stretching conjecture rather too far; and the bare suggestion shows how ready Spiritualists are to be deceived by the "spirits." Why not apply the same rule to the communications of "spirits" as to those of our world, and assume, in such a case, that the writing is by some ignorant creature?

Mrs. W. had been investigating Spiritualism; had held her arm, in a passive condition, for the purpose of having "spirits" write with it; and, like all other mediums, had some low being *en rapport* with her, who, in some way—probably from her mind—had learned the name of her late suitor. Mrs. W. assured Mr. Owen that she could not recollect having thought of the gentleman for several years previous to the occurrence; but it would be very strange if she had not; and a name very familiar occurs to the mind without producing any decided impression ; so that afterward we have no rec-ollection of having thought of it.

Although Mr. Owen has doubts as to whether the error in the grammatical construction of the sentence was from design, he has none whatever as to the object of the " spirit " in writing backward. He says:

" Whence, again, the writing backward ? In that the will had no agency. As little had expectation. Mrs. W., in her normal state, had not the power so to write. By diligent practice she might, doubtless, have acquired it. But she *had* no such practice. She had *not* acquired it. And, not having acquired it, it was as much a physical impossibility for her, of herself, so to write, as for a man, picking up a violin for the first time, to execute thereon, at sight, some elaborate passage from Handel or Beethoven.

" Again, whence the intention to write after so unex-ampled and impracticable a manner ? Where there is an intention there must be an intelligence. It was not Mrs. W. who intended ; for the result struck her with awe—almost with consternation. It was not her intel-ligence, therefore, that acted. What intelligence was it?

" Nor can we reasonably doubt what the intention was. Had Mrs. W.'s hand written forward, she would, in all probability, have remained in uncertainty whether, half unconsciously perhaps, the words were not of her own dictation. The expedient of the backward writing precluded any such supposition ; for she could not of herself do unconsciously a thing which she could not do at all. And this expedient seems to have been in-geniously devised to cut off any supposition of the kind. Then here we have the invention of an expedient, the display of ingenuity. But who is the inventor? Who displays the ingenuity? I confess my inability to answer these questions."

There was no ingenuity of the kind exercised. The invisible being wrote backward, or from right to left, solely because it was easier for him to write thus than from left to right. I have explained this matter in the proper chapter.

If these two narratives are not the only ones of the kind that Mr. Owen has been able to procure, we may assume that they are, in his opinion, the most convincing. We have, then, as instances of "ultramundane aid and spiritual protection" by such of the invisible world as can produce the physical phenomena, the good advice of *Gaspar*, after annoying the family for several weeks, and the gift of a Newfoundland dog. The ultramundane aid does not appear to be very valuable, even upon the assumption that this gift of a dog was owing to the influence of the "spirits." But, as the dog was brought on the morning succeeding the afternoon on which Mrs. W. felt a desire for one, and by a gentleman living in a neighboring town who had decided not to keep dogs, most persons will conclude, I think, that the gentleman had formed the determination to give her the dog before she expressed her wish for one, and, consequently, that the "spirits" had nothing to do with the gift.

I will copy from this chapter one narrative showing, as I believe, good accomplished through the agency of a dream, or, of *impressions*, produced in an individual of our world by one of the invisible world, who could communicate in no other way. The following narrative

I have read in a work by Rev. Dr. Bushnell, entitled "Nature and the Supernatural," from which Mr. Owen has taken it:

"*Help Amid the Snow-Drifts.*"

"'As I sat by the fire, one stormy November night, in a hotel parlor, in the Napa Valley of California, there came in a most venerable and benignant-looking person, with his wife, taking their seats in the circle. The stranger, as I afterward learned, was Captain Yount, a man who came over into California, as a trapper, more than forty years ago. Here he has lived, apart from the great world and its questions, acquiring an immense landed estate, and becoming a kind of acknowledged patriarch in the country. His tall, manly person, and his gracious, paternal look, as totally unsophisticated in the expression as if he had never heard of a philosophic doubt or question in his life, marked him as the true patriarch. The conversation turned, I know not how, on spiritism and the modern necromancy; and he discovered a degree of inclination to believe in the reported mysteries. His wife, a much younger and apparently Christian person, intimated that probably he was predisposed to this kind of faith by a very peculiar experience of his own, and evidently desired that he might be drawn out by some intelligent discussion of his queries.

"'At my request he gave me his story. About six or seven years previous, in a mid-winter's night, he had a dream in which he saw what appeared to be a company of emigrants arrested by the snows of the mountains and perishing rapidly by cold and hunger. He noted the very cast of the scenery, marked by a huge perpendicular front of white rock cliff; he saw the men cutting off what appeared to be tree-tops rising out of deep gulfs of snow; he distinguished the very features of the persons and the look of their particular distress. He woke profoundly impressed with the distinctness and apparent reality of his dream. At length he fell asleep and dreamed exactly the same dream again. In the morning he could not expel it from his mind. Falling in, shortly, with an old hunter comrade, he told him the story, and was only the more deeply impressed by his recognizing, without hesitation, the scenery of the dream. This comrade had come over the Sierra by the Carson Valley Pass, and declared that a spot in the pass answered exactly to his description. By this the unsophisticated patriarch was decided. He immediately collected a company of men with mules and blankets and all necessary provisions. The neighbors were laughing, meantime, at his credulity. "No matter," said he: "I am able to do this, and I will; for I verily believe that the fact is according to my dream." The men were sent into the mountains, one hundred and fifty miles distant, directly to the Carson Valley Pass. And there they found the company in exactly the condition of the dream, and brought in the remnant alive.'

"Dr. Bushnell adds, that a gentleman present said to him, 'You need have no doubt of this; for we Californians all know the facts and the names of the families brought in, who now look upon our venerable friend as a kind of Savior.' These names he gave, together with the residences of each; and Dr. Bushnell avers that he found the Californians everywhere ready to second the old man's testimony. ' Nothing could be more natural,' continues the doctor, 'than for the good-hearted patriarch himself to add that the brightest thing in his life, and that which gave him the greatest joy, was his simple faith in that dream.' "

Had the facts been, simply, that Captain Yount, in a winter's night, dreamed that a party of emigrants were perishing in the snows of the mountains, and it was afterward learned that such a party were thus perishing at the time of the dream, the coincidence might reasonably be considered accidental, for both the dream and the fact would be events likely to occur. But, in this case, peculiar scenery, which he had never seen, was presented to the dreamer's vision so distinctly and correctly that another person recognized the description as being that of a certain spot which he had seen ; and the emigrants were found· at this precise spot. This is not all ; exactly the same dream was repeated—which is very unusual in the case of natural dreams—and the impression made upon the dreamer was so great that it induced ·him to send, at considerable expense, a rescuing party to a spot one hundred and fifty miles distant. I do not believe that a dream occurring from ordinary causes would have such an effect; assuming that the dreamer was of sound mind.

This dream could not have been produced by the action of the mind of one of the emigrants upon that of Captain Yount; for it appears that the party were all strangers to him ; besides, the dream would not, probably, have been repeated from such a cause. As the narrative appears to be authenticated beyond reasonable question, I believe the dream to have been produced by a being of the other world. The vision, it will be observed, differed entirely from those narrated by Captain Norway and Captain Clarke. There was no long-continued succession of events, lasting through a considerable interval of time, presented to the mental vision of Captain Yount; all that he perceived might have been the impression of a moment. It is hardly necessary to state that this narrative is far better authenticated than the two others referred to.

The attempt to produce such an impression may have been, and probably was, made with a number of individuals before success crowned the effort. Dr. Bushnell's decription of Captain Yount conveys the idea of a susceptible person. The effort of the invisible being would not cease with the production of the dream. The influence upon the mind of Captain Yount, acquired while he was asleep, was, undoubtedly, continued until he sent the rescuing party; and this explains his extraordinary action.

Now, those of the other world able to produce the physical phenomena, and communicate at any time through mediums, have been in daily communication with our world for the past twenty years; and yet, during all this time they have not done as much good as was accomplished by this dream. In fact, I have been unable to learn of a single well-authenticated instance of substantial benefit conferred by the class referred to, or by communication through a medium.

But the instances of annoyance by this class are numerous; several instances of the kind being given in Mr. Owen's work; and the use of the electricity of an

individual of our world, in the production of the phenomena is, in itself, a positive and serious injury to the
individual. The mediums for the production of these
phenomena, so far as I have information, universally
complain of poor health.

It here occurs to me that before closing my review
of this work, it may be well to make a few remarks
relative to the last narrative; and having a bearing
upon the whole subject.

Some of my readers may have read the work of Dr.
Bushnell; others may have seen reviews of it; and
those not inclined to belief in the supernatural may conclude the credulity of Dr. Bushnell is such that he is
very poor authority for any narrative of the kind.

There is no more coincidence between the views of
Dr. Bushnell and my own, than between those of the
former and the most sceptical (in reference to this whole
subject) individual living. In fact, his explanation—if
it can properly be called such—of this very narrative,
differs entirely from that I have given. In reference to
it he says:

"Let any one attempt now to account for the coincidences of that dream by mere natural causalities, and
he will be glad enough to ease his labor by the acknowl-
edgment of a supernatural Providence."

In short, Dr. Bushnell believes it was a miracle;
though why a miracle should have been performed in
this case, and not in thousands of other similar ones, he
does not attempt to explain. Without discussing this
question, I feel bound to state, after reading Dr. Bushnell's work, and especially the chapter headed, "Mir-

acles and Spiritual Gifts not Discontinued," from which the above narrative is taken, that if we were obliged to rely upon his *judgment* for the authenticity of the narrative, I should not think of citing it. But I endeavor to discriminate, by the use of *my own* judgment, between authentic and fictitious narratives; and all I ask of the reader is, that he will do the same. To show that this is not, in most cases, so very difficult, I will copy from Dr. Bushnell's work a narrative immediately following that of Captain Yount.

"I fell in, also, in that new world, with a different and more directly Christian example, in the case of an acquaintance whom I had known for the last twenty years; an educated man in successful·practice as a physician; a man who makes no affectations of piety, and puts on no airs of sanctimony ; living always in a kind of jovial element, and serving everybody but himself. He laughs at the current incredulity of men respecting prayer, and relates many instances, out of his own experience, to show—for that is his doctrine—that God will certainly hear every man's prayer, if only he is honest in it. Among others, he gave the following :—He had hired his little house, of one room, in a new trading town that was planted last year, agreeing to give a rent for it of ten dollars per month. At length, on the day preceding the rent day, he found that he had nothing in hand to meet the payment, and could not see at all whence the money was to come. Consulting with his wife, they agreed that prayer, so often tried, was their only hope. They went, accordingly, to prayer, and found assurance that their want should be supplied. That was the end of their trouble, and there they rested, dismissing further concern. But the morning came, and the money did not. The rent owner made his appearance earlier than usual. As he entered the door, their hearts began to sink, whispering that now, for once, they must give it up, and allow that prayer had failed. But before the demand was made, a neighbor coming in called out the untimely visitor, engaging him in conversation a few minutes at the door. Meantime a stranger came in, saying, 'Dr. —— I owe you ten dollars for attending me in a fever at such a time, and here is the money.' He could muster no recollection either of the man or of the service, but was willing to be convinced, and so had the money in hand, after all, when the demand was made."

Let us assume, as I think we may, that the *veracity* of Dr. Bushnell is not to be questioned. The circumstances stated in Captain Yount's narrative—with the exception of the dream—must, if they occurred, have been generally known throughout the vicinity. Dr. Bushnell states that they were known, as he ascertained. The only question then is, whether Captain Yount sent the rescuing party in consequence of a dream. Dr. Bushnell omits to state whether he conversed with any of the neighbors who laughed at the credulity of Captain Yount in fitting out an expedition upon the impulse of a dream. But how could the situation of the emigrants have become known to Captain Yount through any ordinary channel? If one or more of the emigrants had succeeded in getting through, or if any other individual had arrived through the pass and reported the situation, the fact would have been known to other Californians. In short, the circumstances did occur as stated, or Dr. Bushnell is not a man of common veracity.

Let us now examine the story of the physician ; *for which there is no corroborating testimony.* The practice of the physician was, at the time, so small that he was obliged to hire a house of only one room, at a rent of ten dollars per month, and was unable to pay even that amount. Yet, according to his story, he had attended a man through a fever without having any recollection of the fact; and, which is still more incredible, he could not recollect having attended the man after the latter called on him and stated the fact; and had, as it appears, no charge against the patient on his books. Such an instance never occurred ; not even with a physician of the largest practice. Besides, how could the man have known, or assumed, without making the inquiry, that he owed the physician just ten dollars ? Setting aside altogether the question of miracles, the story is an utterly absurd one. And look at the character of the narrator. He stated that he could, at any time, get whatever he wanted by praying for it. Every one of common sense knows that this was false ; and knows, therefore, that the man was a liar or a fool.

But what I wish more particularly to point out is, that if we reject the narrative of Captain Yount, we must impeach the *veracity* of Dr. Bushnell ; while in rejecting that of the physician, we only doubt the soundness of his *judgment* as to the character of the narrator.

The accounts of apparitions which I have taken from Mr. Owen's work, I have treated as having been merely instances of hallucination. But in " Explanations of

Phenomena," I have stated that it was possible for those of the other world to produce a tangible apparition—one that could be actually seen and felt; that is, that a dress and mask, originally invisible to us, could be made visible and sensible to the touch. Mr. Owen's work does not contain a narrative which I feel fully warranted in citing as an instance of this kind; I will, therefore, take such from another work.

In the London *Spiritual Magazine*, a monthly publication, I find the correspondence—including extracts from the diary—of a gentleman residing in New York. The name of the gentleman is not here given; but as, since the publication of this correspondence, it has been given—presumably with the assent of the gentleman—in at least two works, there would be no propriety in my withholding such a voucher for the truth of the accounts. The author of the correspondence, then, is Mr. C. F. Livermore,* late of the well-known banking-house of Livermore, Clews & Co.

The correspondence appears to have been carried on for several years. When it commenced, or when Mr. Livermore commenced his investigations, I do not know;

---

* I would here state—and I intend to be very guarded in statements of this kind—that the full name was given me by my invisible informants when writing the former work. I have no acquaintance with Mr. Livermore, and never, to my knowledge, ever saw him; the banking-house having been organized about the time I left New York. And until the name was thus given me, I had never heard that he was interested in Spiritualism. It was not until some time—I think at least a year—after the name was given me, that I learned it was the correct one. I mention this to show how generally extraordinary occurrences of this kind are known in the other world; and also as in some measure a voucher that my informants know how these apparitions were produced.

but I find it stated in a letter dated, "New York, March 17, 1862," that success "only crowned months of pa tient watching." The medium for the production of these apparitions was Miss Fox. How often, during these months, Mr. Livermore sat with Miss Fox for the purpose, is not stated ; but I infer from subsequent correspondence that they sat at least once every week, and during some weeks oftener. Mr. Livermore, then, sat, by direction of the "spirits," with the same medium— an excellent one for the purpose—at least once a week for several months before he witnessed an apparition. Evidently, these apparitions must have been of a differ ent character from those I have considered hallucinations.

I have before me the number of the Magazine for January, 1866, from which I will give a few extracts. As Mr. Livermore had been sitting with Miss Fox for several years, it may be assumed that the invisible beings would have their materials and arrangements for producing the phenomena perfected as far as possible.

In explanation of the following letter, it is stated that Mr. Livermore first met the lady (called Estelle) who became his wife, at Baden-Baden, in the year 1851. In the summer of 1865 Mr. Livermore was again at Baden-Baden, his wife having in the meantime died ; and he happened to occupy the same room that Estelle occupied when he first met her. When in London, on his way home, he mentioned the incident to Mr. Coleman, author of a work from which I have given an extract in the chapter on "Modern Spiritualism ; " and Mr. Coleman suggested that Mr. Livermore should, on his return home, make the circumstance a test as to the identity of Estelle with the apparition which had frequently appeared to him, claiming to be her.

"NEW YORK, November 20th, 1865.

"MY DEAR MR. COLEMAN:—You will no doubt be interested to learn that my first spiritual manifestation since my return from Europe was in my own house, in the presence of Dr. Gray,* and resulted in the tangible, real, visible presence of my wife in my own room, where there could by no possibility have been any other persons than Dr. Gray, the medium, and myself. This was on Friday evening, November 10th, 1865.

"The atmosphere was moderately electrical, cold and overcast. The medium and Dr. Gray having called to see me, we determined to have a sitting in a room upstairs, there being no persons in the house but the servants, who were three flights below. The door was carefully locked, and after seating ourselves at the table in the middle of the room I turned out the gas. In about fifteen minutes a spirit-light rose from the floor on the side of the table opposite to the medium, and after describing a semicircle over and above the table three times consecutively, it rested upon Dr. Gray's head and disappeared. The medium and myself were then requested to stand up. Upon our doing so the light again made its appearance between us and the window, pressing us back a little, as though to give it more room. Vigorous rustlings succeeded this movement, and the next instant the figure of my wife stood before us, holding a single flower in her hand, with every

* A physician and prominent Spiritualist of New York.

feature radiant, and vividly visible. She was dressed in white gossamer, which enveloped her head, a transparent veil falling just before her right eye, but thrown back. The veil was subsequently removed altogether. Her dress, or robe, was carefully plaited around the neck, but with that exception it was loose and flowing. It was of thicker material than that about her head, and seemed to be of the texture of silk and gossamer. As Dr. Gray was seated during this time (we standing between him and the spirit), he saw only the light and drapery as she came and glided away, which she did five or six times during a period of about three-quarters of an hour. For some cause unknown to me, the spirit could not on this occasion remain visible to me when Dr. Gray approached.

"You will, perhaps, remember a suggestion you made to me in London, that upon my return I should make certain interesting circumstances which occurred to me on the Continent, the subject of a spiritual test. I am happy to say that it has been done with a most satisfactory result. I had mentioned the circumstances to no one on this side of the ocean. At a second *séance* two days after that which I have just described, I applied the test as follows:—I wrote two questions without the medium's knowledge. The questions and answers were as follows:

"'My Dear Wife:—I desire you this morning to write me a word about your appearance on Friday night last, also something in reference to the interesting circumstance now on my mind, which occurred on the Continent during my last visit to Europe.'

" Answer (written on a card by the spirit):

"' MY DEAR HUSBAND:—I was most happy to come
to you in form in our own house.   It gave me joy
greater than words can express.   The next time I wish
to wear a different dress—one entirely covered with
violets and roses, so that you may perfectly see their
color.   I was with you at Baden-Baden, and saw your
thoughts of me while there.   I was very near you—as
near as at the time when I there promised to be yours
forever.   I was near you when this thought came.   I
heard the echo go forth from your heart, and my spirit
was drawn at once to your side.   Sacred memories are
attached to that place.   Do you remember, dear Charles,
how happy we both were then ?   Be happy now, for I
am ever near you.

"' ESTELLE.'"

I give this "test," which Mr. Livermore thought
"most satisfactory," and which is as satisfactory as any
I have seen in the correspondence, for the purpose of
showing what evidence—aside from the resemblance—he
had that the apparition was his wife.   If the "spirit"
was unable to read his mind she could not have known
what was on his mind, or what the question referred to.
If she could read his mind the question was, of course,
no test at all.   But the "spirit" stated that she could,
and did at Baden-Baden, perceive his thoughts; that is,
she saw them, and heard the echo of one go forth from his
heart.   It is not easy to understand how any sane
man could consider this a test of identity, but it is a
very fair sample of the tests generally instituted by
Spiritualists.

"*Extracts from Diary. First evening:*—Cold and clear. A bright fire was burning in the grate. I turned the gas down partially, but still sufficient to make all objects distinctly visible. I then opened the table about six inches in the middle, placing a large musical box across one side, and the table-cover across the other, leaving an opening of about six inches square in the centre. After a few minutes a white fleshy hand rose, pointing its fingers upward through this opening. A snow-white envelope encircled it from the wrist downward. It was natural in shape, size, and color. A few moments elapsed, when the hand again made its appearance, but now held a flower, which, with its stem, was about three inches in length. I reached out my hand to touch it, and the instant it came in contact with the flower there was a snap, like the discharge of electricity. By request I now turned up the gas, making the room fully light. The hand again rose, holding the flower, which it placed upon a sheet of white paper which I had placed next the opening. I lifted the paper and examined the flower, which was to all appearance a lovely pink rose-bud, with green leaves. Miss Fox took it in her fingers and held it up for examination. It was damp, cold, and glutinous. As expressions of dissatisfaction, from the unseen agents of this wonder, were here manifested, she replaced the flower upon the paper, when the hand rose, seized and took it away instantly. Various flowers of different sizes, shapes, and colors were presented. One was a small white flower, like a daisy. By raps it was said, 'Obey directions; you wither the flowers by your touch.'"

" *Third evening:*—Cold and clear. The spirit-light soon rose, divided into two, and discovered before us standing the beautiful spirit-form of my wife, so often described. She was vividly visible, but differently dressed from her usual style, apparently typical of something which I did not understand. A kind of turban was wreathed about the head, of gossamer and gold, sparkling with bright points, like diamonds, her head resting upon her right hand.

"After remaining visible for some time, we crossed the room, when she again appeared, similarly dressed. The shining head-dress was entirely new. After she had disappeared the light floated about, as answering questions by rapid circular motions. The light then rose near to the ceiling, describing revolutions the reverse of its previous motions. At times these revolutions described circles of six to eight feet in diameter. I asked that the light might pass around us, which was immediately done with great rapidity.

" A large roll of drawing paper was taken up during these gyrations and carried with the light. The light itself, as well as the envelope, was heard occasionally to strike against the table or ceiling with considerable force, as it passed about."

"*Fourth evening:*—Cold and overcast, with threatened storm. Shortly after the gas was turned out heavy rustlings were heard, a brilliant electric light rose, and the well-known countenance of Dr. Franklin beamed upon us. No words can convey an idea of the calm, peaceful serenity, the dignity, the spirituality which shone out from that face. Although I have so often before seen it, yet on this occasion I was more than ever impressed, for his every feature was radiant. The light was very powerful, rendering him distinctly visible. He appeared in four different parts of the room, and each time differently draped, or dressed. My hat, which had been left upon the bureau, was worn by him a portion of the time, and then taken from his head in full view, and placed upon mine by the spirit. Immediately afterward, while my hat was still upon my head, he was seen wearing a three-cornered hat, a ruffled shirt, white neckerchief without a collar, his gray hair behind the ears. He was enveloped in a dark robe, which passed down by the side of his face, partially shielding that side, and was drawn across his breast about six or eight inches below the chin. This mantle I examined both by sight and touch, and found that it resembled in fabric rather coarse dark flannel or worsted stuff. Beneath this his dress was perfect, the cravat and ruffler were spotless white, and the vest and coat real, for I pulled aside the mantle with my own hand. His face was like the crystallization of expression, the expression changing during the intervals of invisibility. The formation being instant and temporary, no doubt lacks the nerves and muscles of the human physical organization, and hence can of necessity only exhibit one attitude, or phase of expression, for each crystallization (or naturalization) during which the features and expression are *en permanence*."

" *Sixth evening:*—Atmosphere clear. A bright coal fire and gas burning, the latter about half turned off.

" Opened the table about the width of six to eight

inches. Soon a white female hand rose through the opening; answered my questions by significant movements. It touched my own hand, took hold of my fingers, etc. I placed my handkerchief upon a large musical box on the table. The hand rose, grasped it, and carried it away. This hand was at times amorphous, or clumsily shaped. Again it would appear perfect, or more nearly so. At times the fingers were widely spread, seemingly stiff, and moving with difficulty; again flexible and natural. It was fleshy in color and to the touch, but unnaturally white. I did not see it beyond the wrist. I had frequently, by the spirit-light, seen that the formation ended at the mist."

" *Seventh evening:*—Weather clear and cold. At the conclusion of a message, a light rose from the floor, discovering to us the spirit of my wife standing before us in all her beauty. My hat was asked for to shield the light. I held it with the opening toward the spirit, the light being shaken quickly inside the hat (by the spirit) threw out brilliant radiations until her face was radiant. A delicate veil of gossamer (white) depended from above her forehead, which we took in our hands for examination. I held it myself before her face, found it transparent, and of such delicate tissue that it heightened her beauty, and made her seem still more ethereal. We now crossed the room to a sofa. The spirit said (by raps), 'I wish to recline on the sofa.' Loud rustlings and movements were heard, when we found that a sofa-pillow, forming one end of the sofa, was in the process of being detached, and afterward we saw it placed on end in the corner of the sofa, against which she was now seen reclining. We bent over, and examined with great care her face and dress. The dress was white, a narrow ribbon was across her forehead, over which was a small white rose, a bunch of violets over her left temple, and a pink rose behind her ear. Her hair fell loosely, so that I took locks of it and placed it over the white robe, which I also took hold of and examined carefully. It was neatly trimmed with a narrow ruffle, and plaited in front."

When the gas was lighted, Estelle, as Mr. Livermore believed it to be, invariably got under the table; yet, so far as I have read the correspondence, it does not appear that Mr. Livermore ever inquired the reason for such a strange proceeding; and it is a remarkable fact, that I never knew a Spiritualist who appeared to think it at all strange that the spirits, when certain phenomena are produced, get under a table if the room is lighted.

It will be perceived from the description of the face supposed to be that of Dr. Franklin, that nothing but dead matter—in other words, nothing but masks—were seen by Mr. Livermore, whether these masks were produced as I have stated, or not. This being the fact, the reader can draw his own conclusions as to the extraordinary beauty of the one claiming to be his wife, and "the calm, peaceful serenity, the dignity, the spirituality which shone out from the face" of Dr. Franklin.

In the production of these phenomena several of the other world were engaged; and the hands seen on the sixth evening, which varied in appearance, were coverings of the hands of different individuals, some of which had been more perfectly prepared than others. The lights, which Mr. Livermore sometimes calls spirit-lights, and at other times electric lights, were produced by a substance somewhat resembling phosphorus. This substance in its normal condition is not luminous to us; but becomes so when it has undergone the change described. As the masks will not bear critical inspection, the "spirits" prefer exhibiting by a light which is under their own control; and besides, these phosphorescent lights do not so readily disclose the fact that the features are masks as would gas-light.

Since the publication of my former work, from which the preceding portion of this chapter is copied—with a few unimportant alterations, mainly for the purpose of condensation—Mr. Owen has published another work upon the same subject, entitled, "The Debatable Land between this World and the Next." This work, also, contains numerous narratives, which I think it unnecessary to notice, as they do not vary in character from those in the former one. It contains, however, two instances of tangible apparitions witnessed by Mr. Owen himself, in the presence of Mrs. Underhill (sister of Miss Fox) and a Boston medium. The figures produced were not, however, so perfect, or distinct, as those seen by Mr. Livermore, and Mr. Owen did not perceive the features at all, these being concealed in both instances. No further information upon the subject would be given the reader, therefore, by copying the narratives, which are rather lengthy.

But Mr. Owen was permitted by Mr. Livermore to read the latter's record, or diary of phenomena, witnessed

REVIEW OF NARRATIVES. 395

by him, and copies from it, in his last work, some items which, as I think, show conclusively that the features of the apparitions were simply masks. I will take from Mr. Owen's work a few of these extracts.

" ' No. 179. At my own house. I had procured a dark lantern, covered with a cloth-casing, and provided with a valve, so that I could throw a circle of light two feet in diameter on a wall ten feet distant.

" 'I placed this lantern, lighted, on the table, and held the medium's hands. Soon it rose into the air, and we were requested to follow. A form, carrying the lantern, preceded us. The outline of this spirit-form was distinct, its white robes dropping to the floor. The lantern was placed on a bureau, and we stood facing a window which was between that bureau and a large mirror.

" 'Then the lantern again rose, remaining suspended about five feet from the floor between the bureau and the mirror, and by its light we discerned the figure of Franklin seated in my arm-chair by the window, in front of a dark curtain. For fully ten minutes at a time the light from the suspended lantern rested on his face and figure, so that we had ample time to examine both. At first the face seemed as if of actual flesh, the hair real, the eyes bright and so dictinct that I clearly saw the whites; but I noticed that gradually the whole appearance, including the eyes, was deadened by the earthly light, and cease l to wear the aspect of life with which the forms I had seen by spiritual light were replete.' "

This face, then, would not bear examination even by the light of a lantern. The only question is, Was a living face, "including the eyes," gradually deadened

by the "earthly light," or did the observer gradually
notice that it was not a living face? It appears to me
to be a question which no man of common sense can
hesitate a moment in deciding.

During the earlier sittings of Mr. Livermore only
himself and the medium were present; but Mr. Owen
states that he has recorded *ten* sittings at which Dr.
Gray was present, and *eight* at which his (Mr. L.'s)
brother-in-law, Mr. Groute, assisted.

"The first opportunity he" (Dr. Gray) "had of joining Mr. Livermore's circle was during sitting No. 256,
of June 6, 1862. On that occasion the figure of Dr.
Franklin appeared, but evidently with difficulty, and
without the full expression which he had previously
worn. The hair, however, and clothing were both
nearly as usual, and were handled by Dr. Gray.

"Eleven days later Dr. Gray was present a second
time. On this occasion the figure of Dr. Franklin
showed itself several times; but the features, at first,
were not recognizable, and, on another occasion, a portion of the face only was formed, presenting a deformed
and disagreeable aspect. This had not occurred during
any of Mr. Livermore's previous sittings. Estelle did
not show herself on either of these occasions.

"The third time (June 25) the figure of Franklin appeared in perfection, and was recognized by Dr. Gray.

"During the fourth sitting there was a message to
the effect that a piece of the spirit's garment might be
cut off with scissors and examined. Both Dr. Gray and
Mr. Livermore availed themselves of this permission.
For a time the texture was strong, so that it might be

pulled without coming apart. They both had time to examine it critically before it melted away."

"Dr. Gray related to me a still more interesting observation. On one of the last occasions that the figure of Franklin presented itself, the face appeared, at first, imperfectly formed, showing one eye only ; for, in place of the other eye and part of the cheek, there was a dark cavity which looked hideous enough. Kate Fox caught sight of it and screamed out in mortal terror, causing the temporary extinguishment of the light under which the figure appeared."

"This was during one of the last sittings at which Dr. Gray assisted. On several of the earliest occasions, as the doctor informed me, the face, though distinctly marked, seemed sometimes shriveled and as if made of dough, at other times it resembled the face of a corpse."

These extracts are sufficient, I think, to indicate the character of these apparitions. In reference to them Mr. Owen advances the following theory :

"The evidence I have adduced goes to show that a spirit may—under certain conditions, and aided, probably, by other spirits—fabricate an ephemeral *eidolon*, resembling the body it had while on earth ; but evanescent, especially under earth-light; so that the poet's line,

'It faded at the crowing of the cock,'

is in strict accordance with the character of the actual phenomenon.

"By what process this temporary induement (if it be correct to regard it as an induement) is effected, we certainly do not know at this time ; and perhaps we never shall until we learn it, on the other side, from the spiritual artists themselves. All that one seems justified in surmising is that there are invisible exudations from the human organization—more or less from all persons, but especially from the bodies of spiritual sensitives—which spirits can condense, or otherwise modify, so as to produce not only what to the senses of human beings is a visible and tangible form, but also substances resembling earthly clothing and other inanimate objects."

But if Dr. Franklin was one of these "spiritual artists," and communicated for years with Mr. Livermore, why should it be necessary to surmise anything upon the subject? Who, better than Dr. Franklin, could explain the phenomena? assuming, as Spiritualists do, that Franklin has not lost any of his mental powers. This is one of the strangest facts connected with Spiritualism, namely, that men of the intellectual culture of Mr. Owen believe that the most intelligent of the other world can communicate with us, and yet cannot, or will not explain a single phenomenon which they are the agents in producing. A very few words from Dr Franklin, if he was the "artist," would have explained, so far as was essential, how he presented to Mr. Livermore the figure of himself.

The theory that the spirits can manufacture from the invisible exudations of human beings cloth like that described by Mr. Livermore and Dr. Gray, appears to me an absurdity. But assuming that these apparitions were produced as Mr. Owen surmises, it is very evident that most of those which I have treated as hallucinations could not have been produced in the same manner, and, therefore, could not have been of the same character.

To suppose that all the apparitions described in Mr. Owen's two works were of the same character; that the wife of Mr. Livermore communicated with him for years without giving any satisfactory evidence of the identity, always getting under the table when the room was lighted ; that Dr. Franklin also visited him for years without explaining anything or giving any valuable information, would make the whole subject an incomprehensible mystery. But if we assume that most of the apparitions were hallucinations; that those seen by Mr. Livermore were tangible figures, though not produced by his wife or Dr. Franklin, then the whole matter becomes intelligible.

Mr. Owen's first work contains about sixty narratives, which he considers well authenticated. Of these there are nine, of which I have given the substance, which conflict more or less with the theories I have given. Three of these nine were given at least half a century after the occurrences took place by parties who did not witness them. Two were given by a Captain Clarke, whose character for veracity Mr. Owen appears to have known nothing about. One purporting to be given by another sea captain was taken from a comparatively unknown work. One was given by a Mlle. de Guldenstubbé, who, for reasons stated, cannot be considered good authority for the *minute accuracy*—which is the important point—of a narrative of the kind. The remaining two were given by the Baron de Gulden-

stubbé and Mr. S. C. Hall. The former of these does
not conflict with the theories, assuming that the baron
was, like Miss Fox, a suitable medium for the production of these figures. But it does not appear that he
ever before or afterward witnessed anything of the kind,
or any physical phenomena, for the production of which
he appeared to be the medium. The only difficulty I
find in the narrative given by Mr. Hall is the manner
in which "Gaspar" is represented as having exhibited
himself, and the statement that any one could hear him
talk. This narrative was given Mr. Hall about forty
years after the events occurred, who repeated it to Mr.
Owen from recollection. It could hardly be expected,
therefore, that the account, as to minute particulars,
would be strictly accurate. I would here observe that
so far as I have read the accounts given by Mr. Livermore, there is no mention of Estelle or Franklin having
ever spoken a word which to him was audible.

I have not read very carefully the second work of
Mr. Owen; but upon a cursory examination I find it
contains about forty narratives, five or six of which it
would be difficult to explain consistently with the theories I have given. Several of the narratives in this
work relate occurrences witnessed by Mr. Owen himself,
not one of which at all conflicts with these theories.

Of the one hundred narratives contained in Mr.
Owen's two collections, then, only fourteen or fifteen
conflict at all with the theories I have stated; and those
which decidedly confirm these theories are not only the
most numerous, but by far the best authenticated.
The result of this test of the theories is, I think, as

satisfactory as could reasonably be expected. And so far as my information extends, other narratives conflicting with these theories are either of occurrences in darkened rooms or from some other cause of doubtful authenticity.

www.ingramcontent.com/pod-product-compliance
Lightning Source LLC
Chambersburg PA
CBHW031351290326
41932CB00044B/878